Message Mapping for Foodborne Outbreaks and Product Recalls

A handbook for US food industries from farm to fork

By Rusty Cawley, APR | MessageMaps.org

First Printing, 2019

ISBN: 978-0-578-21160-2

MessageMaps.org| Bryan-College Station, Texas

About this handbook

This guide offers a step-by-step process for developing and delivering effective risk messages to consumers and other stakeholders during outbreaks of foodborne illness that result in product recalls. The focus is on companies that produce, manufacture, distribute, or serve food products within the United States. At the heart of this process are three concepts:

- The principles of high-stress communication, as established by the research of risk communications scholar Vincent T. Covello, as well as its primary tool: the message map, which organizes and simplifies the essential task of delivering effective messages to large groups of upset people. You can find his website at centerforriskcommunication.org.

- Hazard = Risk + Outrage, a model created by risk communications consultant Peter M. Sandman to help clients deal more effectively with large groups of upset people, as well as his principles, methods, and strategies of outrage management. You can learn more at his website, psandman.com.

- Best practices for risk communication, as outlined by Timothy L. Sellnow, Robert R. Ulmer, Matthew W. Seeger, and Robert S. Littlefield in their book, Effective Risk Communication: A Message-Centered Approach (2009), a volume in Springer Science+Business Media's Food Microbiology and Food Safety series.

The handbook is supplemented with three case studies that help to demonstrate the handbook's core concepts in the context of an actual foodborne outbreak followed by a product recall. It is designed to help train your company's crisis response team to communicate clearly with angry or upset stakeholders. It also serves as a field guide for use during actual outbreaks and recalls, when tempers run high and the resulting stress can interfere with our ability to think clearly and strategically.

Learn more at MessageMaps.org.

— Rusty Cawley, APR

Table of Contents

About this handbook 1

Introduction: Why you need this handbook 5

Part I: High-Stress Communication for Foodborne Outbreaks and Recalls 9
Section 1: Fundamentals of high-stress communication..11
Section 2: Understanding the foodborne risk controversy 17
Section 3: Understanding stakeholder outrage 21
Section 4: Stakeholder outrage and the foodborne risk controversy 25
Section 5: The primary strategy — acknowledge and improve 31
Section 6: How to deliver three types of news — the bad, the good, and the uncertain...35
Section 7: How to communicate effectively through the news media 39
Section 8: Understanding what outraged stakeholders need from you 45
Section 9: Nine best practices for communicating risk to stakeholders 49
Section 10: Summary of important concepts from Part I..53

Part II: Message Mapping for Foodborne Outbreaks and Recalls 55
Section 11: Building message maps for foodborne outbreaks 57
Section 13: Composing the preamble 81
Section 14: Delivering risk messages to stakeholders..83
Sources for Parts I and II 87
Part III: Case Studies in Message Mapping for Foodborne Outbreaks and Recalls ...91
CASE STUDY: The Blue Bell listeriosis outbreak of 2010-15 and the recall of 2015...93
CASE STUDY: The I.M. Healthy SoyNut Butter E. coli O:157 outbreak and recall of 2017 121
CASE STUDY: The Cadbury Schweppes salmonella outbreak and chocolate recall of 2006 145

About the author 203

Introduction: Why you need this handbook

Jimmy Patton bought a bag of Sam's Choice Backyard Gourmet Burgers from his local Wal-Mart in Springdale, Ark. About a week later, he cooked a burger and ate it. A few days after his meal, Patton says, he began suffering from abdominal cramps, bloody diarrhea and body fatigue (Belson and Fahim, 2007).

Doctors diagnosed Patton with an infection of the E. coli bacteria strain O157:H7, one of the nation's leading causes of foodborne illness. Each year, according to federal estimates, the various infectious strains of E. coli strike an estimated 265,000 Americans, sending 3,600 to a hospital, and thirty to the morgue. The bacteria infect humans through foods that are contaminated with the bacteria. (Centers for Disease Control and Prevention, September 2016)

Patton was among twenty-nine Americans in eight states who reported contracting E. coli from frozen burger patties between July and September 2007. Investigators traced all of the patties to one source: the Topps Meat Company of Elizabeth, New Jersey.

Founded in 1940, Topps posted $8.8 million in annual sales by 2007 and ranked among the largest producers of frozen meat patties in the United States. It employed around ninety workers in its 3,000-square-foot facility.

In early September 2007, the US Department of Agriculture tested Topps products and confirmed the presence of E. coli in some samples. But Topps waited eighteen days before recalling 331,582 pounds of frozen hamburger patties, and did so only at the insistence of the USDA. Four days later, the USDA expanded that recall to 21.7 million pounds of beef.

On Oct. 4, Patton and other victims of the E. coli outbreak filed a class-action lawsuit. That same day, the USDA announced plans to shut down the entire plant. Why? Inspectors had discovered "inadequate process controls" in the company's production lines that extended beyond just ground meat.

On Oct. 5, Topps shut its doors and fired all but ten workers. Here's what the company's CEO had to say: "In one week we have gone from the largest US manufacturer of frozen hamburgers to a company that cannot overcome the economic reality of a recall this large."

Stop and think about the essential facts of this case:

- Investigators held Topps accountable for twenty-nine cases of infection out of an annual US average of 305,000 E. coli infections. That's less than a third of one percent of the average annual total.
- No deaths were attributed to the Topps outbreak.
- Yet the USDA forced Topps to recall 21.7 million pounds of beef.

As a result, the company went from a thriving production operation to a dead corporate shell in just four months.

This is what an outbreak of a foodborne illness, along with the public's reaction to the outbreak and the resulting product recall, can do to any company in the US food industry.

This is a major issue for the food industry, for your company and your career. No company is immune. Scientists have identified more than 250 foodborne diseases, most of which are infections caused by bacteria, viruses, and parasites. Toxins and chemicals cause the rest. Each year, according to federal estimates (CDC, December 2017), foodborne agents both known and unknown result in:

- 48 million illnesses in the United States.
- 128,000 hospital admissions.
- 3,000 deaths.

Moreover, it's clear that Americans are concerned about the safety of the food products they buy. A scientific survey asked Americans, on which of the following would you spend the most federal dollars (Stinson, 2006):

- Preventing terrorists from flying jetliners into skyscrapers?
- Stopping terrorists from releasing poison gas in city subways?
- Thwarting terrorists from contaminating the nation's food supply?

Most of the respondents chose number three: Protect the food supply. Now you may be surprised by that answer. A lot of folks involved in homeland security were amazed. They shouldn't be. Not every American travels in airplanes or by subway. But everybody eats.

Americans love to eat. They expect their food to taste good. They also expect their food to arrive on their tables or in their kitchens free of disease or contamination. That's why taxpayers pay billions annually for the USDA to set standards and conduct inspections. That's why they spend billions more to empower the Food and Drug Administration as well as the Centers for Disease Control and Prevention. That's why cities and states create health departments to license and regulate their local food markets, manufactures, and restaurants. Americans want to serve their families with food that is clean and safe. When they suspect or discover that their food is contaminated, they get anxious, then they get angry, and then they punish anyone they believe responsible for the contamination.

In short: Americans become outraged. In the United States, public outrage rarely manifests as riots, boycotts, or demonstrations. When it comes to foodborne illness, public outrage most often expresses itself as consumer choices, news coverage, class-action lawsuits, overt political pressure, and aggressive government action. Through these means, public outrage may cause serious damage to even the largest companies that manufacture, distribute, or sell food products.

Responsibilities of the company executive

If you are a corporate executive in the food industry, you have a duty to acquire a fundamental understanding of what causes the public to get anxious and angry about outbreaks of foodborne illnesses. You should also learn how to calm that outrage before it destroys your company. You can't leave it to the lawyers, who tend to become so focused on liability and litigation they forget that you can win the legal battle and still lose the war. You can't leave it to your public relations team; few PR professionals understand the strategies and the tactics required to navigate public outrage during a risk controversy. Thus, as a corporate executive, the responsibility is yours to understand why the public gets angry about foodborne illness and how you can mitigate that anger. It is also up to you to understand that you have as much or more to lose in the court of public opinion as you have in any court of law.

There is more to running a successful company than a legal license. Every corporation in the United States also operates with a social license to do business. If the public turns against you, you lose that license, and soon you lose your business. Your legal license may still be intact, but good luck making a profit. You may consider it a paradox, but it is true: The more you help the public to make the right decisions about an outbreak of foodborne illness, the more you help your company. If you want to emerge from a foodborne crisis with your social license intact, you must understand the dynamics of the public's reaction to foodborne outbreaks. And you must be ready to make the right moves and avoid the wrong ones. This is where risk communication comes into play. Risk communication can arm you with sound strategic thinking that will guide your responses to the public's anxiety and anger over an outbreak of foodborne illness. This handbook focuses on one of the most useful and powerful tools in the risk communication arsenal: the message map.

Benefits of the message map

In any risk controversy, our primary communication challenge as an organization is to design messages that stakeholders can understand and accept when they are under high stress. The solution, Covello says, is to develop "a limited number of key messages that are brief, credible, and clearly understood (Covello, Minamyer and Clayton, 2007)."

The tools that help us do this are message maps, which risk communicators like Covello have developed based upon their research into how people process information when under significant stress (NCFPD, 2007). The message map is the organization's best available tool for managing our risk messages to stakeholders during a high-stress event.

A message map organizes the key messages we most need to communicate – quickly, efficiently, and clearly – to stakeholders who are affected by a controversy or an emergency. "It is the template for displaying detailed, hierarchically organized responses to anticipated questions or concerns," risk communicators Regina E. Lundgren and Andrea H. McMakin say in the fourth edition of their book, Risk Communication: A Handbook for Communicating Environmental, Safety, and Health Risks (2013) "Message maps are one way to make sure everyone understands the organization's messages for high-concern or controversial issues."

Once we complete our message maps, we can use them again and again to create a wide range of communications tools, including fact sheets, news releases, advertisements, talking points, scripts, speeches, web sites, and public service announcements. We can also use them as a guide when speaking to the news media or at public events.

The process of developing message maps can also help us to meet several goals before, during, and after a risk controversy. (Covello, Minamyer and Clayton, 2007). These goals include:

- Identify stakeholders, both current and potential, with whom we will need to communicate messages.
- Anticipate their questions and concerns.
- Organize our thoughts and prepare messages that address those questions and concerns.
- Develop key messages and supporting messages.
- Place these messages into a framework that is clear, concise, accurate, transparent, and accessible.
- Encourage an open dialogue about these messages inside and outside the organization.
- Deliver a user-friendly guide to the messages for anyone who represents the organization to stakeholders or the news media.
- Make certain the organization's messages are accurate, consistent, and effective.
- Assure that the organization speaks with one voice. (For a dissenting view on this final point, read Peter Sandman's 2006 column "Speak with One Voice": Why I Disagree," which is available on his web site, psandman.com.)

The language of this handbook

Before we get started, let's establish some key definitions:

- A **risk** is the sum of hazard and outrage.
- **Hazard** is the estimated threat that a risk poses to life, health, and property as determined by subject-matter experts.
- **Outrage** is a community's response to the risk; it is all the things that laypeople worry about that the experts consider irrelevant.
- A **stakeholder** is anyone who cares about a particular risk issue.
- An **outraged stakeholder** is anyone who is angry, upset, or fearful about a risk.
- A **community** is a group of stakeholders who share common values or interests.
- An **organization** is any corporation, company, partnership, institute, collaboration, or agency in the public or private sectors.
- A **risk controversy** is any high-stress situation that brings hazard and outrage into a public conflict between an organization and a community of outraged stakeholders. This includes an outbreak of foodborne illness.
- A **message map** is a tool designed to help an organization communicate effectively with its stakeholders during a risk controversy.

Part I: High-Stress Communication for Foodborne Outbreaks and Recalls

Section 1: Fundamentals of high-stress communication

In this section, we will explore the established basics of how to communicate effectively with stakeholders when they are upset or angry. This section takes about twelve minutes to read.

Most of us understand how communication works between people when their emotional stress is low. However, the rules of communication change drastically when stakeholders are subjected to the high stress of a risk controversy. Researchers in risk communication have boiled these rules down to five principles:

Principle 1: When under stress, people tend to lose at least some of their ability to comprehend, accept, or recall information.

Risk communicators call this the Mental Noise Theory. "Research shows that mental noise can reduce a person's ability to process information by more than 80 percent," risk communications researcher Vincent T. Covello says (Covello, Minamyer and Clayton, 2007). "This is mostly due to trauma and a heightened emotional state during a crisis."

In the traditional low-stress model, communication begins with a sender who transmits a message to a receiver via a channel. For example, if I am talking to you, then I (the sender) am sending a message to you (the receiver) through the air between us (the channel). If you are reading The New York Times, then the reporter (sender) is sending a message to you (the receiver) via newsprint (the channel).

Sometimes, a message is distorted by noise. For example, if you are watching television during a thunderstorm, the signal may cut in and out. This "noise" interferes with the message that the network (the sender) is attempting to send to you (the receiver).

However, noise is not always physical. Sometimes noise is mental.

Let's say that I want to send a message to you. I choose to do this in person, verbally. If I present my message in a calm tone, and I am able to attract your interest in what I have to say, then odds are good that you will receive this message with at least a moderate degree of accuracy.

However, if I put a loaded gun to your head while I deliver my message, what are the odds that you will accurately remember my message? Poor, at best. That's because the loaded gun will probably raise your stress levels and thus create "mental noise" that interferes with your brain's ability to comprehend what I'm saying. In essence, you have lost your capacity to trust me or my message.

High stress causes stakeholders to lose much of their ability to process complex messages. The mental noise created by the stress interferes with comprehension of messages; the higher the stress, the lower the comprehension. According to Covello's research, here's what we can expect from our audiences in low vs. high stress situations (see Fig. 1):

People under LOW STRESS	People under HIGH STRESS
Can process an average rate of seven bits of data (such as a phone number).	Can process an average rate of three bits of data.
Will process data in linear order (as in: one, two, three, etc.)	Will process data in terms of what they hear first and what they hear last.
Can process information at around the eighth-grade level.	Will process at one to four grades lower than the eighth grade.

(Fig. 1) Sources: Covello (2003); NCFPD (2007; 2016)

As a result, in any high-stress situation, our messages must be simple. They must be "dumbed down" to their most fundamental levels. Why? Because if we present a complex message to an audience that is under high levels of stress, our message will get lost in the mental noise. Indeed, if our subject-matter experts complain, "You are oversimplifying the message," then we probably are on the right track.

Principle 2: People under high stress tend to focus their attention less on the positive and more on the negative.

There's a lopsided relationship between how people under stress react to good news and to bad news, as well as to positive words and to negative words. Covello calls this the Negative Dominance Theory, which is based on research that shows one negative word or message is roughly equal to three positive words or messages.

When delivering bad news, an organization should plan to deliver three positive messages for every negative message. This is not to say that the organization should seek to over-reassure its stakeholders about a given risk controversy; as we shall see during our discussion of outrage management, over-reassurance tends to make upset stakeholders even more upset. This principle does mean the organization should emphasize the positive whenever doing so is honest and forthright. This can be a difficult line to walk.

Principle 3: People under high stress place far more value on empathy than expertise.

In high-stress situation, stakeholders want to know that our organization cares about their outrage, Covello says. Only then will they listen to what we know. Covello calls this the Trust Determination Model. We have to be willing to listen to their concerns. We have to be willing to express our empathy. If we fail to meet this standard, we lose their trust and their willingness to heed our advice.

In a low-stress situation, Covello says, the receiver's trust in the sender's message is based largely on the sender's competence and expertise (2003). But when the stress is increased (such as during an outbreak of foodborne illness), the receiver's trust in the sender's message is based on how the receiver perceives the sender's:

- Listening, caring and empathy (50 percent).
- Honesty and openness (15 to 20 percent).
- Competence and expertise (15 to 20 percent).
- Dedication and commitment (15 to 20 percent).

Now here's the really bad news, according to Covello: During a high-stress situation, the sender of a risk message has roughly thirty seconds to establish trust with the receiver.

As senders, if we fail to demonstrate listening, caring, and empathy in the time it takes to watch a television commercial, we're in trouble.

This contradicts traditional public relations, which says we should send in the calm, cool, rational expert to speak to the public: a lawyer, an official spokesperson, or a scientist. In a high-stress situation, our audience will not invest its trust in a spokesperson based on competence and expertise. The public is looking for someone who can communicate simply and clearly with candor and empathy.

Principle 4: People under high stress tend to trust experts and other authorities who acknowledge the situation's uncertainty.

Stakeholders will cast a jaundiced eye on messages that are overly reassuring, risk communication consultant Peter M. Sandman says (1993). Over-confidence tends to provoke acrimony with stakeholders and to destroy our organization's credibility.

Instead, we must learn to talk about risk honestly and forthrightly. We should be ready to clearly distinguish between what we know, what we think we know, and we do not yet know. This means we must often talk to stakeholders about the risk before we are ready to talk about it. "If you're going to communicate about risk, you will need the courage to talk when your information is uncertain," Sandman and psychiatrist Jody Lanard write in a co-authored column about the relationship between risk, communication, and uncertainty (2011, Aug. 14). "And you will need the skill to express uncertainty in ways that guide your audience's decisions and minimize the cost (to you and your audience both) if you turn out mistaken. The communication of uncertainty is a central risk communication capability."

Principle 5: People who are under high stress tend to become far more concerned with their outrage than with any hazard.

During a risk controversy, the subject-matter experts want to talk about the potential for death and injury; meanwhile, the non-experts want to talk about their anger or their fear, Covello and Sandman say (2001). This dynamic tends to generate rancor between stakeholders and organizations in a high-stress situations. It's important to understand why.

As early as 1993, psychology professor Paul Slovic identified two specific trends in how American society was dealing with the perception and management of risk.

First, he noted, as life in the United States has grown healthier and safer since the 1970s, the American public has become more concerned with the risks that may affect its health and safety: "We have come to perceive ourselves as increasingly vulnerable to life's hazards and to believe that our land, air, and water are more contaminated by toxic substances than ever before."

Second, he says, the assessment and management of these risks has become a greater source of contention between the technical experts in those risks and the non-expert public: "Polarized views, controversy, and overt conflicts have become more pervasive."

In frustration, scientists and industrialists often scold the non-expert public for behaving in ways that may appear irrational or ignorant, Slovic says. However, research demonstrates that such criticism is misplaced. The research shows that the non-experts' reactions to risk are often guided by a general sensitivity to technical, social, and psychological qualities of a given hazard that are missing from the technical models. These qualities may include a lack of certainty, a lack of control, a lack of fairness, or just an overall sense of dread (Slovic, 2000).

Stakeholders and experts rarely have similar concerns about a given risk. With all of that in mind, Covello and Sandman say (2001), suppose we generated a long list of risks, and then asked a group of technical experts to rank those risks from the most dangerous to the least dangerous. Next, let's say we took that same list and conducted a survey of non-experts, asking them to rank those same risks from the most upsetting to the least upsetting.

If we compare those two versions of the list, we will find a statistical correlation of about 0.2.

"There is virtually no correlation between the ranking of hazards according to statistics on expected annual mortality and the ranking of the same hazards by how upsetting they are," Covello and Sandman say. "There are many risks that make people furious even though they cause little harm – and others that kill many, but without making anybody mad."

By taking this insight to its logical conclusion, Sandman arrived at a game-changing realization. Most technical experts consider "risk" to be synonymous with "hazard"; however, Sandman says (1993), the 0.2 correlation indicates that non-experts are clearly looking at "risk" very differently.

Recognizing this, Sandman redefined risk. He took what the technical experts call "risk" – that is, anything that presents a tangible threat to life, health, safety or property – and renamed it "hazard." Then, he took what the non-experts call "risk" – that is, anything that communities tend to find upsetting – and re-named it "outrage." Sandman then created a formula to express the overall concept: Risk = Hazard + Outrage.

"The implication for those who are communicating risk (whether in care, consensus, or crisis communication) is that a presentation of the technical facts will not necessarily give most audiences the information they want," Lundgren and McMakin say (2013). "Indeed, the audience will probably not ever listen to those facts until their concerns and feelings have been addressed."

Sandman (1993) recognizes twelve primary factors that tend to trigger outrage among communities of non-experts. He frames the twelve primary factors with the question, "Is it X or is it Y?" If the answer is "Y," then the risk is likely to include high outrage:

1. Voluntary or coerced? When a community believes it has no real choice in accepting a risk, it tends to become outraged.
2. Natural or industrial? A community can accept an act of God far more readily than a man-made threat.
3. Familiar or exotic? If the threat is new to a community's experience, then it is more likely to provoke outrage.
4. Not memorable or memorable? Arguments tend to provoke outrage when they take the form of easily recalled images, metaphors, icons, slogans, or nicknames.
5. Not dreaded or dreaded? A feeling of disgust or fear will tend to provoke outrage. (Sandman sometimes refers to this as the Yuck Factor.)
6. Chronic or catastrophic? If the perceived hazard outweighs any perceived benefit, then people tend to become outraged. (Sandman uses the example of planes vs. automobiles. Cars kill far more people than planes do, but far more people are scared of flying than they are of driving.)
7. Knowable or unknowable? If a perceived hazard exists beyond the perception of the five human senses, then it tends to trigger outrage.
8. Controlled by me or controlled by others? When a community is offered little or no control over a risk, it tends to become outraged.
9. Fair or unfair? When a community shoulders most of the risk, but someone else gets all or most of the benefits, the community will tend to become outraged.
10. Morally irrelevant or morally relevant? If a community can clearly identify a moral issue in the context of the risk, it tends to become outraged

11. Trustworthy or untrustworthy? When the perceived source of a risk is deceitful or dishonest, the community tends to become outraged.
12. Responsive or unresponsive? When the perceived source of a risk fails to respond in a manner the community considers appropriate or effective, then the community tends to become outraged.

Another way to think of these factors, Sandman says (2011), is to divide them into two categories: "safe" and "risky" (Fig. 2). The first item in each row (that is, voluntary, natural, familiar, etc.) represents a "safe" factor when it comes to outrage. These are factors that will leave folks calm, Sandman says, even if it kills them. Each of the second items (that is, coerced, industrial, exotic, etc.) represents a "risky" factor. These are factors that tend to upset people even if they pose no actual threat to their well-being.

Any of these twelve factors may become dominant in a controversy. However, Sandman says (2011), the three factors that most frequently become dominant are a lack of control, a lack of trust, and a lack of response.

Primary factors of outrage	
"Safe"	**"Risky"**
Voluntary	Coerced
Natural	Industrial
Familiar	Exotic
Not memorable	Memorable
Not dreaded	Dreaded
Chronic	Catastrophic
Knowable	Unknowable
Individually controlled	Controlled by others
Fair	Unfair
Morally irrelevant	Morally relevant
Trustworthy sources	Untrustworthy sources
Responsive process	Unresponsive process

(Fig. 2) Source: Sandman (1993)

In addition to the twelve primary factors, Sandman (1993) identifies eight secondary factors.

1. Vulnerable populations: The public is more likely to become outraged if a risk affects the elderly, the very young, the sick, the poor, and the otherwise helpless.
2. Delayed vs. immediate effects: A risk that lies in wait to strike is more likely to trigger outrage than will an immediate threat.

3. Effect on future generations: Stakeholders want to know how a risk might harm their great, great, great grandchildren.
4. Identifiability of the victim: Large numbers of faceless victims will trigger less outrage than will a single, easily recognizable victim.
5. Reduction of risk: Stakeholders want to eliminate the risk, not merely reduce it, whenever possible.
6. Risk-benefit ratio: Stakeholders in general are willing to look at the big picture. If their sacrifice makes sense, they may accept it. If not, watch out.
7. Media attention: The media cannot cause stakeholders to become outraged, but they can amplify existing outrage.
8. Opportunity for collective action: Stakeholders are far more likely to become outraged if they can identify the chance for effective, collective action. For example, calling a neighborhood meeting or marching on city hall.

It is vital to understand that Sandman (2011) considers each of these factors to be a component of risk, and not a misperception of risk. Indeed, he says, this is his "explicit argument," that outrage is just as real and just as measurable as any hazard. "Social scientists can tell you to within three decimal places the impact of most controversial risks on people's opinions; no one can tell you to within three decimal places their impact on people's health," Sandman says. "So if we are going to get into a competition over which of the two is science, I am in grave danger of winning (1993)."

Section 2: Understanding the foodborne risk controversy

Now we will examine the specific relationships between foodborne illnesses, the risk controversies they can spark, and the strategies of outrage management that organizations may employ to help upset stakeholders cope with their fear and anger. This section will take about ten minutes to read.

What is a foodborne risk controversy? For your organization, a foodborne risk controversy is any outbreak of foodborne illness that is or could be blamed on a product your company manufactures, markets, or distributes. Primarily, this means stakeholders are blaming our company (rightly or wrongly) for distributing a product that is infecting consumers with a foodborne pathogen.

A comprehensive list of foodborne diseases is beyond the scope of this book. By itself, the list of identified foodborne diseases tops more than 250 entries (CDC, 2017). What follows is a list of the most common foodborne risks found in the United States as identified by the Centers for Disease Control and Prevention (CDC).

It's not necessary to memorize every item on this list. Rather, you should identify the risks most commonly associated with your company's product line, become familiar with those risks, and keep this list (or a more comprehensive list available from the federal government or your industry association) at hand in case of an outbreak. Official lists compiled by the CDC are available online at /www.cdc.gov/foodsafety/foodborne-germs.html.

Salmonella is a bacterium that is often found in the intestines of birds, reptiles and mammals. It spreads to humans through foods that come from animals, such as meat, milk and eggs. Symptoms include fever, diarrhea and abdominal cramps. In people with poor health or weak immune systems, the disease can invade the bloodstream and cause life-threatening infections.

E. coli O157:H7 is a bacterial pathogen found in cattle and other cloven-hoof livestock. Humans acquire the disease by consuming food or water contaminated with microscopic amounts of livestock feces. Symptoms include severe and bloody diarrhea, painful abdominal cramps, but little fever. In less than five percent of all cases, a form of kidney failure known as hemolytic uremic syndrome (HUS) can develop several weeks after the initial symptoms. Symptoms of HUS include temporary anemia, profuse bleeding, and kidney failure.

Campylobacter is a bacterial pathogen that lives in the intestines of healthy birds and is found on most raw poultry meat. It causes fever, diarrhea, and abdominal cramps. Indeed, it is the most common bacterial cause of diarrhea in the world. The most frequent cause of the disease in humans is eating undercooked chicken or other food that has been contaminated with juices dripping from raw chicken.

Calicivirus, or Norwalk-like virus, causes an acute gastrointestinal illness, usually with more vomiting than diarrhea. Symptoms usually end within two days. Unlike many foodborne pathogens, Norwalk-like viruses spread primarily from one infected person to another. "Infected kitchen workers can contaminate a salad or sandwich as they prepare it, if they have the virus on their hands," the CDC says. "Infected fishermen have contaminated oysters as they harvested them."

Other foodborne diseases are caused by a toxin produced by a microbe within the food. The bacterium **Staphylococcus aureus**, for example, may produce a toxin that causes intense vomiting, while clostridium botulinum produces a powerful paralytic toxin in foods that leads to botulism, which is rare but deadly. "These toxins can produce illness even if the microbes that produced them are no longer there," according to the CDC.

Check with your industry association and see if you can get a chart or other document that describes the most likely foodborne pathogens for your company's products. In addition, develop a list of the man-made toxins and poisonous chemicals that may cause foodborne illness through your product line. This list should include pesticides and other poisons, as well as naturally occurring substances that may be used to prepare products.

Try to identify anything (natural or artificial) that may, under the right circumstances, cause your food products to make people sick. Don't wait for your in-house experts to brief you during a risk controversy. Have a working knowledge of each hazard well before any outbreak occurs.

Hazard, outrage, and the foodborne outbreak

Earlier, we discussed a model championed by Peter M. Sandman, one of the nation's top practitioners, consultants, and theorists in the management of public outrage: Risk = Hazard + Outrage. Let's review that concept, and then apply it to outbreaks of foodborne illness and similar farm-to-fork issues.

In any situation that involves risk, there are two components. One is hazard, the actual threat to the public's well being. The other is outrage, the stakeholders' perception of the hazard and the threat it poses.

The experts (scientists and engineers, for example) tend to focus on hazard only. As far as they are concerned, risk equals hazard—and they get frustrated when stakeholders fail to recognize this.

Stakeholders tend to focus on their outrage: their perception of the hazard. Stakeholders get frustrated with the experts because the experts often fail to look beyond the facts and acknowledge the emotions.

Here's a simple example:

Let's say an outbreak of salmonella is blamed on products from Chicken Little Farms. The experts at Chicken Little tell stakeholders through the company's media relations team: "You have nothing to fear from our chicken as long as you cook the meat well enough to kill the salmonella bacteria." But angry stakeholders want to know, "Why the hell are there salmonella bacteria in our chicken?"

Neither side is wrong. The scientists are talking about the hazard. The stakeholders are talking about their outrage. The scientists are focusing on the facts, but the stakeholders are focusing on their emotional response. As Sandman says, "The risks that kill people and the risks that upset them are completely different (1993)."

Outrage management emphasizes managing or mitigating the stakeholders' fear or anger. It attempts to figure out what makes the public anxious or angry about a specific hazard — in this case, foodborne pathogens or contamination — then seeks to reduce outrage among stakeholders.

In this way, outrage management helps stakeholders to make better, more effective choices in response to a hazard; it also helps to mitigate the damage done to the target of stakeholder outrage. During a foodborne outbreak, that outrage usually focuses on the source of the outbreak. (In this case, that's Chicken Little Farms.)

Americans expect their food to be clean and safe. And they get very upset when they find out that our food products are putting them and their families at risk. This goes beyond the facts and straight to fear:

- "Am I in danger?"
- "Is my family in danger?"
- "What can I do about it?"
- "Why did it happen in the first place?"
- "Will it happen again?"
- "Who should be punished for letting this happen?

When an outbreak of foodborne disease is blamed on our company's product, we must answer these questions quickly and accurately, and in a way that acknowledges and addresses both fear and blame.

If we fail, we are in trouble.

From the moment we become aware of an outbreak of foodborne illness that involves one of our products, we need to start working toward an accurate answer to this question: "How much public outrage is this hazard likely to generate?"

Let's start out with a simple scenario.

You are the CEO for a meat packing plant. The news media have identified your frozen meat patties as the sources for at least thirty illnesses due to E. coli. The USDA and the FDA, so far, are silent on the issue.

You summon your in-house experts. These are the folks who are in charge of understanding the scientific and technical side of food safety. They tell you:

- The E. coli contamination is not a hazard if the public thoroughly cooks the patties.
- The patties that contain the E. coli are most likely already out of the supermarkets and have either been consumed, trashed, or frozen at home.
- Any recall will bring back far more uninfected meat than infected meat.
- A recall is a waste of time from a hazard perspective.

Meanwhile, your lawyer tells you: Until the USDA and FDA point the finger at you, the news media are simply speculating, so don't open your mouth.

OK, so your experts tell you that the hazard is low. And your lawyer tells you your liability is low, at least for now.

Is this a risk controversy?

You bet it is. And here's why.

Outbreaks of foodborne illness are newsworthy. It's a no-brainer for any journalist. Folks are getting sick and the cause is a food product. The only question is: Who's to blame? And if the news media (or the state regulators, or the federal regulators, or an activist group) point to your product as the culprit, you have a big, big problem.

News of foodborne illness is guaranteed to stir up pubic anxiety. It causes customers to question your product. It causes shareholders to question the value of your stock. It puts your employees on the defensive at home and in the community. It causes lenders and suppliers to question your long-term viability. It causes your board of directors to make phone calls to you in the middle of the night asking you, "What the hell are you doing about this? And don't you dare tell me 'nothing.'"

It doesn't matter that our experts say, "There is no hazard." It doesn't matter that our attorney says, "There is no liability." We are in trouble. And we'd better start doing something about it. We had better get to work on reducing the public's outrage, and we'd better start now.

The good news is that outrage among stakeholders will tend to follow a fairly predictable seven-step path:

1. Catalyst: An event or a rumor sparks some level of outrage within a community of stakeholders by offending that community's safety or values.
2. Cause: The community identifies the cause of the offense.
3. Blame: The community assigns blame for the offense.
4. Meme: The outrage evolves into a contagious story that can easily pass from person to person. The basic structure of this story is, "The villain is doing X to the victim." Example: "Cadbury is selling tainted candy to our children." Or, "Taco Bell is selling poisoned beef to its customers."
5. Distribution: The outrage spreads as a story through the community by word of mouth or social media.
6. Amplification: The outrage story is picked up and spread by news media or activists.
7. Propagation: The outrage spreads to stakeholders as well as to the public at-large. The result is often an intense scorn that can affect the ability of the organization to function normally.

What separates foodborne outbreaks from many other risk controversies is the sheer speed by which the outrage can spread. Most outrages take time to develop as the offended community builds alliances with activists and media to spread its story of outrage to the masses. But a suspected outbreak of foodborne illness is by definition news. It affects public health. It is considered an imminent threat. It can hurt anyone, young or old, rich or poor. For the journalist, this is the kind of story you don't have to explain to the editors. It's like a fatal car wreck or a destructive tornado or a hazardous waste spill. It is news by reflex. It is news by default.

Thus, if a single reliable authority (a government official, a health expert, a scientist, even the leader of an activist group) can identify an outbreak of foodborne disease, the news media will not hesitate to move the issue to center stage.

Section 3: Understanding stakeholder outrage

In this section, we will gain a better understanding of outrage and how it can affect our ability to communicate effectively with stakeholders. This section takes about six minutes to read.

Everything we do involves some level of risk. Walking across a street. Chewing a stick of gum. Eating food with a spork. There is no such thing as zero risk. So, to better understand outrage, we require a deeper understanding of how humans perceive risk, how that perception changes with new information, and how that can quickly move stakeholders from anxiety to anger.

In its training programs on risk communication, the Food Protection and Defense Institute at the University of Minnesota uses the example of a fictional new drug it calls "U-phoria" (2007)

Imagine you are in the training class. First, the trainer gives you some background on the drug:

- A leading research university created U-phoria.
- It took sixteen years to develop the drug.
- U-phoria provides the user with a boost in short-term memory.
- It also provides a "pleasant feeling" during times of stress; the feeling lasts for twenty-four to thirty-six hours.
- The drug has undergone multiple trials that suggest potential side effects that are both short-term and long-term.

Next, the trainer allows you and your classmates to ask any question you desire. Every question receives a positive answer. The cost is low. The pill is readily available. The FDA has approved it.

The only question that draws a negative response is, "What are the side effects?" And the answer to that question is: "Severe diarrhea lasting up to 24 hours."

Finally, the trainer asks you and the rest of your class to stand. The trainer says: Remain standing if you would be willing to take the U-phoria pill even if the odds of developing severe diarrhea are:

- 1 in a billion?
- 1 in a million?
- 1 in a hundred thousand?
- 1 in a thousand?
- 1 in 10?
- An absolute certainty; every dose results in severe diarrhea?

The point is: The perception of risk varies with the individual who is considering the risk.

At what point would you sit down?

Peter Sandman (1993) offers another excellent example of risk perception, but this one is tied more closely to the concept of public outrage: Would you send your child to a dentist that you know is HIV-positive?

The probability of contracting HIV from your dentist is less than one in 400,000, Sandman says. Those odds could obviously worsen if your dentist actually has HIV. But if an infected dentist takes proper precautions, the odds remain about the same.

Still not interested in sending your child to see the infected dentist?

What if I told you that the odds of your child contracting HIV from an infected dentist (using proper precautions) are significantly less than their odds of dying from (National Safety Council, 2017):

- Heart disease or cancer (one in seven).
- A motor vehicle accident (one in 114).
- An assault with a firearm (one in 370).
- Firearms discharge (one in 6,905).
- Contact with a sharp object (one in 38,174).
- Cataclysmic storm (one in 66,335).
- Dog attack (one in 147,717).
- Legal execution (one in 119,912).

Understand what this means: Your children are far more likely to die by legal execution than they are to contract HIV from an HIV-infected dentist who takes reasonable precautions. And given that a dentist who is known to have HIV is likely to charge fees that are far less than those of other dentists, you're ready to make that appointment for your kid. Right?

No? Why is that?

The answer is that your personal perception of risk has less to do with the actual hazard (one in 400,000) than with your outrage.

Instead of making your decision based purely on the odds (which is how most organizations decide whether risk is high or low), you are likely making your choice based on one or more of these factors:

- Your dread of AIDS.
- Your distrust of the dentist.
- The loss of control you feel when you send your child to sit in the dentist's chair.
- The horror that a simple dental procedure could cost your child's health.
- Your abhorrence of the lifestyle that may have led the dentist to contract HIV.

When it comes to the personal perception of any risk, the hazard data is simply not enough. Until you accept this, your odds of making the right choice for your company's primary strategy during an outbreak of a foodborne illness are approximately zero.

What forms our risk perception?

There are four factors that shape our perception of risk, according to the Food Protection and Defense Institute (2007):

- Threat: What is the thing that can go wrong?
- Probability: What is the likelihood of the hazard actually happening?
- Consequence: What are the implications of the hazards to the individual as well as the community?
- Value: What do we lose if we fail to take the chance, and how important is that thing to us?

To illustrate this, let's go back to the example of the imaginary drug U-phoria:

- Threat: Severe diarrhea.
- Probability: 1 in 100.
- Consequence: Dehydration, embarrassment, lack of mobility.
- Value: Memory boost and a feeling of well-being.

Now let's consider these factors in light of Sandman's model: Risk = Hazard + Outrage.

Threat and probability fall on the hazard side of this equation. This is also known as the "thinking" or "logic" side. It focuses on the danger and the likelihood of the danger occurring. This is where the scientists, the engineers, and the other subject-matter experts tend to dwell.

Consequence and value fall on the outrage side of the equation. This is also known as the "feeling" or "emotion" side. It focuses on anger, fear, anxiety, revulsion, and other high-impact emotions. During an outbreak of foodborne illness, this is where stakeholders tend to dwell.

All of this information fits neatly into this table (Fig. 3):

Experts Interested in hazard | Respond with logic	Stakeholders Interested in outrage | Respond with emotion
Threat	Consequence
Probability	Value

(Fig. 3) Source: Food Protection and Defense Institute (2007)

Your experts are interested in the logic-based factors of threat and probability on the left side of the table. They "know." They "think." But stakeholders are interested in the emotion-based factors of consequence and value. This is the right side of the table. They "feel." They "believe." And this is exactly how companies get crossways with stakeholders during outbreaks of foodborne illness. They talk about facts when stakeholders want to feel emotions. They speak of threat and probability when they should speak of consequence and value.

The result is that stakeholders become more and more outraged, and the experts become more and more frustrated. Now here are two very important points. First, neither the experts nor the stakeholders are wrong. They are simply speaking different languages. Second, the experts are the authorities on hazard. But stakeholders are always the authority on outrage. If they are outraged, there is a good reason, and that reason has almost nothing to do with the hazard.

Savvy practitioners of outrage management understand these points; they learn to convey the experts' facts in ways that acknowledge and address stakeholder outrage. When they do, two amazing things generally occur. First, stakeholder outrage will tend to decrease. Second, the ability among stakeholders to absorb useful information and respond to the hazard will tend to improve. When that happens, actual communication can begin between your company and your stakeholders.

Section 4: Stakeholder outrage and the foodborne risk controversy

In this section, we look at the factors that contribute to stakeholder outrage and then examine how those factors come into play during an outbreak of foodborne illness. This section takes about fifteen minutes to read.

As we discussed earlier, Peter Sandman (1993) frames the twelve primary causes as the question "Is it X or is it Y?" If the answer is "Y," then the risk is likely to include high outrage. Here's a chart summarizing the twelve primary factors (Fig. 4.):

Is it X?	Or Y?	Indications
Voluntary	Coerced	The public believes it has no real choice.
Natural	Industrial	The public can accept an act of God far more readily than a man-made threat.
Familiar	Exotic	If the threat is new to the public, then it is more likely to provoke outrage.
Not memorable	Memorable	Arguments provoke outrage when they take the forms of images, metaphors, icons, slogans, or nicknames.
Not dreaded	Dreaded	Disgust or fear can provoke outrage.
Chronic	Catastrophic	The perceived risk outweighs any perceived benefit.
Knowable	Unknowable	The threat is beyond the public's perception.
Controlled by me	Controlled by others	The public is offered little or no control over the risk.
Fair	Unfair	The public takes the risk, but someone else gets the benefits.
Morally irrelevant	Morally relevant	The public can clearly identify a moral issue.
Trustworthy	Untrustworthy	The source of the risk is deceitful or dishonest.
Responsive	Unresponsive	The public is left out of the decision-making process.

(Fig. 4) Source: Sandman (1993)

Those are the factors that trigger risk controversies. Let's now apply each to foodborne illness (Fig. 5):

Primary factors	Foodborne disease and contamination
Coerced	Coercion doesn't apply. No one is going to force the public to eat contaminated food.
Industrial	All food products include the human element at some point in production or distribution.
Exotic	The public will never consider salmonella or E. coli as familiar.
Memorable	When the news media tell you that eating a certain food product may cause you to vomit, sweat, shake, enter a coma, or die … you probably will remember.
Dreaded	People dread nausea, convulsions, fever, diarrhea and other symptoms of foodborne disease.
Catastrophic	The risk of illness or death clearly outweighs any benefits.
Unknowable	The public cannot see, hear or touch, and often cannot taste or smell, foodborne disease.
Controlled by others	If the public lacks the information to mitigate foodborne disease, it lacks control over the risk.
Unfair	The company takes the profits from contaminated food while passing the risk of illness to the public.
Morally relevant	Contaminated food may cause sickness and death.
Untrustworthy	The company may lie about a hazard, or attempt to hide it.
Unresponsive	The company may ignore the public or fail to ask the public to participate in mitigating the risk.

(Fig. 5.)

As you can see from the previous chart, outbreaks of foodborne illness touch upon eleven of Peter Sandman's twelve primary factors of outrage. To this, Sandman adds eight secondary factors. These often lead to stakeholder outrage, but not as often as the twelve primary components (Fig. 6):

Secondary causes	Indications
Vulnerable populations	The public is more likely to become angry if the risk affects the elderly, the very young, the sick, the poor and the otherwise helpless.
Delayed vs. immediate effects	A risk that lies in wait to strike at us is more likely to trigger outrage than an immediate threat.
Effects on future generations	The public wants to know: Will this harm our great, great, great, great grandchildren?
Identifiability of the victim	Statistical victims will trigger less outrage than will a single, easily recognizable victim.
Reduction of risk	The public wants to eliminate the risk, not merely reduce it.
Risk-benefit ratio	A community gets angry when its sacrifice outweighs any overall benefit to society.
Media attention	The media cannot cause outrage, but it can amplify existing outrage.
Opportunity for collective activism	If the public can take an effective, collective action against source of a threat to a community, it usually will.

(Fig. 6) Source: Sandman (1993)

Now let's put each of these secondary causes against foodborne risks (Fig. 7.):

Secondary causes	Foodborne disease and contamination
Vulnerable populations	A foodborne disease is especially egregious when it shows up in products made specifically for babies, children, or the elderly.
Delayed vs. immediate effects	Suspense creates outrage. Foodborne outbreaks are generally spread over several months, and thus may build suspense.
Effects on future generations	This hot button does not apply, since foodborne illness is short term and has few if any implications for the future.
Identifiably of the victim	If the news media talk about seven deaths and twenty-three illnesses in fourteen states, that's a statistic. If they talk about the father of three who died from a poisoned peanut butter sandwich, that's an outrage.
Reduction of risk	It's not enough to cut back on the number of contaminated candy bars you produce. You have to find the problem and wipe it out.
Risk-benefit ratio	Is there any benefit to a taco swimming with E. coli bacteria?
Media attention	Any outbreak of a foodborne illness is by definition news, and media are likely to jump on it.
Opportunity for collective activism	The most effective "collective action" is for stakeholders to stop buying your product and to encourage others to do the same.

(Fig. 7)

As you can see from the charts, foodborne illness offers an almost-perfect storm, touching on at least eighteen of the factors that can trigger stakeholder outrage. Much of this boils down to what Peter Sandman calls the Yuck Factor (Sandman and Lanard, 2004). There's something repugnant about eating or drinking anything that is contaminated. For example, the thought of serving your children chocolate that contains salmonella can make the skin crawl. It's not a logical response. It's a visceral, emotional reaction. It comes from the gut, not the brain.

Helping your stakeholders deal with this real, reasonable, and understandable reaction is the major task of outrage management in the farm-to-fork environment. Let's say you are the CEO for Topps Meat Company in September 2007. The USDA has just fingered your company as the culprit for twenty-six illnesses in eight states from an E. coli outbreak that spread through frozen hamburger patties. You fear that the government may force you to recall millions of pounds of hamburger patties.

Your experts tell you, "Hey, just look at the statistics. We're talking about only twenty-six reports of illness spread across eight states over three months. Is that an 'outbreak?' And there have been no deaths, just a few tummy aches. If the patties are cooked properly, there is nothing to fear. One more thing: Any infected patties are now out of the stores. They've been eaten, discarded, or are stored in home freezers. A recall will bring back only the patties we know are uninfected."

The experts declare the hazard officially low. But you know the experts are rarely authorities on stakeholder outrage. And you sense a growing anger out there in the public that is driving the USDA to take action. Let's put this situation on the factors-of-outrage chart and see if we can identify some possible sources of stakeholder outrage (Fig. 8):

Hazard = E. coli in beef patties	Apply the outrage component to the hazard
Coerced	(Coercion does not apply)
Industrial	The presence of the E. coli is a direct result of the meatpacking process, and is due to badly maintained equipment.
Exotic	"E. coli? What the hell is E. coli? And why is it my hamburger?"
Memorable	E. coli consistently ranks among the most dangerous foodborne diseases.
Dreaded	If it doesn't kill you, E. coli will make you miserable with severe and bloody diarrhea with painful abdominal cramps.
Catastrophic	E. coli, if untreated, can lead to kidney failure.
Unknowable	You can't see it. You can't smell it. You can't taste it.
Controlled by others	"I have no idea which box of meat to trust, because Topps has failed to tell me which ones to discard."
Unfair	"Topps takes the profits, but the public takes the risks."
Morally relevant	It is a moral outrage to offer tainted food to the public and fail to address the risk when it is detected.
Untrustworthy	"Topps failed to alert us until the USDA forced it to tell the truth. Why should we trust Topps now?"
Unresponsive	"We've asked Topps to publicly identify the brands to avoid. And they have ignored us."
Vulnerable populations	Children love hamburgers.
Delayed effects	E. coli can take several days to affect your health.
Effects on future generations	(A foodborne outbreak has no effect on future generations.)
Identifiability of the victim	Here is Pete. He ate a Topps meat patty and spent the next four months in a hospital after a kidney transplant.
Reduction of risk	It's not enough to reduce the percentage of E. coli in your meat. You must eliminate it.

Risk-benefit ratio	"There is no benefit to playing Russian roulette with my food."
Media attention	Foodborne illness is ALWAYS news.
Opportunity for collective activism	"Hey, why don't we create an I Hate Topps website and broadcast our outrage around the world?"
Delayed effects	E. coli can take several days to affect your health.

(Fig 8)

Compounding all this is Sandman's Yuck Factor: "The E. coli came from cow feces that fell into my food? Yuck!"

Let's assume that only two or three of the factors are in play. That's more than enough to trigger high outrage, the sort that drives consumer boycotts, investor sell-offs, and government action. If you are the CEO of Topps Meat Company, you now know that you must take action to mitigate the coming public outrage if your company is to survive.

Section 5: The primary strategy — acknowledge and improve

In this section, we will discuss the primary strategy for managing stakeholder outrage during a risk controversy. This section takes about eight minutes to read.

As managers of stakeholder outrage during a foodborne risk controversy, our task is to craft the risk messages and to take the effective actions that are most likely to calm that outrage. What we need is a strategy that will lead us to consistently make the right choices, especially when under pressure. For most folks, "strategy" is at best a vague concept that is often confused with "tactics." So let's start with a working definition. The best one I know comes from David H. McIntyre, former dean of faculty at the US National War College and now a lecturer and an authority on homeland security at the Bush School of Government and Public Service at Texas A&M University: "A successful strategy is a concept of cause and effect that will produce a result you are willing to accept — at a price you are willing to pay." With that in mind, let's think through the strategy of managing outrage during a foodborne outbreak.

So far in this handbook, we have established the following:

- A foodborne risk controversy can involve either a high hazard or a low hazard. In either case, the strategic focus must center on dealing with stakeholder response to the outbreak.
- An outbreak of foodborne illness may include as many as eighteen of the twenty factors that trigger stakeholder outrage.
- Foodborne outbreaks are inherently newsworthy; news of an outbreak will spread quickly to the general public through the news media and will frequently generate a significant level of stakeholder outrage.
- Stakeholders will focus their outrage on whomever they consider to be the source of the hazard.

Our strategic goal is to calm stakeholders to a manageable, constructive level. Why? Because calm stakeholders will probably take actions that are:

- More likely to protect them from any actual hazard.
- Less likely to expose them to unnecessary harm or loss.
- Less likely to cause unwarranted damage to our company, its reputation, or its products.

So what we need is a strategy that achieves the end of calming stakeholder outrage at a price we are willing to pay. Peter Sandman (2017) offers a strategy that fits the bill. During any risk controversy, he says, there are really only four ways to respond to our critics.

1. We can keep a low profile and hope the trouble goes away.
2. We can defend our company and make the case that our critics are wrong.
3. We can attack our critics by making the case that stakeholders should pay more attention to our critics' misdeeds and less to ours.

Each of these is far more likely to increase stakeholder outrage than to calm it. But we have a fourth option: We can employ a strategy Sandman calls "acknowledge and improve."

Let's start with the first part of the strategy: acknowledgement

One key to reducing public outrage whether the hazard is high or low, Sandman says (1993), is to acknowledge "all the bad news." This includes acknowledging that the risk is scary, that your company may not have responded quickly or well enough, or that you may not be able to eradicate the hazard. It also includes conceding that at least some of what your critics say is actually valid (Sandman, 2017).

"Acknowledging (the bad news) might feel terrible," Sandman says, "but it is in fact virtually cost-free. (Your lawyer's instinct will still be to advise you not to, but ask him or her to explain the problem with admitting something people already know and can easily prove.)"

Our antagonists – the activists, the tort lawyers, and the watchdog news media – will certainly acknowledge our faults. The smart strategic move is to steal their thunder.

"Make a list of the other side's strongest points – facts, arguments, emotions, images – and work them into your own communications," Sandman says. "Everything your audience already knows or feels, and everything your opposition is likely to find out and emphasize, belongs in your presentation."

Sandman compares stakeholder outrage to a seesaw. We're on one side; our stakeholders are on the other. We explain that the hazard is low and present the facts. But the stakeholders express their high outrage and demand that we acknowledge the validity of their emotions. The seesaw goes up and down, up and down, ad infinitum. Meanwhile, the seesaw is consuming time and energy we could apply to far more productive and profitable opportunities.

Only by moving toward the fulcrum of the seesaw, by acknowledging the outrage and its components, can we break the cycle. An intelligently run program of outrage management goes beyond simply telling stakeholders the bad news they already know. We should take the additional step of revealing bad news that has yet to become public. We must recognize that all of the bad news is likely to become public, especially if an activist, a journalist, or a community leader starts to study the data and to ask the right questions.

Withholding bad news (or misleading stakeholders in any way) will destroy our credibility. Credibility is the coin of the realm in any risk controversy. Without credibility, we have no chance of mitigating stakeholder outrage. "Far better to release (bad news) at the outset," Sandman says, "and earn credit for candor."

To achieve our end, that is to calm the public, we must acknowledge:

- The validity of stakeholder outrage.
- Our complicity in triggering that outrage (even when the hazard is low, or when we believe we played no part creating a high hazard).
- Our sincere remorse for having caused or contributed to their outrage.
- Our obligation to act in a transparent and trustworthy manner at all times.
- Our commitment to solving the perceived problem.
- Our willingness to let stakeholders help us fix the problem and repair the damage to their satisfaction.
- Our readiness to open the entire process to public scrutiny and measurement.

If we want to achieve our strategic end, we must avoid:

- Treating hazard as more important than outrage.
- Emphasizing facts over emotions.
- Regarding stakeholders as amateurs, troublemakers, or kooks. (Stakeholders are the final authority on outrage. If stakeholders are upset, there's a reason for it.)
- Evading our responsibility.

- Downplaying the hazard.
- Employing euphemisms.
- Hiding or ignoring the bad news.
- Closing the process to stakeholders.
- Ignoring the public's opinions, criticisms, or desires.
- Handling stakeholder outrage as a legal issue instead of risk communication issue.

Now let's consider the second part of the Sandman strategy: improvement.

Words are important. If we want to calm outrage among stakeholders, it is important to express our contrition for any role we play in an outbreak. But it is just as vital for us to take effective actions to end the outbreak and to address the harm that results from the outbreak, whether it's refunding the purchase price or taking care of sickened customers.

As we acknowledge bad news, we should explain how we plan to deal with that bad news. We may have solutions in hand or we may want to consult with stakeholders on the best approach to solving the problems created by a foodborne outbreak. We should present steady and effective progress every time we speak to stakeholders directly or through the news media.

We must acknowledge and improve, over and over again, until the outrage is calmed, the outbreak is under control, the food supply is safe, and stakeholders are dealt with fairly.

There is simply no substitute for effective action.

Section 6: How to deliver three types of news — the bad, the good, and the uncertain

In this section, we look at strategies for delivering updated information to stakeholders during a risk controversy. This section takes about nine minutes to read.

When we speak to the public during a foodborne outbreak that leads to a recall, we are delivering three kinds of news: bad, good, and uncertain. How we present this news can have a significant impact on how well journalists accept and deliver our messages. It can also affect how readily stakeholders accept our messages and how well they respond.

How to deliver bad news

What is bad news? It's not just news about the actual hazard. It's also the news that can raise stakeholder outrage. You have to treat both hazard and outrage seriously, especially if the hazard is low and the outrage is high.

Many companies attempt to avoid bad news. Or, at the very least, they try to bury it in good news. This is a mistake that is almost guaranteed to backfire. If there is bad news, you want to be first to the podium with it. And you don't want to sugarcoat it. During a foodborne outbreak, there is little stakeholders crave more than candor.

There are actually three kinds of bad news, according to Peter Sandman (2005):

- The bad news everyone already knows.
- The bad news everyone is going to eventually learn.
- The bad news you may be able to keep secret.

We get nowhere by ignoring the bad news everyone knows, he says. Indeed, our best strategy is to wallow in the bad news. We must do more than talk about the bad news until we are sick of it. We have to keep talking about it until everyone else (especially the news media) is sick of hearing about it. This is especially true of the information that stakeholders find the most outrageous and you find the most damaging. Talk it to death. We have nothing to lose. Everyone already knows about it.

Next is the information that stakeholders will most likely find out once a sharp reporter or activist or community leader starts asking the right questions of the right people. Don't wait. Beat them to the podium. Be the first to get the information out there. We gain credibility from everyone when we do. And credibility is the coin of the realm during a risk controversy.

Finally, there is the damaging information that we might be able to keep a secret. Don't even try. If we reveal 99 percent of the damaging information, and cover up the other 1 percent, you can bet that last 1 percent will get out. And we'll suffer the full force of stakeholder outrage, just as if we covered up 100 percent.

Besides, there is an upside to revealing the bad news we could have kept secret. Our credibility will shoot through the roof. When we pledge to act in a trustworthy fashion at all times, folks may actually believe us.

Three more quick points about bad news. We should:

- Never fool ourselves that we can tell our friendly stakeholders anything without the news media, the activists, and the public also finding out.

- Always apologize for our role in the outbreak, even if the hazard is low, and even when we believe we are innocent. Apologizing is not the same as admitting liability. We should say we're sorry for the situation and that we'll do our best to make it better. And we should say it in a human voice, not in corporate speak.
- Be willing to say, "We were stupid!" The default position with stakeholders is to believe our organization is evil and outright contemptuous of stakeholder safety, health, and intelligence. Admitting we are a little dumb is certainly better than letting the public believe we are evil. If we say we were stupid, most folks can empathize with us. (Hell, we've all done something stupid, right?)

How to deliver good news

There's always room for the good news, Sandman says (2005), if delivered with an acknowledgement.

The public likes good news. It loves good news. But people are used to being sold "good news" that is little more than "spin." As a result, they have their automatic crap detectors set on high.

By all means, we should deliver good news whenever possible during a foodborne outbreak. But we must temper that good news by acknowledging at least one negative reaction stakeholders are likely to have to that good news.

Here's an example on a small scale.

Let's say you just bought a brand new car. You let your teenage son drive the car and he steers it into a telephone pole. The insurance company sends the car to a repair shop. A month later, the car is delivered to your driveway, looking as good as new. Your son calls you with the good news.

"The car is back and it looks great," he says.

"It should," you reply. "It cost $10,000 to make it look that way."

"But the insurance company paid most of the costs," he says.

"And they charged me a $1,500 deductible," you say.

"I'll pay you back," he says.

"With what?" you say. "Money from your college fund? Are you also going to pay the extra $1,000 per year that your wreck added to my annual premium?"

You get the idea. No matter what good news your son delivers regarding this car, you are going to remind him of your outrage about the wreck.

What if your son took a difference approach when he calls you with the good news?

"I'm sorry about the wreck, and I know it cost $10,000 to fix it. And $1,500 of that came out of your pocket. And it jacked up your premium. But the good news is that the car is back in the driveway and it looks fantastic. The repair shop did a terrific job."

What do you say? "Hey, that is good news. I can't wait to see the car."

Acknowledgment works on both the personal level and the public level. The key is to anticipate stakeholder reactions and objections, and to acknowledge them before we deliver good news.

If the stakeholders are likely to have trouble believing the good news, acknowledge their incredulity: "You may not believe this. Indeed, we have trouble believing it ourselves. But …"

If the good news is self-serving, acknowledge that: "We realize that what I'm about to say may be self-serving, but …"

If you can think of any objection that might be voiced by stakeholders, the news media, the tort attorneys, or the activists, acknowledge it: "Though we understand that there will continue to be concern about the safety of this product, we can report that government inspectors have declared the plant to be free of all contamination."

Even better, let your good news come from a credible source that is beyond your influence. Let the government inspectors tell the public that your plant is clean. Let the food safety experts say your product is now safe, and that you've put safeguards in place to keep it that way.

The best source for good news about your company is an adversary, someone who is willing to say, "Well, I thought this company was the Great Satan, but I have to admit they've now set a new standard for food safety."

That's the ideal. Get as close as you can. It will add credibility, and thus impact, to any good news you want to send to the public.

How to deliver uncertain news

The problem with uncertain news is that it's, well … uncertain. And uncertainty can trigger outrage. Does this mean we should act certain and confident even when we aren't? Absolutely not. That's a recipe for disaster.

During a foodborne outbreak and recall, we are going to spend much of our time dealing with uncertainties. And we are going to be dealing with:

- Anxious stakeholders from outside our organization who are demanding more information about the outbreak.
- News media who could go on the attack at the first scent of deception.
- A pool of internal stakeholders (employees, investors, lenders, vendors, etc.) who want to know what we are doing and how they can help us succeed.

If we act certain, and we are wrong, we tend to provoke outrage. If we wait until we are certain before we announce news, we provoke outrage.

What do we do? Acknowledge the uncertainty (Sandman, 2005; Sandman & Lanard, 2011).

Sellnow, Ulmer, Seeger, and Littlefield say, "Given the inherently dynamic and uncertain nature of risk, messages are most accurate and effective where they are stated in equivocal terms. Remaining equivocal in risk messages means acknowledging that uncertainty exists and framing messages within that inherent uncertainty. Messages that include statements such as 'We do not yet have all the facts,' and 'Our understanding of these factors is always improving," can be use to preface risk messages (2009)."

Again, let's use a personal example. You've just completed your annual physical, and your doctor returns with uncertain news.

"We think you may have a blocked artery," the doctor says. "But we're not sure. Now we could go ahead and insert a stint to open that artery. Or we could move ahead with by-pass surgery. Or we can take the more moderate route of drug therapy and close observation. Therapy may cure the problem without surgery, but there is a risk that you may have a heart attack if I'm wrong. Nonetheless, I'm going to recommend that we try the therapy first."

Here is a medical professional acknowledging to you, the patient, that the news is uncertain. Are you outraged? Probably not. The tone is positive. The explanation is clear and concise. But the news is uncertain.

This also works when delivering uncertain news about a foodborne outbreak and recall. We want to explain the best available options, announce the one we are choosing, and explain why. We also want to explain the potential consequences if we are wrong, and how we will mitigate those consequences if our plan fails.

We want to cover our bases. We want to stake out the middle ground (Sandman, 1993). Above all, we must:

- Demonstrate that we are moderately confident in our plan, but avoid the words "confident" or "certain."
- Never say our plan is "safe" or "foolproof," or anything like that.
- Admit we could be wrong.

Our goal with uncertain news is never to demonstrate that we are in complete control of the situation. No one will believe that, and any attempt to make that the core message will insult stakeholder intelligence and stoke the outrage.

Instead, we should make our goal with uncertain news to demonstrate that we are confronting the uncertainty, that our organization is functioning despite the uncertainty, and that we are working carefully toward achieving certainty (Sandman, 2005; Sandman & Lanard, 2011).

Section 7: How to communicate effectively through the news media

In this section, we will gain a better understanding of traditional news media and how they generally approach coverage of a foodborne risk controversy. This section takes about twelve minutes to read.

Given the dominance of the mainstream news media in communicating messages to the American public, and given the inherent newsworthiness of foodborne outbreaks and recalls, we have little choice but to speak to our stakeholder audiences through the news media.

What about toll-free phone lines, and advertisements, and public meetings? What about our company web sites, weblogs and podcasts? Yes, these are powerful tools that can help us bypass the news media and speak directly to our stakeholders. But they are dwarfed by the power of television, newspapers, magazines, radio, web sites, and social media to gather and distribute news. Our society is trained to turn to the news media for information during a crisis or a controversy. If we fail to provide messages for the news media to pass on to stakeholders, the news media will create their own messages. This will do us far more harm than will working with and through the media.

The truth is, the news media are not the enemy. Indeed, they can become valuable allies during a foodborne outbreak, if we provide them with the materials they need to tell the story. For this reason, it becomes critical for us to thoroughly understand news outlets and to accurately assess our ability to give them what they need to help us.

It's important to understand from the beginning that there is a tri-polar nature to the news media in a free market culture. There are three aspects of the news media's nature that are in constant conflict.

First, there is the inescapable fact that the news business is Big Business. In the United States alone, the mainstream communications media that control the supply of news generate total revenues of about $60 billion each year, according to the Pew Research Center (Holcomb and Mitchell, 2014). That means there's a lot at stake. Big News makes money (and thus pleases stakeholders) by attracting audiences to their stories. But the media are engaged in a zero sum game. The audience for news is limited in size and appears to be shrinking. Thus when revenues begin to shrivel (as they have in recent years) it becomes necessary to trim expenses. The result is that the most experienced (and thus most expensive) reporters get axed, the news hole gets smaller, and the remaining less-experienced reporters are stretched to the limits of their skills, talents, resources, and time. And this affects news judgment.

Several years ago, I watched a morning news program on FOX News. The big story was about an office fire in a government building in Washington, DC, where one person was injured. President George W. Bush was scheduled to speak to a breakfast meeting and FOX cut live to the speech. "We believe President Bush is about to comment on this morning's fire," the anchor said. Instead, the president launched immediately into his speech, which addressed a massive and sweeping energy reform bill then before Congress. About thirty seconds in, FOX cut away from the speech. "It appears," the anchor said, "that the president has chosen not to talk about the fire, so we are now going back to our reporter on the scene."

This anecdote tells you everything you need to know about the news business. Forget that the president is about to comment on a major energy bill that will affect the entire nation. Let's stay with the fire, because it's easy for the audience to comprehend, and it makes for good video.

This approach to news judgment is dominant in every newsroom in the nation every day. If the choice is between an easy-to-get story that will keep an audience versus a more complex but vital story that may lose some viewers, then the news media will take the easy story.

This is an important lesson for risk communicators. Journalists don't want the hard stories. Indeed, they can't handle the hard stories. They no longer have the experience or the time to unravel them. They want the interesting stories that are easy to understand and to report. It is our job to boil down our narratives into their most basic, easy-to-understand elements to make it simple for reporters to do their jobs.

The second aspect of the news media's tri-polar nature is the Objective Reporter.

Journalists portray themselves as the only truly objective players within the public arena. In their worldview: They conduct interviews and research, and combine these with personal observation to produce news stories that are factual, impartial and dispassionate. Their goal is to discover the most newsworthy stories of any given day, then present these to the public without bias.

On the other hand (and this is the third aspect of the tri-polar culture), journalists view themselves as the Public Watchdog who guards the public's interest. They are there to fight for the little guy, to speak truth to power, to demand justice, to set the public agenda, to comfort the afflicted, to afflict the comfortable, and, whenever possible, change the world. This is, of course, in direct conflict with the journalists' self-portrayal as dispassionate observers and reporters of events. Exactly how do you become, much less function, as an objective activist?

So you get the three aspects of the tri-polar culture in constant conflict: Big News vs. the Objective Reporter vs. the Public Watchdog. The result is a cultural personality disorder that takes its toll on the quality of the news that goes out to the public.

So, if there are moments during a risk controversy when you begin to wonder if the news media are insane, the answer is yes. All that said, during a foodborne outbreak and recall, we have no option but to work with the news media's tri-polar culture. And so we have to ask ourselves, how can the news media help us manage public outrage, and how can they hurt us?

If we were dealing only with the Objective Reporter, then the news media could be of enormous help to us and to the public. They can:

- Get our risk messages out to a large audience quickly.
- Reach the audiences that most need our information.
- Provide education in an easily understood format.
- Help to bring outrage to a level appropriate to the hazard.
- Quell rumors.
- Correct misinformation.
- Encourage productive activity.
- Generate support for the overall plan to mitigate the hazard.

Unfortunately, we must also deal with the Public Watchdog: that sanctimonious, overly emotional, and almost paranoid aspect of the tri-polar news culture that believes in its heart that there must be a dark cloud behind every silver lining and an agent of the devil in charge of every business enterprise (except, of course, Big News).

According to crisis consultant James Lukaszewski (2013), intense competition has created a media culture that feels the need to "connect instantly with readers, viewers and listeners." As a result, he says, reporters often abandon objective reporting and instead function as:

- Alarmists
- Allegationists
- Interpreters
- Interveners
- Speculators

This is the Public Watchdog at its worst, eschewing rational journalism for overwrought, self-righteous storytelling that often does the public more harm than good.

During an outbreak of foodborne illness of any significance, we can expect to deal with both the Objective Reporter and the Public Watchdog. We must do our best to appeal to the Objective Reporter that lies within most mainstream journalists, and do what we can to avoid waking the Public Watchdog. Once the Watchdog snaps into action, the Objective Reporter vanishes.

How do we appeal to the Objective Reporter? By following the advice of the Centers for Disease Control and Prevention (2012): Be first. Be right. Be credible. Don't wait for a state agency or an activist group to tell the public that you've sold a product tainted with a foodborne disease to consumers. Don't wait for your in-house experts to assess the hazard. Assume that your product is going to trigger public outrage and move quickly to mitigate that outrage.

Your best initial step is to beat everyone else to the podium and tell your story. Be as transparent as you possibly can. Be penitent. Your essential message is: "Here's how we screwed up, we're very sorry for it, here's what we're doing to solve the problem, and here's what you can do as a consumer to protect yourself until we have this under control."

Once you've admitted your error and you've starting taking steps to correct the error, there's little for the Public Watchdog to do. The Objective Reporter is now free to do its job, which is to help you help the public avoid the hazard.

So what do journalists need from you to allow them to tell your story and deliver your messages?

- Accurate, truthful, transparent information.
- Evidence that you are taking appropriate action.
- Regular updates, preferably on a predictable schedule that gives the reporter plenty of time to make deadline.
- Concise comments ("sound bites").
- Interviews with key players within your company:
  - The CEO.
  - The in-house experts.
  - The executive in charge of solving the problem.
  - Not the lawyers.
  - Not the corporate spokesperson.
- Simple, attractive graphics in electronic formats that reporters can transmit quickly to editors, such as photos, flow charts, and illustrations.
- Key statistics in an easily understood format.
- Context: How does the situation fit into the larger picture?

- Background information, preferably as fact sheets and other easily digested documents.
- Emotion, passion, and empathy that go beyond a mere recitation of the facts.
- A healthy respect for the media's deadlines.

Most reporters are generalists. They may cover a car crash one day, a key piece of legislation the next, and an outbreak of foodborne illness the next. They are like college undergraduates who are constantly cramming for an exam. They have only an hour or so to become experts about foodborne disease and about our company. We want them to pass that exam. So we want to be ready to give them everything they need to tell the story accurately and fairly.

If we hedge, if we hold back, if we fail to cooperate, we risk waking the Public Watchdog. And then we will find out what true misery is.

You can find far more on how to execute all these tactics by downloading handbooks from the World Health Organization and the US Centers for Disease Control and Prevention. Links to these handbooks are available in the sidebar at MessageMaps.org.

How to prepare your messenger

Outrage management requires far more of our company than pointing to the media relations team and saying, "Get ready in case things go wrong." It requires training from the top down.

That includes the CEO.

The public doesn't want to hear from the "company spokesperson" or the corporate attorney. During any risk controversy, the face of the corporation should always be the CEO. If your CEO is incapable of serving as that face, or of learning how to become that face, get a new CEO. In the age of Big News, a CEO who isn't "media savvy" is a dangerous liability. This is especially true in the food industries, where a risk controversy is possible with every bite taken of every product.

That doesn't mean the CEO should go it alone. Every top executive in the company should train to deal with news media, for two reasons. First, there's always a chance that the CEO will be out of position to deal with a risk controversy for twenty-four hours or more. You can't wait that long. If the CEO is on the way, somebody has to get out there and play the media game until the CEO arrives. Second, even if the CEO is on the spot at the moment the controversy hits, the CEO will need folks at hand who are trained to think clearly and express themselves concisely about how to navigate the risk controversy while communicating through the news media.

Unfortunately, most corporations that bother to get training take this approach: Put the executives through a morning boot camp, stick them in front of a video camera for an afternoon, teach everyone forty ways to avoid saying "no comment," and send them home. For most executives who get media training, that's the extent of their experience until a controversy hits.

This is insane, to say the least.

What faith would you have in a paramedic, or a lifeguard, or a firefighter who took this approach? Less than none. So why should your shareholders have faith in an executive team that fails to train, retrain, and re-retrain in something as important as working with the news media during a foodborne outbreak and recall?

42

The only way to get and remain in good physical condition is to adopt cardio and strength training as part of your life, not as something you do only when you have time. As a corporate executive in the food industry, you must take the same approach to media training. It has to become a regular part of your routine. You should undergo intensive training at least twice a year. And you should undergo at least one tabletop exercise per a month.

Not worth the investment? Call the former CEO of Topps Meat Company, and ask him how much his company should have invested in media training.

If we fail to invest in a communication strategy, we have no strategy. Indeed, the budget is the strategy. In other words, it's easy to say we have a strategy. But unless our budget reflects that strategy by providing the ways and means to support the end, then we have no strategy. We are just kidding ourselves and endangering our company, its shareholders, and its employees.

Section 8: Understanding what outraged stakeholders need from you

In this section, we discuss the importance of listening carefully to outraged stakeholders during a foodborne risk controversy and meeting their need for both useful information and well-expressed empathy. This section takes about ten minutes to read.

Acknowledgement isn't just about what we say and do. It's also about how well we listen. Yes, the messages we send and the actions we take are crucial. But it's also vital to be willing to listen. Indeed, we should listen far more than we talk. When outrage is high, stakeholders need to vent that outrage. There are plenty of ways for consumers to express their outrage after a foodborne outbreak. They can avoid our products. They can recommend to friends and family that they avoid our products. They can set up websites to ward off potential customers. They can fire off emails to friends, family, government agencies, or lawmakers. They can set up chat rooms. They can complain to reporters and bloggers. And, if they are victims of the outbreak, they can always file a lawsuit.

The savvy organization will deliberately create venues that allow stakeholders to blow off steam. For many types of risk controversies, this might include public meetings. But a foodborne outbreak tends to spread across a region rather than just a neighborhood or a city. If the outbreak is localized, then a meeting may be an option. But more likely we will need to create and publicize electronic pathways for our stakeholders to express their outrage directly to our company, and for us to respond to their outrage constructively.

The most fundamental path is a twenty-four hour, toll-free number for stakeholders to call to receive information and get advice about responding to the outbreak. We want to be able to perform a triage that separates the worried and the curious from the truly outraged. Our first line of operators should be trained to detect outrage in the caller's message and to pass outraged callers to a "supervisor" who is trained in reducing outrage. If a caller is so outraged that even the supervisor can't satisfy the caller, it may be time for the CEO to take the call personally.

What's that? Have the CEO speak to an angry stakeholder? Sure. What better way is there to demonstrate our company's concern than for the top brass to take a personal phone call or two? We will want to limit these calls to only the most outraged stakeholders. But this kind of selective response should greatly cut down on the number of hate campaigns and lawsuits that follow a foodborne outbreak.

We will also want to monitor the news media and social media for signs of over-the-top outrage. Look for columnists or commentators who attempt to turn our company into a villain. Look for interviews with experts or with consumers that indicate extreme outrage. Scan the web for bloggers and podcasters who are attacking our company or our products.

Reach out to these folks. Listen to their suggestions, and look for ways to incorporate their suggestions (no matter how outrageous) into your plans to mitigate the outbreak and improve food safety.

Above all, let them vent. Don't get defensive. Whenever possible, agree with anything they say. Why they say, "You're an idiot for letting this happen," we should reply, "I agree. That's why I'm talking to you. I need to get smarter."

We want to slow down the seesaw of public outrage with Peter Sandman's techniques (1993; 2001, July 14; 2005, December 13). We want to position ourselves as close as we can to the fulcrum. We want to stake out the middle ground. This can be aggravating. This can be humiliating. But it can also save our company from permanent damage to its brand or its bottom line.

The martial arts master Bruce Lee reduced his entire philosophy to one metaphor: "Be like water." And it's a good one to adopt in a foodborne outbreak or a recall. Lee said, "Don't get set into one form, adapt it and build your own, and let it grow, be like water. Empty your mind, be formless, shapeless — like water. Now you put water in a cup, it becomes the cup; You put water into a bottle it becomes the bottle; You put it in a teapot it becomes the teapot. Now water can flow or it can crash. Be water, my friend (Little & Lee, 2000)."

The point is to be flexible. Bend with the outrage. Absorb the outrage. Dissipate the outrage. This requires us to remain calm, but engaged. We must accept criticism while offering no excuses (even when we believe ourselves blameless).

Above all, it requires us to express empathy.

In any foodborne risk controversy, whether high hazard or low hazard, stakeholders need two things from our company.

The first is useful information. This is the tactical side of risk communication and is largely the job of our risk communication team. We have to move very quickly to answer questions such as:

- How do I know if I'm in danger?
- What do I do with an infected product?
- Who do I call for medical assistance?
- How can I get my money back?
- What are my options if I've already consumed the product?

Most of the questions can be anticipated well before an outbreak. Systems can be set in place to answer the others swiftly. This is not a book about media tactics. If your team needs training, get a copy of the World Health Organization's handbook and field guide to crisis communication. You can download these as PDFs at MessageMaps.org.

The second thing that stakeholders need from us is emotional support: empathy.

Stakeholders need to know that our company understands there is a problem and we are working hard to make it right (even if we don't believe we are to blame). We must show respect and never treat stakeholders like children, morons, or enemies.

If the hazard is high, we should never reassure the public falsely. If the hazard is low, we should never belittle or dismiss the public's anxiety or anger. Remember Peter Sandman's metaphor of the seesaw of stakeholder outrage (1993). If we insist on putting our company on the far end of the seesaw with our stakeholders on the other, we can expect outrage to increase, cooperation to decrease, and our company to suffer as a result.

We rarely can position ourselves on the stakeholders' side of the seesaw. Indeed, it's very dangerous to try. Comments like "We know how you feel" can actually increase the outrage. On the other hand, if we speak objectively and dispassionately about the situation, we will trigger outrage as well. But we can use empathy to position ourselves near the fulcrum and that is often enough to stop the seesaw from rocking. Empathy requires that we feel the stakeholders' anxiety or at least try to feel it. We cannot fake empathy. To get there, we have to walk a mile in our stakeholders' shoes. We must put ourselves through an emotional exercise, such as:

"Gee, what if I had served a pot pie from my freezer to my child for dinner last night, and this morning CNN is telling me that in the next week that pie may put my child in the hospital or the morgue. What would my reaction be? Guilt? Rage? Fear?"

Or: "I've got a freezer full of pot pies. How do I know which ones are dangerous? Should I throw them all out? Will cooking them thoroughly make them safe? And how do I get my money back?"

Except for those of us who are complete sociopaths, we all as individuals have the innate capacity to put ourselves in our stakeholders' positions. The question is, can our company overcome "corporate mentality" long enough to express human emotions rather than dispassionate, robotic legal-speak? Our challenge is to design messages that stakeholders can understand and accept when they are under stress. And there are two types of messages we must communicate: practical information and emotional support.

On the practical side, stakeholders need to get clear, concise answers to these questions:

- Am I in danger? (This extends to friends and family as well.)
- How do I avoid the foodborne pathogen?
- What do I do if I've already consumed the product?

On the emotional side, stakeholders want to know:

- How did this happen?
- What are you doing to solve the problem and to mitigate the damage it has done?
- Do you care?

The answers must be simple. How simple? We must limit each answer to no more than twenty-seven words (or roughly a nine-second sound bite). Let's walk through a brief exercise to illustrate these ideas: You are the CEO for a company that, among other things, produces a popular line of frozen potpies sold in supermarkets across the nation. The government has identified an outbreak of salmonella in the states of Ohio, Indiana and Illinois. The news media are suggesting that your potpies are to blame, but there is no direct evidence. Inspectors, however, are testing samples of your product for contamination. The hazard is undetermined, but likely high. And the stakeholder outrage is moderate but climbing as news travels through the media. You decide to get in front of the story by crafting a message to consumers that you can distribute both through the news media and through your own communication infrastructure.

First, what are the answers to the practical questions?

Am I in danger?	Check your freezer. If you have a Chubby Checker Frozen Pot Pie with the lot number 93874 on the bar code, you may have an infected pie.
How do I avoid the disease?	Throw out the pie. Do not cook it or eat it. We will send you a refund in return for the clipped bar code from the carton.
What do I do if I've already consumed one of the pies?	Visit a doctor or emergency room immediately. Take the carton. Ask the doctor to call this toll free number for information and support.

(Fig. 9.)

Next, what are the answers to the emotional questions?

How did this happen?	We're unsure whether our pies are to blame. Government inspectors should have answers for us in the next seventy-two hours.
What are you doing to solve the problem and to mitigate the damage?	We are recalling the suspected pies and offering refunds to customers. We are also looking at ways to help anyone who may have gotten sick from them.
Do you care?	We're not waiting for the government's verdict. If our customers are concerned, we're concerned and we're taking action right now.

(Fig. 10.)

Now here's a point about answering this last question – "Do you care?" – in a way that effectively reduces stakeholder outrage. There is no substitute for action that signals empathy. We can say we care all day and all night. No one will believe us. If we want to be believed, we have to take tangible actions that go above and beyond what stakeholders would consider reasonable. Which actions? Obviously, we need to pull the suspected products from the market. At the very least, we need to pull the products from the cities, states, or regions where the outbreak has been identified. And we will need a program that reimburses customers in return for proof that they purchased a potentially contaminated product. Better yet, we could refund the purchase price of any of our products that any customer returns to the store. No questions asked. This policy can decrease stakeholder outrage significantly.

Now all of that is a good start. But "above and beyond" requires us to think past the immediate evidence and to anticipate stakeholder outrage. What happens if our product really has made customers ill? What happens if they've been hospitalized? What if they have died? If we wait for all the evidence to pour in, we risk losing the high moral ground to the news media and the tort lawyers. Instead, we should follow the advice of public dispute scholars Lawrence Susskind and Patrick Field (1996): "Offer contingent commitments to minimize impacts if they do occur, and promise to compensate knowable but unintended impacts." In other words, promise now to work things out in a fair fashion with any customers who can show our product made them ill or sent them to the hospital, or with any family that can show our product led to the death of a loved one.

Now the lawyers will have a collective stroke at this idea. And certainly we don't want to accept liability when no one really knows that we are to blame. But a "wait and see" approach will not work during a risk controversy such as a foodborne outbreak or recall. Stakeholders will not wait. They want to know right now that our company cares that it may have put its customers in danger. That's why Susskind and Fields suggest you make contingent commitments. Let the lawyers set the parameters of the contingencies. Just don't let them go crazy with it. Come up with a standard that is fair on its face and defensible in court. The key is to make the commitment early in the process: "If we have done wrong, we'll make it right." That's the clearest message of empathy we can send.

Section 9: Nine best practices for communicating risk to stakeholders

In their 2009 book Effective Risk Communication: A Message-Centered Approach, four communication scholars — Timothy Sellnow of the University of Kentucky, Robert Ulmer of the University of Arkansas, Matthew Seeger of Wayne State University, and Richard Littlefield of North Dakota State University — make the case for managing an organization's risk communication program along nine best practices. In addition to aiding risk communicators in the field, these best practices also lend themselves for use by researchers in the study of risk controversies.

"We describe nine best practices for risk communication that are generated from the research literature on risk communication and from the larger goal of achieving convergence around issues of risk," the authors say. "The view of best practices presented here is also informed by fundamental values of communications including openness, honesty, equity, and fairness. Moreover, these best practices are designed to help build constructive and mutually beneficial relationships with risk stakeholders, acknowledge the complex and multi-dimensional nature of both risk and communication, and respond to the communication and informational needs of diverse and challenging audiences."

In Part III, we will employ these nine best practices to analyze how well certain food companies have performed during foodborne risk controversies and to help identify where those performances fell short in serving the best interests of stakeholders and likely harmed the best interests of the companies.

1. **Infuse risk communication into policy decisions:** Many companies use risk analysis to form policies for risk managers to put into action during a risk controversy. What these companies call "risk analysis" is what Sandman (1993) would likely call "hazard analysis." That is, the analysis focuses on what the experts consider risky while ignoring what stakeholders consider risky. Instead, Sellnow, Ulmer, Seeger, and Littlefield (2009) suggest, companies should deliberately include risk communication in the policy process. By doing so, companies could avoid a great deal of frustration—not to mention a great deal of damage to their brands—during the chaos of a risk controversy.

2. **Treat risk communication as a process:** Communicating risk demands far more from our organization than sending a set of messages. Risk is dynamic. So is uncertainty. As a result, risk communication must work consistently as a multi-dimensional process in which we listen for and respond to the feedback we receive from stakeholders, and in which we watch for and react promptly to new information as it arrives. We should avoid treating communication as a one-time event, but rather approach it as an ongoing conversation in which stakeholders are active participants.

3. **Account for the uncertainty inherent in risk:** "Risk factors interact with other variables in unanticipated, non-linear, and chaotic ways," Sellnow, Ulmer, Seeger, and Littlefield (2009) say. "No given risk assessment, no matter how comprehensive, can account for what has yet to be learned." For that reason, it's important to remain equivocal when delivering risk messages. To remain credible, and to manage potential outrage among our stakeholders, we must recognize that uncertainty plays a role in our attempts to inform and calm our audiences. Prefacing our messages with phrases such as "We do not yet have all the facts" or

"Our understanding of this situation is always improving" becomes a vital part of our messaging process, the authors say.

4. **Design risk messages to be culturally sensitive:** Many factors affect the ability and the willingness of any given set of stakeholders to accept, comprehend, or adopt any given set of risk messages. These factors include race, gender, ethnicity, religion, education, age, or culture. "One strategy involves adapting the location and form of messages to fit the preference and media consumption patterns of the target audience," Sellnow, Ulmer, Seeger, and Littlefield (2009) say. If we fail to carefully analyze our audiences and their preferences, we are likely to fail to communicate risk to them effectively.

5. **Acknowledge diverse levels of risk tolerance:** As Covello and Sandman (2001) said, there's almost zero correlation between the risks that experts find dangerous and the risks that laypeople find upsetting. We must recognize these variations, as well as those between cultures, genders, age groups, education levels, ethnicities, religions, and races. When we ignore these differences, the positions that stakeholders take can become entrenched, making it much more difficult to calm their outrage.

6. **Involve the public in dialogues about risk:** Organizations tend to think of communication as a one-way distribution of information. When dealing with a risk controversy, the one-way approach to communication can endanger the company's social license to conduct business. Risk communication should include an open and honest conversation about risks between governments, industries, any other interested parties, and the general public. If we want to manage their outrage, stakeholders must have an opportunity to express their views and influence the process. Transparency is essential, especially during a risk controversy.

7. **Present risk messages with honesty:** During a risk controversy, and especially during one that involves foodborne illness, it is essential that we provide consumers with the information they need to protect themselves their families, and their community. This is known as self-efficacy information because it empowers stakeholders to select from credible options and take actions to avoid harm. Obviously, ethics require we craft these messages to be open, honest and accurate. When it comes to issues of public health, we must overcome any tendency to put the organization's interests first.

8. **Meet risk perception needs by remaining open and accessible to the public:** In one sense, this best practice is a matter of attitude. When it comes to risk communication, especially during a risk controversy, we should encourage an attitude of openness and accessibility to outraged stakeholders. This is difficult to achieve when an organization feels it is under siege. Yet it is essential for weathering the controversy. In another sense, this practice is a technical and cultural issue. We must remain aware that there is no "one-size-fits-all" solution to delivering risk messages. For example, not all stakeholders have access to the Internet, so we can't simply post our messages to a website and consider the mission as accomplished. Another example: Many cultures trust information only if delivered by a recognized and trusted leader. If we deliver our messages only through our own spokesperson, we are unlikely to calm the members of those cultures.

9. **Collaborate and coordinate about risk with credible information sources:** As an organization, we must become willing to reach across borders and establish working relationships on matters of risk communication with the agencies who regulate us, the industries to which we belong, the researchers who study our practices, and even the issue-based groups who criticize us. When it comes to outbreaks of foodborne illness, we have a responsibility to find common ground on accurate, honest, and effective messaging to stakeholders. Otherwise, in the heat of an outbreak, we risk issuing contradictory information that is likely to confuse and upset consumers.

Section 10: Summary of important concepts from Part I

To wrap this up, let's boil down this section into a short list of concepts we can apply at a moment's notice.

- Put your risk communication in the hands of the top-level executive team; take advice from the public relations staff or the legal counsel, but do not let them control the strategy.

- Recognize that outrage is as real as hazard.

- Accept that outbreaks of foodborne disease are newsworthy, and news coverage can amplify public outrage.

- Assess the outrage among stakeholders by identifying the factors that are causing (or could cause) the public to become anxious or angry about any specific outbreak.

- Use "acknowledge and improve" as your primary strategy for reducing stakeholder outrage.

- Focus your messages on consequences and values, not threats and probabilities. (But be ready to talk about threats and probabilities, if asked.)

- Practice the art of the sound bite: twenty-seven words and nine seconds for each key point, with three key points per message.

- Let your CEO deliver the message.

- Provide practical information to stakeholders on how to respond to the outbreak.

- Demonstrate you know there's a problem, you are working to solve it, and you give a damn.

- Express empathy through actions that protect the public and mitigate any damage.

- Act before you have all the facts.

- Accept uncertainty and ambiguity as part of the process of navigating a foodborne crisis.

- Make it a priority to provide extensive training in risk communication and outrage management to your executive staff at least twice annually.

- Resolve to put your executive staff through a one-day tabletop exercise in foodborne risk communication once each month.

- When in doubt: Talk like humans, act like humans.

- Employ the nine best practices as a guide for preparing for, dealing with, and recovering from a risk controversy.

Part II: Message Mapping for Foodborne Outbreaks and Recalls

Section 11: Building message maps for foodborne outbreaks

In this section, we will discuss the benefits of the message map, its anatomy, and a ten-step process for generating an effective set of message maps for a risk controversy. This section takes about twenty-two minutes to read.

During an outbreak of a foodborne disease that involves our products, our challenge is to design messages that stakeholders can understand and accept even if they are under high stress. The solution is to develop "a limited number of key messages that are brief, credible, and clearly understood" (Covello, Minamyer and Clayton, 2007). The tools that help us do this are message maps, which leading risk communicators like Vincent Covello have developed based on their research into how people process information when under significant stress (NCFPD, 2007). The message map is our primary tool for managing our risk messages to stakeholders during a high-stress event like a foodborne outbreak.

Benefits of the message map

A message map organizes the key messages we most need to communicate—quickly, efficiently, and clearly—to stakeholders who are affected by a risk controversy, in this case an outbreak of foodborne illness. "It is the template for displaying detailed, hierarchically organized responses to anticipated questions or concerns," Lundgren and McMakin say (2013). "Message maps are one way to make sure everyone understands the organization's messages for high-concern or controversial issues."

Once we complete our message maps, we can use them again and again to create a wide range of communication materials, including fact sheets, news releases, advertisements, talking points, scripts, speeches, web sites, and public service announcements. We can also use them as a guide when speaking to the news media or at public forums.

The process of developing message maps can also help us to meet several goals before, during, and after a public dispute (Covello, Minamyer and Clayton, 2007). These goals include:

- Identify stakeholders, both current and potential, with whom we will need to communicate messages.
- Anticipate their questions and concerns.
- Organize our thoughts and prepare messages that address these questions and concerns.
- Develop key messages and supporting messages.
- Place these messages into a framework that is clear, concise, accurate, transparent, and accessible.
- Encourage an open dialogue about these messages inside and outside the organization.
- Deliver a user-friendly guide to the messages for anyone who represents the organization to stakeholders or the news media.
- Make certain the organization's messages are accurate, consistent, and effective.
- Assure that the organization speaks with one voice. (For a dissenting view on this point, read Peter Sandman's 2006 column "Speak with One Voice": Why I Disagree, which is available on his web site, psandman.com.)

Anatomy of the message map

To be effective, a message map must follow the Rule of Three (NCFPD, 2007; Covello, 2003), which says in a high-stress situation the organization should:

1. Present three key messages.
2. Repeat each key message three times.
3. Prepare three supporting messages for each key message.

An effective message map also will conform to Covello's 27/9/3 Rule:

- Each map will include three key messages.
- We will limit our key message to a total of twenty-seven words or fewer.
- This will allow us to deliver each message as a sound bite in nine seconds or fewer.

The message map is organized using a template developed by Covello and his research team. The template remains essentially the same today as when introduced in 2003. You can easily create a message map in standard word-processing software, such as Microsoft Word. Use the Tables function to design a table with three rows and nine columns, and then merge the top row. This looks like this (Fig. 11):

Category of stakeholder: Question or concern:		
Key message 1	**Key message 2**	**Key message 3**
Supporting information 1.1	**Supporting information 2.1**	**Supporting information 3.1**
Supporting information 1.2	**Supporting information 2.2**	**Supporting information 3.2**
Supporting information 1.3	**Supporting information 2.3**	**Supporting information 3.3**

Fig. 11 (Covello, 2003; NCFPD, 2007)

As you can see, the message map has three tiers:

1. **The top tier** identifies the category of stakeholders we will target with our messages as well as the question or concern that the message map will address.
2. **The middle tier** contains the three key messages that we want stakeholders to take away from the communication.
3. **The bottom tier** contains three sets of supporting information for each key message.

Message mapping: a ten-step process

Vincent Covello and his research team established a step-by-step process to develop a set of message maps during any risk controversy (Covello, 2002; Covello, 2003). In this section, we will apply Covello's approach with a slight variation on his original seven-step process to the task of developing a set of message maps to manage risk communication during a product recall prompted by a foodborne outbreak. Along the way, we will also apply some of the concepts from Part I, especially those of risk communication consultant Peter M. Sandman.

Step 1: Assess stakeholder outrage

In a foodborne outbreak that in any way involves our company, it is safe to assume we are dealing with a risk controversy that will require us to develop a set of message maps. If the outbreak leads to a recall of one or more of our company's products, we are definitely caught in a risk controversy and must assess the potential outrage among stakeholders. As we saw in Part I of this handbook, foodborne outbreaks touch almost every factor that Peter Sandman associates with stakeholder outrage (1993). When confronted with an outbreak that has any chance of affecting our company, we should move forward with the message mapping process, even if we are not sure that our product is to blame. Waiting is dangerous. Immediate and effective action to inform stakeholders and mitigate their outrage is the safest route.

Step 2: Identify stakeholders who are affected by or could be interested in the foodborne outbreak

Every risk controversy creates its own distinctive set of stakeholders. "Risk communicators must adjust their messages to fit the needs and capabilities of an audience," risk communicators Ivy Lin and Dan D. Peterson of the Environmental Protection Agency say (2007). "A situation where stakeholders are children/laypeople would yield a very different message map than a message map where the stakeholders are doctors or health workers." As risk controversies, foodborne outbreaks and recalls create a set of stakeholders that tends to remain consistent from case to case. The most obvious are these external stakeholders:

- Customers who purchase our food product regularly, frequently, or occasionally.
- Prospects who may consider trying our product.
- Victims who may have consumed a tainted product and suffered some degree of harm.
- Families and friends of victims.
- Distributors such as supermarkets and convenience stores who sell our product directly to customers.
- Outlets who serve our products, such as restaurants, hospitals, or schools.
- Regulators at the local, state, or federal levels who are charged with establishing and enforcing the standards that keep our product safe to consume.
- Legislators and policymakers at all levels who write and pass the laws that govern the quality and safety of our food product.
- Investors whose decisions may affect the price of our public stock on the markets.
- Lenders whose decisions may affect our access to capital.
- Suppliers whose decisions may affect our access to ingredients or technology.
- Competitors who may be waiting to exploit our company's situation during a foodborne outbreak.

Not all external stakeholders are necessarily antagonists. Many, such as lenders and investors, will likely support our company and we should avoid alienating them.

We also have to consider our internal stakeholders. These include our rank-and-file employees, our management team, and our top executives. We have to keep them informed, but we must tell them the same honest, straightforward story we are telling our external stakeholders. Everything must be consistent. If we are inconsistent, the media will notice and change rapidly from Objective Reporters to Public Watchdogs, and we will have a difficult time regaining their trust.

It's also important to distinguish "stakeholders" from "publics." Stakeholders care about our dispute; publics generally don't. Peter Sandman (2003, June 12) breaks down audiences for a risk controversy into four categories:

- **Fanatics** are the handful of people who are consumed, even obsessed, with our risk controversy. "Your issue is their main preoccupation in life," Sandman says, "second only to job and family (and sometimes not that)."
- **Attentives** are highly concerned about the situation, but are living without allowing our controversy to distort their lives. This is what separates attentives from fanatics: Attentives will participate in the outrage by going to a meeting, or keeping up with the dispute in the news, or joining an organization. However, our issue is far from the most important thing on their minds.
- **Browsers** keep up with our controversy in the news, but have no desire to participate.
- **Inattentives** simply don't know or don't care about our issue.

Fanatics and attentives are stakeholders; browsers and inattentives are publics. What separates them is what Sandman identifies as their levels of arousal. The first two are either outraged or merely concerned. The second two are somewhat interested or just apathetic. This can change swiftly. It is possible for folks to shift from one category to another as the risk controversy evolves. How we define any given community—as stakeholders or publics—all comes down to where their emotions fall on the outrage-to-apathy scale (Fig. 12):

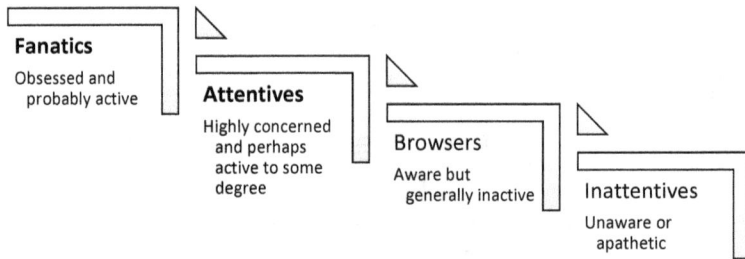

(Fig. 12) Source: Sandman (2003)

In a foodborne outbreak, fanatics and attentives are likely to include victims, their families, consumer advocates, food safety experts, tort attorneys, regulators, policymakers, and lawmakers (especially politicians). As a general rule, outrage management should pay far more attention to stakeholders than publics. There are some risk controversies in which we may ignore the browsers and the inattentives entirely. However, a foodborne outbreak presents a situation where we cannot afford to ignore browsers or inattentives. As long as we have a food product on the market that might cause harm if ingested, we have an obligation to get the attention of stakeholders and publics alike. This is a reality we must recognize as we prepare our message maps. Our best chance of reaching these inattentives with our messages is generally through traditional news media backed with social media. The same goes for the browsers and to some degree the attentives.

As for the fanatics, they have the most influence over how long our risk controversy remains controversial. Our goal, Sandman says, is to persuade the fanatics to declare victory under conditions our organization finds acceptable. Our approach is to identify and apply a combination of messages and actions that will cause our harshest critics to say, "The organization has realized it made a mistake and is now on the right path." Unfortunately, top executives too frequently allow their egos to hinder this approach. They will avoid the actions that will cut the controversy short and spare the organization's reputation.

Keep in mind that not all fanatical stakeholders are critics. Many are also our most ardent supporters: employees, investors, and customers. We must take their feelings into account, but not to the point of perpetuating the dispute. Sandman says it best: "Managing stakeholder controversies successfully requires you to make concessions to critics— concessions your supporters are not going to like. It's important not to blindside your supporters; if you're going to say something self-critical, give them a heads-up first. It's important to bring your supporters in on your strategic thinking, so they understand why you plan to acknowledge the negatives. Above all, it's important to bend over backwards to make sure supporters don't feel scapegoated. (2003, June 12)"

Step 3: Anticipate the concerns of stakeholders

Once we have a list of the stakeholders who are or might be affected by the foodborne outbreak, it's time to anticipate the specific concerns each group of stakeholders is likely to express. These concerns are driven by stakeholder outrage and are often expressed as questions. Covello (2002) says these questions fall into three categories:

1. Overarching questions, which focus on the essentials of what stakeholders will need to know to avoid, identify, or manage the tainted food product or the pathogen itself, such as "How do I know if I have purchased a tainted product?" or "What do I do if I have consumed the product?" These questions generally deal with some level of self-efficacy. That is, "How can I protect myself, my family, and my community?"

2. Informational questions, which seek relevant answers that may not be essential to coping with the situation, but which stakeholders and news media are likely to ask, such as "How and why did this happen?" or "When did you discover the problem?"

3. Challenging questions or statements that express outrage. For example, "Why should we trust anything you say given your long track record of misleading the public?"

In advance of a possible recall, we can identify these concerns and generate specific questions by:

- Organizing focus groups of stakeholders.
- Conducting surveys of stakeholders and publics.
- Analyzing content from media reports.
- Reviewing complaint logs from email, phone, mail, or the web.
- Interviewing our subject-matter experts.
- Studying records and transcripts from public meetings, public hearings, and legislative sessions.
- Listening to our frontline employees, vendors, and anyone else who deals with our stakeholders every day.

This can be a daunting task. Here's the good news: Covello estimates that we can anticipate at least 95 percent of the questions we will receive before we are asked them (2003). His research shows that strong concerns generally fall into no more than twenty-five categories. These include practical concerns, such as safety, human health, pet health, processes, and legal issues; broad concerns, such as economics, religion, and ethics; and emotional concerns, such as trust and fairness. This gives us time to prepare for those questions. The message map is an essential tool in making those preparations.

Step 4: Identify the questions stakeholders are most likely to ask

In the case of a foodborne outbreak and recall, these questions and concerns are fairly predictable.

- Overarching questions
    - What do we most need to know about this recall?
    - What product are you recalling?
    - Why are you recalling this product?
    - What actions should consumers take?
    - Why are you recalling your product?
    - What pathogen was found in your product?
    - Is your product causing an outbreak?
    - What actions are you taking?
    - What are the effects of the pathogen and its disease?
    - How does the pathogen enter the body?
    - What symptoms does it cause?
    - How dangerous is the disease?
    - What can sick people do to manage the disease and its symptoms?
    - What are the early warning signs?
    - When should an otherwise healthy person seek medical treatment?
    - Which populations are most at risk?
    - What can we do to avoid the pathogen or manage the disease?
    - Which products should we avoid?
    - What do we do with purchased products?
    - What do we do if we have consumed the product?

- Informational questions
    - How did this happen?
    - What led to the contamination?
    - How did your factory miss the contamination?
    - What are you doing to make sure this doesn't happen again?
    - Who detected the contamination?
    - How was it detected?
    - Are you searching for additional contamination?
    - What are you doing to avoid future contamination in your products?
    - How are you improving the manufacturing process?
    - How are you improving detection in the plant?
    - Which agencies are monitoring your progress?
    - What are you doing to make things right?
    - Are you refunding products?
    - Are you cooperating with health agencies?
    - How are you addressing the victims?

- Challenging questions
    - Why wasn't more done to prevent this?
    - Why did you hide the facts from the public?
    - What are you not telling us?
    - Do you accept responsibility for what is happening?

o   Why should we trust you?

Step 5: Craft your key messages

Our key messages will fill in the second tier of our message maps (Covello, Minamyer and Clayton, 2007). We want to develop three key messages for each question or concern that is covered within a message map. In general, our messages will fall into one or more of three categories (Covello, Minamyer and Clayton, 2007):

1.   What do we want our audience to know?
2.   What would our audience like to know?
3.   What is our audience likely to get wrong?

Each key message will serve at least one of three purposes (NCFPD, 2007):

1.   Assist in the execution of an immediate response to the situation.
2.   Provide background, technical information, or educational information.
3.   Support recovery with the goal of returning to normalcy.

In addition, each key message should focus on just one of three components.

The first component is information content:

- Here's what we know.
- Here's what we don't know and we're trying to find out.
- Here's what we are doing, or trying to do, to resolve the situation.
- Here's when we will provide the next update.

For example: "We are recalling 16-ounce packages of Aloha Bill's Frozen Shredded Coconut. These packages were made at our San Diego plant. You can identify them with a code on the back panel: SD-19-A45. We are unsure how the bacteria got into our product. We are cooperating with state and federal health officials to investigate. If you have purchased this product, please return it to where you bought it. You will receive a complete refund. We will provide an update on Friday at noon Eastern time."

The second component is self-efficacy content. These statements are the key messages that explain actions that stakeholders can take to avoid the hazard or to deal with its effects:

- Here's what you must do.
- Here's what you should do.
- Here's what you could do.

For example: "To avoid salmonella bacteria, stakeholders must avoid consuming the food product responsible for the outbreak. They should dispose of any of the food product they might have around their home or office. They could add an extra layer of safety by washing their hands thoroughly after handling any suspected food products."

The third component is the empathetic expression. These are the messages that help stakeholders manage their outrage. Unfortunately, they are also the expressions that many organizations find difficult to convey. They include (Sandman, 1993; 2007):

- Apologizing for whatever role our company played in the risk controversy.
- Accepting moral responsibility for the situation, even if our attorneys advise the company to avoid taking legal responsibility.
- Staking out the middle ground in the dispute.
- Acknowledging our uncertainty.

For example: "We are sorry for any role our product may have played in this outbreak. We are unsure to what extent we are legally liable. However, we have a moral responsibility to our customers to provide wholesome, healthy, safe products. We take that responsibility seriously. We will work closely with federal and state health officials to assess our part in this outbreak and to make things right."

In addition, as we compose our key messages, we should consider what is known as "meta-messaging." These are the hidden-but-implicit messages that are encoded into every message. Sandman (2007) explains it this way: "Meta-messaging is content about your audience and content about yourself—especially your thoughts and attitudes and feelings about each other and about the crisis you are facing together."

These include:

- How we view our stakeholders: as trusted allies who can help us solve the problem, as hapless victims who are likely to ignore our instructions, or as troublesome meddlers who cannot be trusted and should be held at arm's length?
- How we say things (rather than what we say). This is a matter of tone, not content.
- The non-verbal signals we send through our attitudes and body language.
- How well we listen to our stakeholders' concerns.
- How well we demonstrate that we care by taking honorable and effective action.

In any risk controversy, our ability to gain trust from stakeholders depends almost entirely on how well we listen, how much we show we care, how well we express our empathy, and how well we manage our meta-messaging.

Step 6: Develop three supporting messages to support each key message

At this stage, we will generate the supporting messages that belong in the third tier of our message maps (Covello, Minamyer and Clayton, 2007). Each key message will get three of these supporting messages, which are designed to add information, credibility, or empathy to each key message.

For example, let's say that one key message concerning the bacteria salmonella is, "Symptoms occur within six hours to seventy-two hours after consumption."

Our three supporting messages could be:

1. Illness lasts from two to seven days.
2. Symptoms may include fever, diarrhea, nausea, vomiting, and abdominal pain.
3. Symptoms are generally mild and require no specific treatment, in most cases.

Generally, we will develop these supporting messages with the help of subject-matter experts or through access to authoritative materials in print or online, such as desk-reference manuals.

Step 7: Test our messages

Once we draft our messages, we should then test them systematically for clarity, accuracy and effectiveness (Covello, Minamyer and Clayton, 2007).

First, we should present our messages for review to subject-matter experts who were not involved in the drafting. These experts should review the text for accuracy. However, we must beware experts who want to make our messages more complex at the expense of clarity.

Second, we should present the messages to focus groups that represent the audiences that are most likely to be affected by a risk controversy; for example, parents of small children. Here we want to test the messages for clarity and for effectiveness. Do our audiences understand the instructions? Can they execute them? Will they execute them?

Ideally, we will have prepared and tested our messages before we must deal with a recall connected to a foodborne outbreak. In practice, this seldom happens. We often must test our messages in the field. We need to carefully observe stakeholder reaction to our messages and be prepared to amend the messages as needed. As a general guide, we should steer all of our messages toward the middle ground. We should avoid extreme statements of any kind, remaining publicly "hopeful" even if privately we are "totally confident." We can recuperate easily from misplaced hope, but we can suffer badly if our confidence is perceived as corporate hubris.

Step 8: Build the message maps

For many risk controversies, companies will want to develop a set of seven message maps (Covello, Minamyer and Clayton, 2007).

However, for a product recall associated with a foodborne illness, we should plan to develop nine message maps. This set of message maps will systematically deal with the questions we are mostly likely to hear from stakeholders as well as journalists. Two of the nine can be built well in advance of any potential event.

These maps will organize the questions we identified in Step 3, the key messages we developed in Step 4, and the supporting messages we developed in Step 5. This step brings all of these concepts together into a single tool for effective risk communication. Later in this handbook, we will introduce you to nine templates that will help you work through these steps more quickly and more effectively, and we will demonstrate how all of this works by applying the templates to three case studies, each drawn from actual outbreaks and recalls.

Step 9: Deliver the messages through the appropriate outlets, with an emphasis on print, broadcast, and online news media.

When caught in a situation where we may have to recall a product and admit to that to some degree our product is responsible for an outbreak of a foodborne disease, we may be tempted to quietly post an announcement on our website and hope no one notices. We must resist this temptation. As the producers of the recalled product, we have a moral responsibility to warn anyone who could possibly stand in harm's way. Our best available means for reaching a mass audience with our risk messages remains the traditional daily news media: newspapers, television, radio, and their online outlets.

In some of the case studies we will examine later in this handbook, we will see examples of companies that put statements on their websites, issued a news release, and perhaps posted a public letter or even an online video from the company's chief executive. This is fine, but it is hardly enough. We need to do as much as we can to frame the story honestly and accurately. If we dodge questions from the news media, we leave it to our critics to frame the story.

Announcing a recall that is associated with a foodborne illness should be a public event, not a clandestine maneuver. It should include a news conference that allows reporters the chance to measure your candor as well as your sincerity. The news conference is your town hall with your stakeholders. It should be approached seriously and honestly. "The media are a prime transmitter of information on risks," Covello and Sandman say (August 2004). "They play a critical role in setting agendas and in determining outcomes."

In addition, we will want to issue news releases, backgrounders, fact sheets, infographics, and other supporting materials to assist the news media in doing their job. Each of these documents should be built directly the message maps and should follow the rules of high-stress communication, as outlined in Part I.

Managing the news media is well beyond the scope of this handbook. However, the World Health Organization offers both a handbook and a field guide to working with news media during a risk controversy. You can find the links to these documents at MessageMaps.org.

Step 10: Listen to your stakeholders, especially your critics

Delivering our messages is hardly the end of this process. Once we issue our messages, we must listen carefully to our stakeholders respond to our messages and be prepared to tweak or alter our messages to better inform them and to help them cope with the outbreak.

We should consider our risk messages as the start of a dialogue with our stakeholders and not merely as an announcement. "These dialogues generally involve a collaboration between government, industry, and citizens that are open, inclusive, and deliberative," Sellnow, Ulmer, Seeger, and Littlefield say (2009). "They may take the form of community meeting, working groups, focus groups, or community forums designed to involve diverse stakeholders in discussions about risk."

Such dialogues are essential if we hope to end the risk controversy as soon as possible with as much of our reputation intact as possible. "If people feel that they are not being heard, they cannot be expected to listen," the National Risk Management Laboratory at the US Environmental Protection Agency says. "Effective risk communication is a two-way activity (Lin and Peterson, 2007.)"

Better yet, we should invite our stakeholders to help us find a solution. We should be more than willing to consult with outside experts and government agencies, as well as with any victims and their families. Doing so helps to mitigate one of the most frequent factors that drive stakeholder outrage: a lack of stakeholder control. The answer is to share control through heeding advice from and encouraging collaborations with experts, agencies, and even our critics. The problem, Sandman says (1993), is not thinking up ways to share control, but rather to want to share control. "You cannot keep all the control for yourself," Sandman says, "and simultaneously reassure other people. Outrage reduction requires finding ways to share control you can live with."

In addition, we should also carefully listen to what our critics—such as government regulators, consumer advocates, grandstanding politicians, and tort attorneys—tell the news media once the story breaks. Critics are frequently (by Sandman's definition) fanatics. They eat, breathe, and sleep food safety. If we want to mitigate stakeholder outrage toward our company and our product, we must manage their criticism positively and constructively. This comes back to our primary communication strategy: acknowledge and improve. We have to steal their thunder. We must analyze their arguments, select the ones that are in any way valid, and include those points in our messaging.

Sandman (1993) says, "Make a list of the other side's strongest points—facts, arguments, emotions, images—and work them into your own communications. Everything your audience already knows or feels, and everything your opposition is likely to find out and emphasize, belongs in your presentation." As the outbreak develops over the coming days and weeks, we should pay attention to any criticism we have missed – and co-opt them. The goal, Sandman says, "is to leave your critics with nothing to say, except for things you have already admitted, and things that are flat-out lies. (2011, January 2)."

We must resist the urge to engage in rebuttal. Now is the time for utter contrition, even if we believe we are blameless. Why? Because it remains our best strategic play to protect the company's reputation and therefore shareholder value.

Section 12: Working with the message map templates

In this section, we will introduce templates for putting together nine message maps that should prove useful during a product recall prompted by a foodborne outbreak. These nine maps will cover the most frequent overarching and informational questions we are likely to be asked by journalists and stakeholders. This section takes about twelve minutes to read.

The message map templates are designed to help us move more quickly through the ten-step process by identifying and organizing answers to the questions we are most likely to encounter from news media and many stakeholders; encouraging us to express appropriate empathy and to accept moral responsibility for the situation; and position us to employ the strategy of acknowledge and improve, with the goal of calming stakeholder outrage so we can focus on managing our role in the outbreak.

If you read case studies about product recalls that involve foodborne outbreaks, you will see certain patterns in the information both journalists and stakeholders demand of the companies involved. This insight allows us to work with templates designed to extract and organize this information with greater speed and effectiveness. In Part III, we will demonstrate how to work with each template through case studies of three actual recalls.

The nine templates fall into two categories: pre-event templates and mid-event templates.

Pre-event templates can be completed in advance of a potential recall. They involve information that is readily available from subject-matter experts and published resources. These templates generally involve information about a foodborne disease and its underlying pathogen. To get started, we should make a master list of all the common pathogens that are likely to contaminate our lines of food products. We should then create a set of pre-event message maps for each pathogen and file them where we can readily find them in a recall situation. There are two pre-event templates:

- What are the effects of the pathogen and its disease?
- What can sick people do to manage the disease and its symptoms?

Mid-event templates must generally wait for the actual events that prompt the recall. The information is too specific to a given risk controversy. However, we can build a database of information we may need to fill out the templates. For example, names and locations of factories; lists of diagnostic tests, procedures, and protocols; lists of specific products; the types of outlets in which each product is distributed; and the cities, states, or regions where each product is sold. Gathering all of this information in one place, and keeping it updated, will save us a lot of time during an actual recall.

There are seven mid-event templates. The first is what Covello calls the Overarching Message Map, which answers this question: What does the public most need to know about this recall?

The other templates answer these questions:

- Why are you recalling your product?
- How did this happen?
- How did you discover the contamination?
- What can people do to avoid the pathogen?

- What are you doing to avoid future contamination in your products?
- What are you doing to make things right?

The templates should serve as guides to help you put together a set of message maps under the stress of a risk controversy. Each foodborne risk controversy is its own beast, but research shows that we can expect stakeholders and journalists to ask common questions. However, you should feel free to follow, alter, or ignore the prompts in each template as best fits your situation, but with an eye to following the guidelines and best practices established by risk communication research.

Map 1: The Overarching Message Map

This map contains our core messages and generally supports our opening statement at a news conference or stakeholder meeting. It also provides core messages for a news release, a fact sheet, a letter to shareholders, and other documents. When we are asked challenging questions designed to provoke outrage, the Overarching Message Map (Fig. 13) gives us a soft place to land by using "bridging" techniques we will discuss later. It is especially important for this map to adhere to Covello's 27/9/3 Rule: We want to deliver the three key messages in twenty-seven words (or fewer) to create a nine-second sound bite.

Map 1: The Overarching Map

Stakeholders: General public and news media

Question: What does the public most need to know about this recall?

Key Message 1	Key Message 2	Key Message 3
What product are you recalling?	Why are you recalling this product?	What actions should consumers take? Return or destroy the product?
Supporting information 1.1	**Supporting information 2.1**	**Supporting information 3.1**
How do consumers identify the exact product?	Tell us briefly about the pathogen or its disease.	Avoid consuming or serving the product?
Supporting information 1.2	**Supporting information 2.2**	**Supporting information 3.2**
Where is the product sold or served?	Who is most at-risk from the pathogen?	Where to check for stored products? Shelf life?
Supporting information 1.3	**Supporting information 2.3**	**Supporting information 3.3**
Are you working with health officials? Which ones?	Who should be on high alert for these products?	Call a hotline or visit a web site?

(Fig. 13)

Map 2: The Recall Map

Our next map (Fig. 14) answers the question, "Why are you recalling your product?" The key messages should convey the name of the pathogen, how your product may be connected with any perceived outbreak, and what actions you are taking other than the recall. This is all part of the strategy of acknowledge and improve. We want to acknowledge that there is a real cause for the recall; that health officials believe there is a connection between our product and an outbreak of some degree (even if your in-house experts disagree); and we want to take clear, effective actions that respond to those concerns. This combination of acknowledging the problem and taking concrete actions to improve the situation will tend to lower outrage among your customers, retailers, regulators, shareholders, and other key stakeholders.

Map 2: The Recall Map

Stakeholders: General public and news media

Question: Why are you recalling your product?

Key Message 1	Key Message 2	Key Message 3
What pathogen was found in your product?	Have health officials connected your product to an outbreak?	What important actions are you taking (other than the recall)?
Supporting information 1.1	**Supporting information 2.1**	**Supporting information 3.1**
Describe the pathogen (virus, bacteria, parasite, toxin).	Where is the outbreak located?	Action 1
Supporting information 1.2	**Supporting information 2.2**	**Supporting information 3.2**
Describe in brief how the pathogen got into the product.	How many are ill; how many are dead?	Action 2
Supporting information 1.3	**Supporting information 2.3**	**Supporting information 3.3**
How dangerous is the pathogen?	What is the evidence of your product's involvement?	Action 3

(Fig. 14)

Map 3: The Situation Map

Our next map (Fig. 15) answers the question, "How did this happen?" It should explain the most important aspects of how we arrived at this situation: the combination of outbreak and recall. Again, we employ the strategy of acknowledge and improve. We acknowledge the factors that led, or we have good reason to believe led, to the contamination. If we are uncertain about the cause, we should say so, with the caveat that we are investigating the cause with health officials and will continue to report progress. Then we present the actions we are taking, preferably in concert with health officials, to solve the issue. Again, treat each of the prompts as guides for building a map that best fits your situation while sticking to the strategy of acknowledge and improve.

Map 3: The Situation Map

Stakeholders: General public and news media

Question: How did this happen?

Key Message 1	Key Message 2	Key Message 3
What led to the contamination?	How did your factory fail to detect the contamination?	What are you doing to ensure this doesn't happen again?
Supporting information 1.1	**Supporting information 2.1**	**Supporting information 3.1**
Failure of technology?	Identify the process your company used.	Are you disinfecting the manufacturing plant?
Supporting information 1.2	**Supporting information 2.2**	**Supporting information 3.2**
Failure of procedure?	Explain how or why the process missed the contamination.	Are you upgrading training, technology, protocols, policy, or procedures?
Supporting information 1.3	**Supporting information 2.3**	**Supporting information 3.3**
Failure of protocol or policy?	How do you plan to change the process to improve detection?	Are third-party agencies monitoring your progress?

(Fig. 15)

Map 4: The Contamination Map

Our next map (Fig. 16) answers the question, "How did you discover the contamination?" The goal is to explain to stakeholders through the news media how we became aware that our product might be tainted. We should give away as much credit to health officials as we can. Thank them for bringing the situation to our attention. Acknowledge their contribution to tracking down the outbreak and helping us to protect our customers and to make things right again. Then we should outline the actions we are taking to track down the contamination and eradicate it from our production process.

Map 4: The Contamination Map		
Stakeholders: General public and news media		
Question: How did you discover the contamination?		
Key Message 1	**Key Message 2**	**Key Message 3**
Who first detected the contamination?	Is the evidence conclusive?	Are you inspecting the plant that produced the product?
Supporting information 1.1	**Supporting information 2.1**	**Supporting information 3.1**
When and where did they detect it?	Is there diagnostic evidence?	Are you inspecting your other plants or processes?
Supporting information 1.2	**Supporting information 2.2**	**Supporting information 3.2**
When did they alert you?	Is there epidemiological evidence?	Are you testing for contamination in other products?
Supporting information 1.3	**Supporting information 2.3**	**Supporting information 3.3**
What immediate actions did you take? How did you respond?	Is there additional evidence?	Are you working with health officials or other third-party experts?

(Fig. 16)

Map 5: The Pathogen Map

Our next map (Fig. 17) answers the question, "What are the effects of the pathogen and its disease?" This is a pre-event map we can prepare well before any outbreak or recall, as the information is readily available from reference materials and subject-matter experts. We should prepare a pathogen map for every pathogen that could realistically threaten our company's supply or production chains. This map does not apply the strategy of acknowledge and improve. It is strictly informational.

Map 5: The Pathogen Map

Stakeholders: General public and news media

Question: What are the effects of the pathogen and its disease?

Key Message 1	Key Message 2	Key Message 3
What is the scientific name of the pathogen?	How do people acquire the pathogen?	How many infections are reported in the United States each year?
Supporting information 1.1	**Supporting information 2.1**	**Supporting information 3.1**
Is it a bacterium, a virus, a toxin, or something else?	What are the most common vectors?	How many people die annually from this infection?
Supporting information 1.2	**Supporting information 2.2**	**Supporting information 3.2**
Is human-to-human transmission possible? Animal-to-human?	How long is the incubation period before onset of symptoms?	Chances of hospitalization? Rare, frequent, certain?
Supporting information 1.3	**Supporting information 2.3**	**Supporting information 3.3**
Anything unusual about the pathogen?	How long do symptoms generally last?	Chances of death? Rare, frequent, certain?

(Fig. 17)

Map 6: The Avoidance Map

Our next map (Fig. 18) answers the question, "What can people do to avoid the pathogen?" This is a self-efficacy map designed to help customers and the public at-large cope with the outbreak. By necessity, it repeats some information from previous maps, but puts the information in a different context. The map simultaneously acknowledges the outbreak and provides effective choices stakeholders can employ to improve their situation. Much of this map can be created pre-event.

Map 6: The Avoidance Map		
Stakeholders: General public and news media		
Question: What can people do to avoid the pathogen?		
Key Message 1	**Key Message 2**	**Key Message 3**
Should people avoid consuming or serving the product?	What should they do with the product?	What should people do if they've consumed the product?
Supporting information 1.1	**Supporting information 2.1**	**Supporting information 3.1**
What is the brand and product name?	Can customers return the product for a refund?	Should they watch for key symptoms?
Supporting information 1.2	**Supporting information 2.2**	**Supporting information 3.2**
Where was it sold? Cities? States? Specific outlets?	Should they destroy it? Throw it out?	When should they get medical attention?
Supporting information 1.3	**Supporting information 2.3**	**Supporting information 3.3**
Describe any key identifiers, like numbers or codes.	How can they safely dispose of the product?	Should they ask for a specific test or treatment? (Cite sources like CDC or FDA)

(Fig. 18)

Map 7: The Disease Management Map

Our next map (Fig. 19) answers the question, "What can sick people do to manage the disease and its symptoms?" It is a self-efficacy map as well as a map that can be created pre-event. It simultaneously acknowledges both the outbreak and the chance that the outbreak may continue and perhaps widen, while also providing information stakeholders can use to mitigate an infection.

Map 7: The Disease Management Map

Stakeholders: General public and news media

Question: What can sick people do to manage the disease and its symptoms?

Key Message 1	Key Message 2	Key Message 3
What are the early warning signs?	When should people who are generally in good health seek medical treatment?	Which populations are most at risk?
Supporting information 1.1	**Supporting information 2.1**	**Supporting information 3.1**
What are the most common mild symptoms?	What tests should they ask for?	What special risks do these populations face?
Supporting information 1.2	**Supporting information 2.2**	**Supporting information 3.2**
What causes the disease to become more serious?	What treatments or therapies are available?	When should they see a doctor?
Supporting information 1.3	**Supporting information 2.3**	**Supporting information 3.3**
How often does the disease become more serious?	Which later-stage warning signs should they watch out for?	How can they best manage symptoms until they see a doctor?

(Fig. 19)

Map 8: The Future Map

Our next map (Fig. 20) answers the question, "What are you doing to avoid future contamination in your products?" This map more fully addresses the actions we are taking to learn from our mistakes and to make sure that our product remains pathogen-free in the future. It simultaneously acknowledges that we are taking the problem seriously and we are cooperating with health officials; it also outlines the actions we are taking to improve our ability to protect the public in the future.

Map 8: The Future Map

Category of stakeholder: General public and news media

Question or concern: What are you doing to avoid future contamination in your products?

Key Message 1	Key Message 2	Key Message 3
How are you improving your manufacturing process?	How are you improving your ability to detect pathogens?	Which health agencies are working with you?
Supporting information 1.1	**Supporting information 2.1**	**Supporting information 3.1**
Technology?	New or improved testing?	Will they inspect or certify your plant's safety?
Supporting information 1.2	**Supporting information 2.2**	**Supporting information 3.2**
Procedures?	New or improved protocols?	Will they monitor your progress?
Supporting information 1.3	**Supporting information 2.3**	**Supporting information 3.3**
Industrial hygiene?	Advanced training?	Will they report on your progress to the public?

(Fig. 20)

Map 9: The Make-It-Right Map

The final map (Fig. 21) answers the question, "What are you doing to make things right?" In essence, this is our acceptance of moral responsibility, even if we have yet to accept legal responsibility. Of the nine maps, this is likely the most difficult to complete. Our lawyers and many of our shareholders will want us to wait until we are proven absolutely guilty before we give an inch. This makes sense in the court of law. But in the court of public opinion, this is a deadly game to play. As communicators of risk, we have two important tasks. First, protect the public's health. Second, rescue our reputation from utter destruction. This map will help us take a great step towards achieving this second goal.

Map 9: The Make-It-Right Map		
Stakeholders: General public and news media		
Question: What are you doing to make things right?		
Key Message 1	**Key Message 2**	**Key Message 3**
Are you offering refunds or other compensation?	Are you working with health agencies?	Are you addressing the needs of outbreak victims?
Supporting information 1.1	**Supporting information 2.1**	**Supporting information 3.1**
How do customers identify products that are eligible for refund?	Action 1?	Acknowledge the situation and apologize for your company's role in the outbreak.
Supporting information 1.2	**Supporting information 2.2**	**Supporting information 3.2**
Where can customers take products for refunds?	Action 2?	Accept moral (if not legal) responsibility toward your customers and the public.
Supporting information 1.3	**Supporting information 2.3**	**Supporting information 3.3**
Where can they go for additional information (such as a toll-free number or web site)?	Action 3?	How are you compensating victims of the outbreak?

(Fig. 21)

Section 13: Composing the preamble

In this section, we will explore how to use the preamble to help manage and mitigate stakeholder outrage during a foodborne outbreak and recall. This section takes about five minutes to read.

We will deliver our risk messages in three stages: an introduction, followed by our three key messages from our overarching map, followed by a question-and-answer session in which we deliver messages from our situational, informational and self-efficacy maps (Covello, Minamyer and Clayton, 2007). In this section, we will focus on preparing the introduction, which we will call the preamble. By expressing our organization's contrition to our stakeholders, this first stage sets the tone for the second and third stages of our delivery.

An effective preamble rolls out in three steps, according to Covello, Minamyer and Clayton (2007): a statement of concern, followed by a statement of intent, followed by a statement of purpose for the event or meeting at which we have chosen to deliver our messages.

First, the statement of concern is our opportunity to convey our meta-messages, with a very strong emphasis on acknowledgement, empathy, and contrition. Even if our company and its lawyers decline to accept legal responsibility for the situation, the CEO should be prepared at this time to accept what Sandman calls "moral responsibility," if only because this is the company's best strategy for easing its conflict with its stakeholders and their representatives.

According to Sandman, "You have to accept responsibility. If a child breaks a lamp, 'I'm sorry your lamp broke' won't do the job; 'I'm sorry I broke your lamp' is the apology that's called for. Even if you decide you shouldn't accept legal responsibility, you can still accept moral responsibility. Here's a formulation my clients sometimes find useful: 'Our lawyers tell us it's not our fault. But we feel like it's our fault, and we're going to act like it's our fault (Sandman and Burrow, 2005).'"

The fundamental goal of our statement of concern is to stake out the middle ground in the dispute. If we are smart, we take this opportunity to position ourselves from the outset near the fulcrum of Sandman's seesaw.

We must look for ways in our statement of concern to acknowledge:

- Our role (as we currently understand it) in the outbreak and the recall—explicitly and without euphemism.
- How and why the outbreak occurred.
- The validity of outrage among our stakeholders.
- Our complicity in fueling their outrage (even when we believe the hazard is low or when we believe we are innocent of causing a high hazard).
- Our prior misbehavior, if it exists and is relevant to the current dispute.
- Our remorse for having caused or contributed in any way to their outrage.

"Keep in mind that you have to behave compassionately, with empathy and sympathy, as well," crisis consultant James E. Lukaszewski (2013) says. "It takes more than words, but the words are crucial because no one may describe your acts of compassion or empathy unless you do." Lukaszewski suggests using words such as ashamed, concerned, disappointed, embarrassed, empathize, failed, humiliated, "let you down," mortified, regret, saddened, shocked, surprised, sorry, tragic, unfortunate, unhappy, unintended, unintentional, unnecessary, or unsatisfied.

The next step in the preamble is our statement of intent. This is our opportunity to reduce stakeholder outrage by expressing:

- Our obligation to act in a transparent and trustworthy manner as we resolve the dispute.
- Our commitment to solving the issue and ending the dispute to the satisfaction of our stakeholders.
- Our willingness to let stakeholders help us fix the problem and repair the damage to their satisfaction, including victim compensation and policy improvement.
- Our readiness to open the response and recovery process to stakeholder scrutiny and measurement, and to provide a means for stakeholders to monitor our performance in the future.

In the third step of our preamble, we make our statement of purpose for the event (such as a news conference or a public meeting) at which we are delivering our key messages. If the event is a news conference, then our purpose is to provide details about the outbreak or the recall to reporters, and provide them with a chance to ask questions. If it's a public meeting, then our purpose (in addition to delivering our key messages) may be to hear from stakeholders as well as to answer their questions. The point of this statement is to establish the parameters and set expectations for the event.

In Part III, we will work through preambles for each of the case studies.

Section 14: Delivering risk messages to stakeholders

In this section, we will first examine a wide range of tactics for successfully delivering our risk messages while avoiding the pitfalls that are common to news conferences and public meetings. This section contains takes about eight minutes to read.

A full introduction to the details of delivering a message to stakeholders through mass media, social media, news conferences, or public meetings is well beyond the scope of this handbook. However, we will now cover certain basic tactics and strategies for delivering your risk messages in ways that are more likely to manage community outrage.

For an in-depth guide to delivering risk messages via mass media during high-stress situations, consult The World Health Organization's Effective Media Communication during Public Health Emergencies, available online or through MessageMaps.org.

Basics of delivering risk messages

In any risk controversy, we should deliver the initial information in three stages, according to Covello, Minamyer and Clayton (2007).

First, we want to deliver our preamble, which should focus on communicating empathy and gaining trust while also preempting the most damaging points our critics are likely to make. (We discussed this in detail in Section 5.)

Next, we will present our key messages and supporting data from our overarching message map. We will want to stress our three key messages, using the supporting data to amplify, clarify, or bolster these messages. This is a case where less is more. Keep the focus on the most essential information that stakeholders will need to respond effectively to the outbreak.

Covello's model for delivering the overarching message map is known as the Triple T Model:

- Tell your audience what you are going to tell them: State your key messages from your overarching message map. Keep in mind you want to keep this message at less than nine seconds for broadcast media and twenty-four words for print media.
- Tell them more: State the first key message and then state the three supporting messages. Do the same with the second and third key messages and their supporting messages.
- Tell them what you just told them: Repeat your three key messages.

Finally, we should be prepared to answer questions from stakeholders and journalists. For this, we should rely upon our eight other message maps, which should anticipate most of the questions the spokesperson will field. Remember: If you don't know the answer to a question, say so. If you are uncertain about the answer, say so. If you need to bring forward a subject-matter expert to clarify your answers, do it.

The question-and-answer section is absolutely fundamental to the reduction of stakeholder outrage during a foodborne outbreak and product recall. We must answer questions, relying on our message maps to guide our responses, and on bridging techniques to steer the discussion back to our maps as needed. But we must also stand in the dock and allow stakeholders to vent their outrage toward us, in person or through the news media. What's more, we must respond with total contrition.

"You have to be humiliated, ashamed—and it has to show," Sandman says. "This is the secular equivalent of the Roman Catholic doctrine of penance—the final step in forgiveness. The dynamics of apology/forgiveness hinge on shame. If you don't visibly mean your apology, if it looks calculated, brazen, and unashamed, it doesn't count (Sandman and Burrow, 2005)."

A Q&A session is difficult for anyone, and especially for the CEO. However, in any risk controversy, the company must own the situation, and the face of the company is usually the CEO. To send a proxy to deal with hungry reporters and outraged stakeholders will signal a lack of courage as well as a lack of leadership. It is also likely to stoke the outrage, not calm it.

Using visual aids

Visual aids such as charts and graphs are often highly effective, especially if they are tailored to the preferences of our audiences (Covello, Minamyer and Clayton, 2007).

"If the information about risk being conveyed involves data and numerical ratings of risk, numerical visuals or charts are the best choice," safety consultant Pamela (Ferrante) Walaski says in her book, Risk and Crisis Communications: Methods and Messages (2011). "The effects of the risk that … can be seen are best presented through the use of photographs or illustrations."

Everyone in the room must easily see our visuals, so a projected image is usually best, Walaski says. Posters may work if the information is very simple and could easily fit on one side of a letter-size handout. The judicious use of color also tends to enhance charts, graphics, illustrations, photos, and other visual elements.

Preparing the primary spokesperson

Selecting the primary spokesperson should depend upon his or her ability to convey caring and empathy, and not necessarily on expertise and status. Keep Covello's research in mind during the selection process: Stakeholders under stress are far more concerned with issues of listening, caring, empathy, honesty, and openness than they are in competence and expertise (Covello, 2003).

Training and practice for the key spokesperson should emphasize repetition of the key concepts that are vital to conveying essential information to our audiences. This is especially true of the overarching message map.

In addition, the main spokesperson should diligently practice the art of the bridging statement.

At first, it may seem difficult to transition from one set of information back to information you need to repeat. It's not. Covello has identified at least thirty-three phrases that will allow a spokesperson to move smoothly from map to the next (2003). These phrases are known as bridging statements because they allow us to build rhetorical bridges that carry our audience from one statement to the next or to steer the discussion back to the message maps.

Among the most common bridging statements are:

- "And what's more important to know is …"
- "However, the real issue here is …"
- "Let me point out again that …"
- "Before we continue, let me emphasize that …"
- "Let me put all this in perspective by saying …"

Practicing these statements will allow our spokespeople to easily and seamlessly transition back to our key messages. For a more extensive list of bridging statements, download Covello's essay on bridging, available through a link at MessageMaps.org.

In addition to general bridging statements, like the ones above, the skilled spokesperson will practice bridging statements for more specific situations. Among them are:

Bridging over questions you cannot answer: In almost any risk controversy, there will come a moment when we are asked a question we cannot answer. Reasons will vary. It could be that we don't know the answer right now, but will know later. It could be that we are prohibited by law, policy, or circumstance from answering. It could be that we are not the best source to provide an answer to that question. Or it could be that the answer is unknowable. In this situation, Covello, Minamyer, and Clayton (2007) suggest a six-step approach:

1. Restate the question as accurately as you can, but leave out any negatives.
2. Bridge with:
   o "I wish I could answer that."
   o "My ability to answer is limited."
   o "We're still looking into that."
   o Or, if there's no other choice, "I don't know."
3. Explain, as best as you can, why you cannot answer the question.
4. Promise to follow up with an answer by a deadline.
   o "I expect to be able to tell you more by …"
5. Bridge again to what you can say:
   o "What I can tell you is …"
6. Return to your message maps.

Bridging over requests for guarantees: Sometimes a stakeholder or a journalist will ask our spokesperson to guarantee a result. This is, of course, dangerous territory. Covello, Minamyer, and Clayton suggest handling the question this way:

- State that the question requires you to predict the future.
  o "You've asked me for a guarantee, to promise something about the future."
- State that the past and the present may indicate the future.
  o "The best way I know to talk about the future is to talk about what we know from the past and the present."
- Bridge to what you do know (your message maps)
  o "Here's what we do know …"

Bridging over hypotheticals: Sometimes a stakeholder or a journalist will ask the spokesperson a hypothetical: "What if this happens?" According to Covello, Minamyer, and Clayton, the best response is usually:

1. Repeat the question as best you can, without the negatives.
   o "You've asked me what might happen if …."
2. Now bridge to "what is."
   o "I believe there's value is talking about what we know now."
3. Go back to your message maps.
   o "What we know is this …"

Bridging over hostility: In a risk controversy, a spokesperson will frequently face a hostile question, a false allegation, or a critical statement. According to Covello, Minamyer, and Clayton, the best response is usually:

1. Paraphrase the question while leaving out the negatives by adding the opposite language, or an underlying value, or neutral language.
   o "You've raised a serious question about X."
2. Indicate that the issue is important.
   o "X is important to our company."
3. State what has been done or will be done to address the issue.
   o "We have done the following to address X …"
4. Return to the appropriate message map.

The advanced spokesperson also will want to master strategies for reducing outrage during public meetings. These are complex strategies that require much practice and training, and are well beyond the scope of this handbook. For initial guidance, look for a 2005 article by Peter Sandman, available online at his web site (psandman.com): "Games Risk Communicators Play: Follow-the-Leader, Echo, Donkey, and Seesaw."

Sources for Parts I and II

Belson, K. and Kareen F. (2007, October 6). "After Extensive Beef Recall, Topps Goes Out of Business." The New York Times. Retrieved 2017, June 13. http://www.nytimes.com/2007/10/06/us/06topps.html

Centers for Disease Control and Prevention (2012). Crisis Emergency + Risk Communication. Retrieved January 15, 2018 from https://emergency.cdc.gov/cerc/resources/pdf/cerc_2012edition.pdf

Centers for Disease Control and Prevention (2016, September). "Escherichia coli (E. coli)." Retrieved 2018, January 5. https://www.cdc.gov/ecoli/pdfs/CDC-E.-coli-Factsheet.pdf

Centers for Disease Control and Prevention (2017, December 20). "Foodborne illnesses and germs." Retrieved 2018, January 5. https://www.cdc.gov/foodsafety/foodborne-germs.html

Covello, V. (2002). "Message Mapping, Risk and Crisis Communication: Invited Paper Presented at the World Health Organization Conference on Bio-terrorism and Risk Communication, Geneva, Switzerland." Retrieved April 25, 2016, from http://rcfp.pbworks.com/f/MessageMapping.pdf

Covello, V. (2003). "Risk and Media Communication (PowerPoint slides)." Retrieved April 25, 2016 from http://www.ecy.wa.gov/programs/tcp/tools/risk_communication.pdf

Covello, V. and Allen, F. (1988). Seven Cardinal Rules of Risk Communication. Retrieved January 5, 2018 from https://archive.epa.gov/care/web/pdf/7_cardinal_rules.pdf

Covello, V., Minamyer S., and Clayton K. (2007). "Effective Risk and Crisis Communication during Water Security Emergencies: Summary Report of EPA Sponsored Message Mapping Workshop." Retrieved April 25, 2016, from http://www.slideshare.net/patricecloutier/messagemapping-7092499

Covello, V., and Sandman, P. (2001). "Risk communication: Evolution and Revolution." Retrieved February 26, 2016, from http://www.psandman.com/articles/covello.htm

Covello, V. (2003). "The 33 Most Frequently Used Bridging Statements Employed by Communications Professionals in Media Interviews." Retrieved May 9, 2016, from https://www.adph.org/ALPHTN/assets/322BridgingStatements.pdf

Dezenhall, E. (2014). Glass Jaw: A Manifesto for Defending Fragile Reputations in an Age of Instant Scandal. New York City: Twelve.

Elliott, G. (2006, May 20). "Master of sorry management." The Australian. Retrieved March 25, 2015, from http://www.psandman.com/articles/ausoil12.htm.

Food Protection and Defense Institute (2007; revised 2016). Risk Communicator Training for Food Defense Preparedness, Response & Recovery. Retrieved February 24, 2016, from http://www.foodinsight.org/Risk_Communicator_Training_for_Food_Defense_Preparedness_Response_Recovery

Lampel, K., ed. (2012). Big Bug Book: Handbook of Foodborne Pathogenic Microorganisms and Natural Toxins. Washington, D.C.: US Food and Drug Administration.

Lin, Ivy and Dan D. Peterson (2007), Risk Communication in Action: The Tools of Message Mapping. Cincinnati, Ohio: US Environmental Protection Agency.

Little, John and Bruce Lee, directors. Bruce Lee: A Warrior's Journey. Warner Home Video, 2000.

Lukaszewski, J. (2013). Lukaszewski on Crisis Communication. Brookfield, Conn.: Rothstein Associates Inc.

Lukaszewski, J. (July/August/September 1996). "Selective Engagement." Retrieved April 2, 2015. http://e911.com/exec/selective_engagement_surviving_corporate_crises.pdf.

Lundgren, R. E., and McMakin, A. H. (2013). Risk communication: A handbook for communicating environmental, safety, and health risks. John Wiley & Sons.

Mead, P. S., Slutsker, L., Dietz, V., McCaig, L. F., Bresee, J. S., Shapiro, C., Griffin, P.M., and Tauxe, R. V. (1999). "Food-Related Illness and Death in the United States. Emerging Infectious Diseases," 5(5), 607-625. https://dx.doi.org/10.3201/eid0505.990502.

National Safety Council (2017). "What Are the Odds of Dying From …" Retrieved on January 8, 2018, at http://www.nsc.org/learn/safety-knowledge/Pages/injury-facts-chart.aspx

Ries, A., and Trout, J. (1997). Marketing Warfare. New York City: McGraw-Hill.

Sandman, P. (2002, October 28). "Accountability." Retrieved March 20, 2015, from http://www.psandman.com/col/account.htm.

Sandman, P. (2001, July 14). "Advice for President Bartlet: Riding the Seesaw." Retrieved March 13, 2015, from http://www.psandman.com/col/westwing.htm.

Sandman, P. (2011, January 2). "Components of Outrage and a Sample Outrage Assessment. "Retrieved February 26, 2015, from https://vimeo.com/18367074.

Sandman, P. (2004, April 15). "Crisis Communication: A Very Quick Introduction." Retrieved June 9, 2016, from http://www.psandman.com/col/crisis.htm.

Sandman, P. (2010, June 8). "Empathetic Communication in High-Stress Situations." Retrieved March 13, 2015, from http://www.psandman.com/col/ empathy2.htm#no11.

Sandman, P. (2011, January 2). "First Outrage Management Strategy: Stake out the Middle." Retrieved March 18, 2015, from https://vimeo.com/18373982.

Sandman, P. (2017, May 28). "Four Ways to Respond to Criticism: Why 'Acknowledge and Improve' is Usually Wiser than 'Low Profile,' 'Defend,' or 'Counterattack.'" Retrieved January 17, 2018, from http://www.psandman.com/articles/mulesing.htm

Sandman, P. (2013, December 9), "Fracking Risk Communications," Retrieved March 20, 2015, from http://www.psandman.com/col/fracking.htm#add-8.

Sandman, P. (2005, December 13). "Games Risk Communicators Play: Follow-the-Leader, Echo, Donkey, and Seesaw." Retrieved March 13, 2015, from http://www.psandman.com/col/games.htm.

Sandman, P. (2006, December 12). "Giving Away the Credit: Managing Risk Controversies by Claiming You're Responsive (though maybe not responsible)." Retrieved April 1, 2015, from http://www.psandman.com/col/credit.htm.

Sandman, P. (2006, April 20). "How Safe is Safe Enough: Sharing the Dilemma." Retrieved March 26, 2015, from http://www.psandman.com/col/enough.htm.

Sandman, P. (2005, February 21). "Laundry List of 50 Outrage Reducers." Retrieved March 19, 2015, from http://www.psandman.com/col/laundry.htm#collaborate.

Sandman, P. (1998). "Reducing Outrage: Six Principal Strategies." Retrieved March 18, 2015, from http://www.psandman.com/handouts/sand42.pdf.

Sandman, P. (1993). Responding to Community Outrage: Strategies for Effective Risk Communication. Fairfax, Va.: American Industrial Hygiene Association.

Sandman, P. (2001, May 4). "Saying You're Sorry." Retrieved April 1, 2015, from http://www.psandman.com/col/sorry.htm.

Sandman, P. (2003, June 12). "Stakeholders." Retrieved April 28, 2016, from http://www.psandman.com/col/stakeh.htm.

Sandman, P. (2001, January 29). "The Stupidity Defense." Retrieved March 26, 2015 from http://www.psandman.com/col/stupid.htm.

Sandman, P. Talking about "'What Happened': Post-Event Risk Communication (Part 2)." Industrial Safety and Hygiene News: 26 May 2005. Print.

Sandman, P. (2010, December 31). "Third Outrage Management Strategy: Acknowledge Current Problems." Retrieved March 26, 2015, from https://vimeo.com/18326386.

Sandman, P. (1991), "Twelve Principal Outrage Components." Retrieved February 27, 2015, from http://www.psandman.com/handouts/sand58.pdf.

Sandman, P. (2012, April 17). "Why do so many people still refuse to eat seafood from the Gulf of Mexico." Retrieved March 2, 2015, from http://www.psandman.com/articles/seafood.htm.

Sandman, P., and V. Burrow. (2005, June 28). "The Role of Apologizing in Crisis Situations, Organizational Preparedness for Reputational Crises, and How an Apology Might Have Affected Australia's AWB Controversy." Accessed June 8, 2016. http://www.psandman.com/articles/busters.htm.

Sandman, P., and J. Lanard. (August 14, 2011). "Explaining and Proclaiming Uncertainty: Risk Communication Lesson from Germany's Deadly E. coli Outbreak." Accessed November 15, 2016. http://www.psandman.com/col/GermanEcoli.htm

Sandman, P. and J. Lanard. "Misleading toward the Truth: The U.S. Department of Agriculture Mishandles Mad Cow Risk Communication." The Peter Sandman Risk Communication Website. March 18, 2004. Accessed February 14, 2018. http://www.psandman.com/col/madcow.htm.

Sandman, P. and Vigileos, G. (2010, December 10). "Prospects for persuading activists and public health officials to be more honest." Retrieved March 1, 2015, from http://www.psandman.com/gst2010.htm.

Sellnow, T. L., R. R. Ulmer, M. W. Seeger, and R. S. Littlefield (2009). Effective risk communication: A message-centered approach. Springer Science & Business Media.

Slovic, P. E. (2000). The perception of risk. Earthscan Publications.

Stinson, T., Kinsey, J., Degeneffe, D., and Ghosh, K. (2006, March). "How Should America's Anti-Terrorism Budget Be Allocated? Findings from a National Survey of Attitudes of US Residents about Terrorism." The Food Industry Center, University of Minnesota. Retrieved 2017, June 13. http://ageconsearch.umn.edu/record/14351/files/tr06-01.pdf

Sun Tzu and S.B. Griffith. (1971). The Art of War. Oxford University Press.

Susskind, L. and P. Field (1996). Dealing with an angry public: The mutual gains approach to resolving disputes. Simon and Schuster.

Walaski, P. (2011). Risk and Crisis Communication: Methods and Messages. Wiley.

Part III: Case Studies in Message Mapping for Foodborne Outbreaks and Recalls

CASE STUDY: The Blue Bell listeriosis outbreak of 2010-15 and the recall of 2015

Executive summary

During spring 2015, federal and state health officials informed one of the largest makers of ice cream products in the United States that the company had triggered an outbreak of listeriosis dating back to 2010. The outbreak covered four states, sickened ten, and killed four, according to the Centers for Disease Control and Prevention (CDC). Blue Bell Creameries responded with a series of recalls that attempted to minimize its financial damage while limiting the useful and actionable information the company provided to the nation's consumers. Only when faced with overwhelming external and internal evidence of its role in the outbreak did Blue Bell recall all of its products from the market. This case study examines the events that led to the April 20 complete-market recall. The study then suggests a series of risk messages that Blue Bell executives could have delivered to help calm stakeholder outrage while also meeting their moral responsibility to protect consumers.

Section 1: Background

1-A. The company: Blue Bell Creameries, LP

Founded in 1907 and still privately owned, the "Little Creamery in Brenham" is a Texas icon by any standard imaginable. Texans love their Blue Bell ice cream like they love the bluebonnet, the Lone Star Flag, and the Alamo. The company may have expanded to twenty-three states, and may have production facilities in Oklahoma and Alabama, as well as sixty distribution centers throughout the South and Southwest—but Blue Bell as a cultural phenomenon remains pure Texas.

However, in early 2015 Blue Bell was also a large corporation with annual revenues estimated at $400 million and a workforce of 2,800, ranking third in sales among the nation's ice cream brands, despite its reputation as a regional brand. The company's primary focus is ice cream, offering roughly twenty flavors all year and another thirty-five flavors on a rotating basis. It also makes frozen yogurt, sherbet, and novelties like ice cream sandwiches and fruit pops. The company has maintained this focus since 1930, when the Kruse family took control of the company, and has carefully controlled its expansion. As of 2015, a member of the Kruse family had always served as the company's chief executive.

Like many privately held companies, Blue Bell in early 2015 had no mission statement, no communications plan to manage a foodborne risk controversy, and no one at the executive level prepared in respond to a foodborne outbreak or a recall. The company had gone 108 years without a recall.

1-B. The pathogen: Listeria monocytogenes

A pathogenic bacterium that can survive without oxygen, Listeria monocytogenes is the cause of the infection listeriosis, which sickens a reported 1,600 Americans each year and kills 260. The infection ranks third among the deadliest foodborne diseases, outpacing salmonellosis and botulism. The germ is found throughout nature, including soil and water. Animals also spread the germ.

Generally, people acquire the germ by eating foods or liquids contaminated with Listeria monocytogenes. Epidemiologists have linked recent US outbreaks to soft cheeses, celery, sprouts, cantaloupe, and ice cream. An estimated 85 to 95 percent of all cases begin with a foodborne transmission. There are no known cases of human-to-human transmission, other than mother to fetus. Babies may be born with the infection.

Diagnosis is achieved with a bacterial culture using body tissue or fluid. The infection is treated with antibiotics.

An otherwise healthy person must ingest a huge number of Listeria bacteria to acquire the infection: somewhere between 10 million and 100 million viable bacteria. Even if infection ensues, a healthy person generally will suffer only fever, diarrhea, and other gastrointestinal symptoms. Few of these cases are diagnosed or reported to health authorities. Symptoms develop between two and seventy days. A past infection does not appear to lead to immunity from the germ.

The disease can become particularly deadly in high-risk populations—pregnant women and their newborns, adults aged 65 or older, and people with weakened immune systems. There is a fatality rate of up to 30 percent among these high-risk groups. These fatalities involve invasive listeriosis, where the infection spreads beyond the gut and into other parts of the body. Symptoms include headache, stiff neck, confusion, loss of balance, and convulsions in addition to fever and muscle aches. In pregnant women, the infection may lead to miscarriage, stillbirth, premature delivery, or life-threatening infection of the newborn. About 90 percent of these serious cases involved high-risk populations.

Since the late 1980s, the US Centers for Disease Control and Prevention have maintained a surveillance program for outbreaks of Listeria monocytogenes. To identify an outbreak, health officials use whole genome sequencing, a process that can compare cultures from several infected people and help determine if their infections come from a common source. This process can take between two and ten weeks, sometimes longer. As a result, infections can continue to occur as the investigation takes place. As we will see in the Blue Bell case, it took four years to connect the dots that identified Blue Bell's ice cream as the source of a deadly outbreak.

1-C. The outbreak

The story of the Blue Bell listeriosis outbreak of 2010-15 is highly complex. It involves multiple frozen products, three production plants in three states, at least two federal agencies and two state health agencies, and takes place over a five-year period. All of these pieces came into focus for investigators during three months in early 2015.

One of this outbreak's great lessons for food industry executives is this: Epidemiologists can now use advanced technology to identify listeriosis outbreaks that are spread over a wide geography and a broad timeline. One test is called pulse-field gel electrophoresis, or PFGE; the other is called whole genome sequencing, or WGS. Each is an example of DNA "fingerprinting" technology that scientists can conduct on bacteria samples from people who are made ill. The information is then uploaded to a national databank—PulseNet—which provides epidemiologists with a library for comparing outbreaks from different times and locations.

"With the implementation of whole genome sequencing to fingerprint harmful microbes obtained from patients, food and food processing facilities, the CDC can now do the unthinkable and connect cases of listeriosis that occurred three to four years ago with a current outbreak," Michael P. Doyle, a professor and director of the Center for Food Safety at the University of Georgia, said. "This is what happened with the recent listeria outbreak associated with Blue Bell ice cream. (O'Neil, 2015)."

Time and distance can no longer hide an outbreak of listeriosis from health officials or the publics they serve. That's a lesson Blue Bell learned the hard way.

Here is how detection of the outbreak unfolded from February 2015 to April 2015, according to the CDC's public summary, Blue Bell's public announcements, and reports from news media outlets.

February 2015

As part of a routine sampling of products from a distribution center, the South Carolina Department of Health and Environmental Control conducts tests that found Listeria monocytogenes hiding in two products manufactured in Blue Bell's plant in Brenham, Texas, located about seventy-five miles northwest of Houston. The products are single-serving items generally served in institutions and sold at convenience stores: Chocolate Chip Country Cookie Sandwiches and Great Divide Bars.

In response, the Texas Department of State Health Services tests a sample of products taken directly from the Brenham production line. The Texas agency finds listeria in samples of the two products identified by South Carolina, plus in a sample of a third product called Scoops. The information, which comprised seven distinct PFGE patterns of listeria bacteria, is then uploaded to PulseNet.

On February 13, Blue Bell executives are informed about South Carolina's discovery of listeria germs in two products. On February 16, without alerting the public, Blue Bell begins the process of pulling ten of its products from the marketplace. Each of the products was produced at the same Brenham factory as the products identified in South Carolina. Neither the CDC nor Federal Drug Administration require Blue Bell to make a public announcement.

March 2015

Health officials in Kansas investigate an outbreak of listeriosis occurring between January 2014 and January 2015 among five patients in a Wichita hospital. Each of the five patients acquired the disease while hospitalized for unrelated health issues. Three died as a result of their infection. Tests of samples from each patient reveal that four of the five infections share the same PFGE pattern as the bacteria found in the ice cream products that were tested in South Carolina and Texas. Investigators find that all four infections resulted from consuming milkshakes made with Blue Bell's Scoops product. The sample from the fifth patient does not reveal any connection to the listeria found in the other patients or in the Blue Bell products. However, the fifth patient also consumed milkshakes made with Scoops. As a result, Kansas health officials include the fifth patient as part of the outbreak.

On March 9, Blue Bell executives learn about the evidence linking the strain of listeria germs found in tainted products in South Carolina with the 2014 illnesses and deaths at the Wichita hospital. A day later, the company shuts down production at the Brenham plant.

On March 13, the company announces its recall of "a limited number" of products manufactured at the Brenham plant. The statement emphasizes this is Blue Bell's first recall in its 108-year history, that the action involves a relatively small number of products that have the potential for listeria contamination, and assures the public that the situation does not involve any other Blue Bell products. The statement does not connect the recall with the 2014 outbreak at the Wichita hospital.

Blue Bell's problems increase on March 22 when Kansas health officials report finding listeria in another single-serving product at the same hospital in Wichita. This product was made at the company plant in Broken Arrow, Oklahoma, which means the bacteria is now active in two plants separated by 475 miles.

For the first time, in a news release on March 23, Blue Bell acknowledges the connection between its products and the Wichita outbreak, and it expresses regret. The company recalls three products identified as contaminated, plus seven others that were manufactured on the same line in Brenham, from twenty-three US states. Blue Bell also provides consumers with UPC numbers with which to identify the recalled products, and phone number to call with questions, but only on Monday-Friday, 8 a.m. to 5 p.m. CEO Paul Kruse expresses the company's regrets for its part in the illnesses and the deaths. "This recall in no way includes Blue Bell half gallons, quarts, pints, cups, three gallon ice cream or the majority of take-home frozen snack novelties," the announcement adds.

On March 27, CEO Paul Kruse issues an open letter to consumers and retail customers offering a personal apology "for any anxiety or inconvenience caused by the recent recalls of certain Blue Bell products." There is no mention of listeria. There is no mention of the illnesses and deaths in the Wichita hospital.

April 2015

In early April, the CDC uses the PulseNet database to link the listeria bacteria that Kansas health officials discovered twelve days ago with six more cases of listeriosis dating back as far as January 2010: four in Texas, one in Oklahoma, and one in Arizona. Meanwhile, Blue Bell announces it will shut down the Broken Arrow plant in Oklahoma to inspect for contamination: "We are taking this step out of an abundance of caution to ensure that we are doing everything possible to provide our consumers with safe products and to preserve the trust we have built with them and their families for more than a century." Around this time, Blue Bell hires crisis communications consultant Gene Grabowski, a partner at the public relations firm kglobal, to serve as its buffer with news media.

Three days later, on April 6, Blue Bell "withdraws" all products made at the Broken Arrow plant as the CDC tells the public to avoid eating any product made there. The company's statement makes it clear "these products HAVE NOT BEEN RECALLED." But, on April 7, the US Food and Drug Administration, or FDA, tells Blue Bell its scientists have found listeria in yet another product made in Oklahoma. Blue Bell announces a recall of seven products it said it was only "withdrawing" the day before. On April 8, the CDC reports that it has used whole genome sequencing to confirm that three isolates taken from the four hospital patients in Texas are nearly identical of the listeria found in ice cream samples produced at the Broken Arrow plant. Meanwhile, Blue Bell's in-house tests find listeria in half-gallon tubs of Chocolate Chip Cookie Dough ice cream that were produced on March 17 and March 27.

1-D. The recall

On April 20, faced with the mounting evidence inside and outside the company, Blue Bell recalls all products on the market, an action that covers twenty-three states and the international market. The recall covers an estimated 8 million gallons of ice cream, frozen yogurt, sherbet, and frozen snacks, (Dinges and Grisales, 2015).

As The New York Times reports, "On Monday, two tubs of cookie dough ice cream at the Brenham plant prompted a somber meeting of top Blue Bell officials. The tub had tested positive for listeria. Paul Kruse, the chief executive and grandson of one of Blue Bell's first executives, huddled with (advertising and public relations manager) Joe Robertson and Ricky Dickson, the vice president for sales and marketing, in a conference room and decided that the company would recall all its products (Abrams and Tabuchi, 2015)."

Blue Bell issues a news release with the headline: "Blue Bell creameries voluntarily expands recall to include all of its products due to possible health risk." The news release says Blue Bell is recalling all of its products "because they have the potential to be contaminated with Listeria monocytogenes, an organism which can cause serious and sometimes fatal infections in young children, frail or elderly people, and others with weakened immune systems."

In addition, the news release:

- Lists the states in which the products are sold.
- Says Blue Bell chose to recall the products after its own tests found listeria bacteria in a sample of ice cream.
- Admits the company now has several positive tests in different plants, but does not mention the involvement of the CDC or the FDA.
- Reports that five people in Kansas and three in Texas have been treated for listeriosis, but fails to make an specific connection between Blue Bell products and the illnesses.
- Fails to say three of the five patients in Kansas died, though news media across the nation reported this fact back in March.
- Avoids using the word "outbreak."
- Says the company will implement a test-and-hold procedure for all products. It does not say where Blue Bell learned of the procedure or why it had not implemented it in the past.
- Reports the Broken Arrow facility will "remain closed as Blue Bell continues to investigate." There is no mention of the CDC or FDA investigations.
- Provides a list of other procedures and tests the company is implementing to upgrade food safety.
- Says the company plans to resume production and distribution once it is satisfied the products are safe. There is no mention of whether health officials will have a say on when production resumes.
- Urges customers to return their purchased products to the point of sale for a full refund. There is no mention about what consumers should do if they no longer have the sales receipt.

The news release also includes:

- A phone number for consumers to call; the number is active only on weekdays during normal working hours in the Central time zone.
- A link to Frequently Asked Questions, none of which have anything to do with the recall or the outbreak.
- A phone number and an email address for journalists to contact the company's publicist.

In a statement, CEO and President Paul Kruse says: "We're committed to doing the 100 percent right thing, and the best way to do that is to take all of our products off the market until we can be confident that they are all safe. We are heartbroken about this situation and apologize to all of our loyal Blue Bell fans and customers. Our entire history has been about making the very best and highest quality ice cream and we intend to fix this problem. We want enjoying our ice cream to be a source of joy and pleasure, never a cause for concern, so we are committed to getting this right.

"At every step, we have made decisions in the best interest of our customers based on the evidence we had available at the time. At this point, we cannot say with certainty how Listeria was introduced to our facilities and so we have taken this unprecedented step. We continue to work with our team of experts to eliminate this problem."

In Kruse's statement:

- There is no apology to the sick or to the families of the dead.
- There is no mention of compensation.
- There is no mention of cooperation with CDC, FDA or state health officials.

(Blue Bell has since deleted the April 20, 2015, news release from its website. The full release is reprinted as an appendix to this case study. The company apparently has also expunged any mention of the outbreak, the recall, listeria or listeriosis from its website.)

In a 38-second video posted on the Blue Bell web site, Kruse essentially repeats the statement from the news release. He makes no mention of what consumers should do. He offers no details about the outbreak or the recall. (The company has since deleted the video from its website.)

Meanwhile, the FDA warns consumers and institutions to recheck their freezers for recalled Blue Bell products, and to get rid of any such products they find.

Blue Bell assembles a team of food safety experts and is working with the FDA and health departments, but fails to mention this in any public announcements (Abrams and Tabuchi).

"It appears Blue Bell's strategy throughout the Listeria case was intended to minimize its financial loss," according to a 2016 case study by DePaul University. "However, the strategy may have cost more in the long run. The timing of the recall has had a devastating effect on Blue Bell's production and placement within the ice cream industry. Rather than taking a proactive approach by doing the recall when Listeria was first discovered—when the company arguably could have been more in control of its own production—the recalls happened much later, backing Blue Bell in a corner and putting the company in a reactive position from a sales and reputational perspective (Barrett, Ericson, and Hanes, 2016)."

The company appears to have had no communications plan for a recall until after the 2015 all-products recall began, when it hired the company hired kglobal from Washington, D.C., and Burson-Marstellar in New York City. Communication seems to focus on the status of products returns to stores and less about the issue and how it was being resolved, according to the DePaul study. For example, there is this passage from The New York Times: "Blue Bell is still making ice cream at its two Texas plants and one Alabama plant, although its products have been stripped from store shelves. All new products will be tested for listeria before being shipped, Mr. Robertson said, and the company hopes to have ice cream back in stores in two to three weeks (Abrams and Tabuchi, 2015)."

Joe Robertson, Blue Bell's director of public relations and advertising, tells the Austin-American Statesman: "Every decision we've made throughout this, we've had the consumer in mind (Dingus and Grisales, 2015)." A New Mexico newspaper spoke to Blue Bell spokeswoman Jenny Van Dorf, who said any customers with Blue Bell products in their freezers should throw the products out or return them to the point of purchase for a full refund. "The majority of Blue Bell products are not contaminated," she said, "but the safe thing, the right thing, is to dispose of it and start fresh." She said didn't know how long the recall would last, but limited distribution could start soon (Ramirez, 2015).

Most retailers are waiting for Blue Bell drivers from the company's sixty-two national distribution centers to pick up the products. A few opt to throw it out on their own (Dinges and Grisales, 2015).

The day after the April 20 announcement, the CDC delivers more bad news: New tests confirm that the sick people in Arizona and Oklahoma are also part of the outbreak. The total now is ten sick customers, with three dead, in four states. Meanwhile, the FDA warns consumers and institutions to recheck their freezers for recalled Blue Bell products and to get rid of any such products they find (CDC, 2017).

In summary: Blue Bell had five chances to recall its products as evidence of contamination steadily mounted, the DePaul case study says. Instead, executives chose to downplay the risk and to reassure the public that its factory was clean and its products were pure. The company left it to federal and state health officials to provide self-efficacy information about the pathogen and the disease. "Blue Bell failed to communicate the whole contamination truths from 2013 through to the full recall in April of 2015. In essence, Blue Bell omitted key facts to its Listeria contamination by not providing an accurate picture of the company's characters, ideals, and practices (Barrett, Ericson, and Hanes, 2016)." Nowhere in its communication to stakeholders did Blue Bell express remorse for endangering its customers, or for its role in the ten confirmed illnesses or the three deaths. Instead, the company apologized for the lack of products in stores.

The company's share of the national market for ice cream fell from 6.5 percent to zero by July 2015, the DePaul case study says. Losses were estimated at more than $180 million. The company laid off thirty-seven percent of its workforce (1,450 employees) and furloughed another thirty-six percent (1,400). The company appeared ready to fold until July 2015, when it received a $125 million loan from Fort Worth billionaire Sid Bass. A letter from CEO Paul Kruse to company shareholders said Blue Bell accepted Bass's investment after it failed to raise money from its existing shareholders (Newman, 2015).

1-E. Stakeholder reaction

"While some corners of the public are vividly outraged," the DePaul study says, "the general public perceptions of Blue Bell in the aftermath of the listeria outbreak is positive. Comments on the company social media pages and elsewhere range from elation for the company's return, to disgust in the company's breach of trust. (Barrett, Ericson, and Hanes, 2016)

The Austin American-Statesman spoke to Dwight Hill, a partner with retail consultancy McMillan-Doolittle: "Limited communication from Blue Bell CEO Paul Kruse—who has posted two open letters to consumers and a 38-second video posted on the company's website—isn't cutting it when it comes to maintaining consumer confidence, Hill said. Instead, Hill said that Kruse should be highly visible, discussing the recall's status and its progress. 'That would really do a lot to help maintain customer confidence,' he said. 'They have lost a lot of confidence (Dinges and Grisales, 2015)."

The New York Times wrote: "Blue Bell took the drastic step as it scrambled to contain the spread of listeria, while trying to reassure its loyal customer base that it would impose stringent testing standards for any new products. But analysts voice concerns that Blue Bell had acted too late, as the recalls eroded customer confidence. Restoring trust as the summer sales season approaches will be difficult, they say. 'When there's a recall and somebody does something quickly and when they handle it properly, we forgive it,' said Phil Lempert, food industry analyst for SupermarketGuru.com. 'When it's the entire product line or the entire company,' he said, 'people are very concerned (Abrams and Tabuchi, 2015).'"

The Houston Chronicle wrote: "Blue Bell Creameries ignored critical parts of federal recommendations aimed at preventing exactly the kind of foodborne illness that thrust the Texas institution into crisis this year. Among the most straightforward: If listeria shows up in the plant, check for it in the ice cream (Colette, 2015)."

Bill Marler, a personal injury lawyer and food safety advocate, told the Times, "Limiting the recall might seem like a good idea. But then if you keep expanding your recall, it's a death by a thousand cuts. You look like you're dragging your feet (Abrams and Tabuchi)."

In the end, two things appear to have saved Blue Bell from oblivion: Its deep emotional connection with its customer base, especially in Texas, and the deep pockets of a Fort Worth billionaire whose family is known for its public philanthropy.

1-F. Timeline (February through November 2015)

- February 12—During a routine sampling, South Carolina health officials discover strains of Listeria monocytogenes in two ice cream products made at the Brenham facility of Blue Bell Creameries: Chocolate Chip Country Cookie Sandwiches and Great Divide Bars.
- March 13—The US Centers for Disease Control and Prevention, or CDC, announces it has found a link between five Kansas cases of listeriosis (including three deaths) and the strain found in the Blue Bell products. At the same time, Blue Bell launches a limited product recall to remove Scoops ice cream and other products made on the Brenham production line. Blue Bell traces the contamination to a machine that wraps ice cream sandwiches and other products. The machine and the room are sterilized and production resumes.
- March 22—Kansas health officials report conducting a positive test for Listeria monocytogenes on a single serving cup taken from a hospital in Wichita, Kansas. Blue Bell's plant in Broken Arrow, Oklahoma, produced the product in April 2014. Using its national PulseNet database, the CDC identifies six hospital patients infected in 2010-14 with a strain of Listeria monocytogenes indistinguishable from the strain found in the single serving cups.
- March 23—Blue Bell recalls three flavors of the single-serving cups.
- April 3—Blue Bell temporarily shuts down its Broken Arrow plant.
- April 6—Wal-Mart, Sam's Club, and Kroger take Blue Bell products off their freezer aisles.
- April 7—In addition to the five cases in Kansas, the CDC reports three cases of listeriosis in Texas, one in Arizona, and one in Oklahoma between January 2010 and January 2015. Meanwhile, the FDA tells Blue Bell it has detected Listeria monocytogenes in pint samples of its Banana Pudding ice cream taken during a March 23 inspection of the Broken Arrow plant. In response, Blue Bell expands its recall.
- April 20—Blue Bell recalls all products made at all facilities and halts all production.
- April 23—Blue Bell revises protocols and retrains its staff for cleaning its plants.
- May 7—The FDA publishes its findings from recent inspections at the Blue Bell production facilities in Brenham, Broken Arrow, and Sylacauga, Alabama. The report finds seventeen separate positive tests for listeria from March 2013 through February 2015 at the Broken Arrow plant.
- May 14—Blue Bell signs a pact with health officials in Oklahoma and Texas that requires the company to tell the states about any positive test for Listeria monocytogenes in its products or ingredients.
- May 15—Blue Bell lays off 750 full-time plus 700 part-time workers, furloughs 1,400 workers on partial pay, and reduces salaries for remaining full-time employees.
- July 13—A high-profile billionaire from Fort Worth, Sid Bass, loans $125 million to Blue Bell Creameries after existing investors decline to re-invest.
- November 19—Blue Bell reopens its flagship plant in Brenham

Section 2: Mapping the messages

2-A. Assessing the outrage

Any foodborne outbreak that leads to a product recall will generate some significant level of outrage among our stakeholders. For Blue Bell, the combination of an outbreak and a recall created an almost-perfect storm for a serious risk controversy by triggering as many as nineteen of Peter Sandman's twenty primary and secondary actors of community outrage.

As Blue Bell Creameries prepared to announce its recall of April 20, 2015, company executives should have considered this as well as their additional errors in judgment since mid-February, each of which clearly had the potential to stoke outrage and spread mistrust among stakeholders:

- The February 16 decision to pull ten products from the market without alerting the general public.
- The announced March 13 recall of "a limited number" of products, which overly reassured the public, focused on the company's previous 108 years without recalls, and ignored the connection between the recall and the outbreak at the hospital in Wichita, Kansas.
- The March 23 news release in which Blue Bell finally acknowledges the link between its product and the Wichita outbreak, but fails to express regret or empathy.
- CEO Paul Kruse's open letter of March 27 in which he apologizes for "any anxiety or inconvenience" cause by the recall, yet makes no mention of listeria or the outbreak.
- Blue Bell's April 3 announcement that it is shutting down the Broken Arrow plant "out of an abundance of caution" and to preserve consumer trust.
- An April 6 announcement in which Blue Bell "withdraws" all products made at Broken Arrow, while insisting "these products HAVE NOT BEEN RECALLED."
- An April 7 announcement that says the company was recalling the seven products Blue Bell withdrew from the market on April 6.

Each of these actions served to damage Blue Bell's credibility with its stakeholders. In addition, when putting together their April 20 recall announcement, Blue Bell executives either ignored or failed to consider the very real chance that the news would get much worse, as it did on the day after the April 20 recall.

2-B. Identifying the stakeholders

For any foodborne outbreak coupled with a recall, the primary audience is the general public (at least in the geographic areas affected by the outbreak) and the primary media are traditional news outlets: newspapers, radio, and television, as well as their websites and social media. We have an obligation as the manufacturers of a suspected product to make a substantial and sustained effort to alert anyone who might have purchased or consumed the product.

As we warn and inform the public, we must also keep in mind more specific stakeholders. For Blue Bell, that would have included its regular customers, potential customers, retail outlets, institutional outlets, regulators, employees and their families, and—as it turned out—its pool of current and potential investors.

2-C. Building the nine maps

Map 1: The Overarching Map

Of the nine maps, this is the most crucial as it is the one you will use most often. It includes the most important information for the public to know. Keep the language tight, crisp and to the point. Avoid getting wrapped up in detail, euphemism, or legalese. Tell the public what it needs to know about the situation.

For the April 20 recall, the focus for Blue Bell should have been on helping consumers protect themselves from the outbreak:

Map 1: The Overarching Map		
Stakeholders: General public and news media		
Question: What does the public most need to know about this recall?		
Key Message 1	**Key Message 2**	**Key Message 3**
Blue Bell is recalling all products from the market.	Tests show these products may contain listeria bacteria.	Consumers should return all purchased products for refunds.
Supporting information 1.1	**Supporting information 2.1**	**Supporting information 3.1**
This includes ice cream, frozen yogurt, sherbet, and frozen snacks.	Listeria can be deadly to high-risk populations.	Please avoid consuming or serving our products.
Supporting information 1.2	**Supporting information 2.2**	**Supporting information 3.2**
These were sold in 23 states and internationally.	These include newborns, seniors, and persons with weak immunity.	Please also check your freezers for our products.
Supporting information 1.3	**Supporting information 2.3**	**Supporting information 3.3**
We are working with federal and state health officials.	Hospitals should be on high alert for these products.	For questions, visit bluebell.com or call 1-800-BLUEBELL.

(Fig. 1)

To deliver the overarching map, we use Covello's Triple T Model:

1. Tell your audience what you are going to tell them: State your key messages from your overarching message map. Keep in mind you want to keep this message at less than nine seconds for broadcast media and twenty-four words for print media.
2. Tell them more: State the first key messages and then state the three supporting messages. Do the same with the second and third key messages and their supporting messages.
3. Tell them what you just told them: Repeat your three key messages.

Here how a spokesperson might deliver the overarching message map using the Triple-T Rule:

- Step 1: Tell your audience what you are going to tell them. Read Tier Two from left to right

- o "Blue Bell is recalling all products from the market. Tests show these products may contain listeria bacteria. Consumers should return all purchases products for refunds.
- Step 2: Tell them more. Read each column from top to bottom.
  - o "We are recalling all products, including ice cream, frozen yogurt, sherbet, and frozen snacks. These were sold in twenty-three states and internationally. We are working with state and federal health officials.
  - o "Tests show these products may contain listeria bacteria, which can be deadly to at-risk populations: newborns, seniors, and persons with weak immunity. Hospitals should be on high alert for these products.
  - o "Consumers should return all purchased products for refunds. They should avoid consuming or serving our products. Also, they should check their freezers. For questions, visit BlueBell.com or call 800-BlueBell.
- Step 3: Tell them again. Read Tier Two from left to right.
  - o "To repeat: Blue Bell is recalling all products from the market. Tests show these products may contain listeria bacteria. Consumers should return all purchased products for refunds."

Map 2: The Recall Map

This is an opportunity for us to acknowledge the situation and our role in it by connecting the dots between the recall and the outbreak. It's also an opportunity to demonstrate that we are cooperating with government health officials, we are listening to what they say, and we are taking effective actions. Once again, the emphasis should be on protecting public health.

Map 2: The Recall Map		
Stakeholders: General public and news media		
Question: Why are you recalling the product?		
Key Message 1	**Key Message 2**	**Key Message 3**
Diagnostic tests have found listeria in samples.	Health officials have connected our products to an outbreak.	We are taking actions recommended by food safety experts.
Supporting information 1.1	**Supporting information 2.1**	**Supporting information 3.1**
Listeria are bacteria that contaminate food products.	The outbreak includes Kansas, Texas, Oklahoma, and Arizona.	We are disinfecting our production plants.
Supporting information 1.2	**Supporting information 2.2**	**Supporting information 3.2**
We found the bacteria in two of our production plants.	So far we have ten confirmed cases, including three deaths.	We are retraining staff in new safety methods.
Supporting information 1.3	**Supporting information 2.3**	**Supporting information 3.3**
Listeria can be deadly to high-risk populations.	Government tests indicate our products are responsible.	We are stopping production until cleared by government officials.

(Fig. 2)

Map 3: The Situation Map

Once we are past the essential details, one of the first questions we must answer is obvious: How did this happen? We need to quickly explain how the pathogen entered our supply chain, acknowledge the seriousness of the situation, and then indicate how we are improving the situation. It is helpful to let the public know we are working closely with their government representatives to solve the problem. It also helps to indicate we are consulting with third-party experts. These messages tend to calm stakeholder outrage; they tell the public that we know we have erred and we are humble enough to consult and collaborate with others.

Map 3: The Situation Map

Stakeholders: General public and news media

Question: How did this happen?

Key Message 1	Key Message 2	Key Message 3
Listeria bacteria contaminated our plants and entered our products.	We should have held all products until cleared by testing.	We are working with experts to update our processes.
Supporting information 1.1	Supporting information 2.1	Supporting information 3.1
These bacteria are particularly difficult to disinfect.	Instead, we trusted pasteurization to kill the bacteria.	We are now disinfecting our production plants.
Supporting information 1.2	Supporting information 2.2	Supporting information 3.2
They tend to hide in cracks and crevices.	We are upgrading to a "test and hold" policy.	The plants are offline until they are completely clean.
Supporting information 1.3	Supporting information 2.3	Supporting information 3.3
They also tend to multiply even under refrigeration.	We will hold all products until testing clears them.	FDA and CDC are monitoring our progress.

(Fig. 3)

Map 4: The Contamination Map

This example pursues our acknowledge-and-improve strategy. We acknowledge that our tests and government tests show contamination, and we are responding with effective action to address the situation in consultation with experts in food safety. Blue Bell consulted with experts, but failed to communicate this fact in its public announcements.

Map 4: The Contamination Map		
Stakeholders: General public and news media		
Question: How did you discover the contamination?		
Key Message 1	**Key Message 2**	**Key Message 3**
Our tests detected listeria in a recent sample.	Government tests also indicate contamination.	We are working with experts to eliminate the bacteria.
Supporting information 1.1	**Supporting information 2.1**	**Supporting information 3.1**
We found bacteria in ice cream made in mid-March.	Health officials in three states detected listeria in our products	We are taking expert advice on new tests and procedures.
Supporting information 1.2	**Supporting information 2.2**	**Supporting information 3.2**
We are uncertain exactly which products are contaminated.	CDC connected the strain with ten cases in four states.	We are adopting a test-and-hold policy for all products.
Supporting information 1.3	**Supporting information 2.3**	**Supporting information 3.3**
So, we are recalling all products from the market.	FDA says consumers should avoid eating our products.	We will retrain our staff in advanced hygienic procedures.

(Fig. 4)

Map 5: The Pathogen Map

Blue Bell will want to emphasize that listeria bacteria can endanger high-risk populations. Note how this information is presented as the third key message, making it more likely that audiences will remember it (Covello, 2003). Also note the use of equivocating language like "generally," "roughly," and "usually." Equivocation is important in managing stakeholder outrage (Sellnow, Ulmer, Seeger, and Littlefield, 2009).

Map 5: The Pathogen Map

Stakeholders: General public and news media

Question: What are the effects of the pathogen and its disease?

Key Message 1	Key Message 2	Key Message 3
People acquire listeria generally by eating contaminated foods.	Symptoms usually appear within several days.	Listeria can cause meningitis and endanger high-risk groups.
Supporting information 1.1	**Supporting information 2.1**	**Supporting information 3.1**
These foods contain the bacteria Listeria monocytegenes.	Mild symptoms include flu-like symptoms.	These groups include pregnant women, fetuses, and newborns.
Supporting information 1.2	**Supporting information 2.2**	**Supporting information 3.2**
They may include dairy, deli meats, or raw fruits and vegetables.	CDC says to wait for symptoms before seeing a doctor.	Also, seniors and persons with weak immune systems.
Supporting information 1.3	**Supporting information 2.3**	**Supporting information 3.3**
Unlike other germs, listeria multiply easily in refrigerated foods.	Most confirmed cases require hospitalization.	Roughly 20 percent of infected patients die.

(Fig. 5)

Map 6: The Avoidance Map

This is primarily a self-efficacy map that provides useful, actionable information for consumers. Note how the map cites information from CDC to enhance its credibility.

Map 6: The Avoidance Map		
Stakeholders: General public and news media		
Question: What can people do to avoid the pathogen?		
Key Message 1	**Key Message 2**	**Key Message 3**
CDC recommends avoiding eating recalled Blue Bell products.	CDC suggests checking freezers for Blue Bell products.	If you recently ate Blue Bell, watch for symptoms.
Supporting information 1.1	**Supporting information 2.1**	**Supporting information 3.1**
These include ice cream, frozen yogurt, sherbet, and frozen snacks.	This advice includes homes, retailers, and institutions.	These may include headache, fever, diarrhea, or a stiff neck.
Supporting information 1.2	**Supporting information 2.2**	**Supporting information 3.2**
These products were sold in 22 US states.	When in doubt, throw it out.	Seek medical attention if you develop symptoms.
Supporting information 1.3	**Supporting information 2.3**	**Supporting information 3.3**
Visit our website, BlueBell.com, for details.	Discard in a closed plastic bag inside a sealed trashcan.	Symptoms generally appear within three to seventy days.

(Fig. 6)

Map 7: The Disease Management Map

This one is also largely a self-efficacy map. Its goal is to give consumers the information they need to manage the effects of listeriosis. Note the emphasis on pregnant women, who are far more likely to contract listeriosis than any other population, according to CDC.

Map 7: The Disease Management Map		
Stakeholders: General public and news media		
Question: What can sick people do to manage the disease and its symptoms?		
Key Message 1	**Key Message 2**	**Key Message 3**
Mild symptoms generally appear within a few days of exposure.	CDC recommends waiting for symptoms before seeing a doctor.	Listeriosis primarily affects pregnant women.
Supporting information 1.1	**Supporting information 2.1**	**Supporting information 3.1**
These include headache, fever, stiff neck, diarrhea, loss of balance, and confusion.	This includes pregnant women, seniors, and persons with low immunity.	Pregnant women typically experience non-specific symptoms.
Supporting information 1.2	**Supporting information 2.2**	**Supporting information 3.2**
The disease becomes more serious if it enters the bloodstream.	Doctors identify listeriosis with a bacterial culture.	Infection can lead to miscarriage, stillbirth, or premature delivery.
Supporting information 1.3	**Supporting information 2.3**	**Supporting information 3.3**
This rarely happens in otherwise healthy people.	The disease is treated with antibiotics.	Infection can also threaten the life of newborns.

(Fig. 7)

Map 8: The Future Map

In this map, we are attempting to point toward a future after the outbreak ends and we regain control of our production process. Again the strategy here is to acknowledge and improve. We want to be seen as working closely with third-party experts to correct our errors.

Map 8: The Future Map

Stakeholders: General public and news media

Question: What are you doing to avoid future contamination in your products?

Key Message 1	Key Message 2	Key Message 3
We are consulting leading experts in food safety.	We are listening closely to their advice.	We are also working closely with government health agencies.
Supporting information 1.1	**Supporting information 2.1**	**Supporting information 3.1**
We are looking at any technology that will make us better.	We have adopted a test-and-hold policy.	They will tell us when our plants are ready to reopen.
Supporting information 1.2	**Supporting information 2.2**	**Supporting information 3.2**
We are considering new procedures and policies.	Products will remain in the plant until cleared by testing.	They will monitor our progress at each step.
Supporting information 1.3	**Supporting information 2.3**	**Supporting information 3.3**
We are looking at new methods of industrial hygiene.	We are also adopting enhanced training for employees.	And they will report their findings to the public.

(Fig. 8)

Map 9: The Make It Right Map

"Making it right" means just that: Compensating those who have paid a price for our mistake. This ranges from simply refunding the purchase price to negotiating compensation for the ill and the families of the dead. This is no time to hide behind the lawyers. We must be ready to refund money to consumers who may not have a receipt. We must be ready to approach the sick and the grieving, and to find a level of compensation that both sides find acceptable. This is a time for human empathy, not for legal hardball. Otherwise, we risk the media portraying our company, our brand, and our executives as sociopathic villains unworthy of a social license to conduct business. And that can be fatal to our enterprise.

Map 9: The Make It Right Map

Stakeholders: General public and news media

Question: What are you doing to make things right?

Key Message 1	Key Message 2	Key Message 3
We are offering refunds on all Blue Bell products.	We are collaborating with FDA, CDC, and state officials.	We know we have a moral responsibility to make things right.
Supporting information 1.1	**Supporting information 2.1**	**Supporting information 3.1**
Return your products to the place of purchase.	Our immediate goals are to make sure the outbreak is over.	We are sorry for our role in this situation.
Supporting information 1.2	**Supporting information 2.2**	**Supporting information 3.2**
If you lack a sales receipt, call 1-800-BLUEBELL.	To speedily retrieve all products from the market.	We want to meet with victims and their families.
Supporting information 1.3	**Supporting information 2.3**	**Supporting information 3.3**
Visit our website, BlueBell.com, for details.	And to make sure this never happens again.	We want their advice on how to make things better.

(Fig. 9)

You probably noticed some repetition from map to map. This is inevitable as each map looks at the same situation from a different perspective. It is also appropriate to have some repetition to improve the chances of cutting through the mental noise. Remember, the template prompts are there to suggest an approach to framing our messages. Each risk controversy has its own specific contours. And there is never a perfect message map. As you study these examples, note how each follows the rules of high-stress communication:

- The key messages are arranged as sound bites of twenty-seven words or fewer.
- Each key message is reinforced by three supporting messages.
- Each message is written for a grade-school reading level.
- Each map attempts to emphasize the positive over the negative without overly reassuring stakeholders.
- As appropriate, each map admits uncertainty.
- Each map aims to put the most important information first and last, following Covello's Primacy Rule.
- The messages avoid words like "no," "not," and "never."
- When possible, each map cites expert sources to enhance the credibility of the risk messages.
- The majority of the maps employ the acknowledge-and-improve strategy to calm stakeholder outrage.

Section 3: Composing the preamble

The preamble helps us to set the stage for our message maps. We use the preamble to open a news conference or a town meeting in which we will discuss the outbreak and the recall. Such public events are crucial to managing stakeholder outrage. We must have the courage to answer questions directly from journalists or stakeholders. Instead, Blue Bell attempted to manage the outrage through a series of announcements and news releases, plus the occasional one-on-one interview between a spokesperson and a journalist. CEO Paul Kruse evaded such scrutiny by releasing a brief video, which merely parroted the company news release, and an open letter to consumers that failed to address many of the important issues surrounding the outbreak and the April 20 recall.

In addition, a well-crafted preamble provides our communications teams with pre-vetted language that they can use in other communications, such as news releases, backgrounders, open letters, advertisements, websites, and videos.

Using the three-part template established by Covello, Minamyer and Clayton (2007), and applying risk communication concepts from Covello and Peter Sandman (1993), here is a version of a preamble that CEO Kruse might have delivered at a news conference to announce the April 20 recall.

Part 1: The statement of concern

"Good morning. My name is Paul Kruse and I am the chief executive officer for Blue Bell Creameries.

"Since 1951, my family has owned and operated Blue Bell. We take pride in serving a quality product that our customers enjoy. Unfortunately, as we have learned over the last few weeks, we have failed our customers. As we continue to investigate the current situation, in partnership with federal and state health officials, it is clear that we have underestimated how difficult it is to keep listeria bacteria out of our products. We have also underestimated the overall impact listeria contamination has had on our customers and their families. For this, we are deeply sorry and embarrassed. We ask for your forgiveness as we move forward with ending this outbreak and driving listeria bacteria out of our facilities and our products. We understand that we have a moral responsibility to do what we can to make things right."

Part 2: The statement of intent

"As we move forward, we believe it is our obligation to act as transparently as possible. Our most important goal right now is to re-earn your trust. We are committed to ending this outbreak and to make sure it never happens again. We are cooperating fully with the US Centers for Disease Control and Prevention, the US Food and Drug Administration, and state and local health officials in Kansas, Texas, Oklahoma, and Arizona. We are working closely with some of our nation's leading experts in food safety. We are listening to their advice and we have asked them to monitor our progress and to report back to the news media and the general public as they feel appropriate. We have clearly failed to protect our products and our customers. We must learn to do better."

Part 3: The statement of purpose

"We are here to announce that, as of today, Blue Bell is recalling all products from the market. Tests show these products may contain listeria bacteria. Consumers should return all purchases products for refunds. We are recalling all products, including ice cream, frozen yogurt, sherbet, and frozen snacks. These were sold in 23 states and internationally. We are working with state and federal health officials. Tests show these products may contain listeria bacteria, which can be deadly to at-risk populations: newborns, seniors, and folks with weak immunity. Hospitals should be on high alert for these products. Consumers should return all purchased products for refunds. They should avoid consuming or serving our products. Also, they should check their freezers for products. For questions, visit BlueBell.com or call 800-BlueBell. To repeat: Blue Bell is recalling all products from the market. Tests show these products may contain listeria bacteria. Consumers should return all purchased products for refunds.

"We are now ready to answer as many of your questions as we can."

Section 4: Conclusion—An analysis based on best practices

As a final step, we will now consider Blue Bell's messages and actions during the outbreak and recall through the lens of nine best practices for risk communication, as outlined in the 2009 book Effective Risk Communication: A Message-Centered Approach, written by four communication scholars – Timothy Sellnow of the University of Kentucky, Robert Ulmer of the University of Arkansas, Matthew Seeger of Wayne State University, and Richard Littlefield of North Dakota State University. These best practices are based on extensive research and are designed to lead a risk controversy toward mitigation and eventual resolution.

Did Blue Bell infuse risk communication into policy decisions?

No. It's clear that Blue Bell never seriously considered the potential effects of an outbreak and recall on its reputation before the spring of 2015. Despite having several public relations firms on its payroll, none were apparently charged with putting together a risk communication plan. The company hired a crisis communication consultant only after the start of the April 20 recall. The result was a chaotic series of mismatched messages that almost sank the company. However, it appears from later episodes of outbreaks and recalls, the company must have organized its risk communication at some level. More than a year after the 2015 outbreak and recall, Blue Bell announced yet another listeria recall of two ice cream products sold in ten southern states. The company immediately blamed a supplier for the problem (Robinson-Jacobs, 2016). Fortunately for Blue Bell, the FDA backed up Blue Bell's claim a few months later, the CDC detected no related outbreak, and there were few repercussions (Blunt, 2017). However, assigning blame to others rather than accepting moral responsibility is rarely a formula for mitigating stakeholder outrage, especially so soon after an outbreak caused by our own failures.

Did Blue Bell treat risk communication as a process?

No. Blue Bell attempted to treat every recall and every announcement as a final event. The emphasis was put on minimizing the information about the outbreak and the company's role in that outbreak, and on fixing the public's attention on how quickly the company could return products to store shelves. With each new recall and each new announcement, Blue Bell lost credibility.

Did Blue Bell account for the uncertainty inherent in risk?

Yes, to some extent. For example, in its news release of April 20, the company admitted it remained unsure about how the bacteria entered the production process. For the most part, however, Blue Bell maintained a public façade of control over the situation and of confidence in the future—right up until the point that its current investors refused to put more money into the company. Executives were then forced to turn to a Texas billionaire for the funds to sustain the company while executives trimmed its workforce by about two-thirds.

Did Blue Bell design messages to be culturally sensitive?

No. Given that Blue Bell lives in one of the nation's most culturally diverse states, one that has at one time or another flown the flags of Spain, Mexico, and France in addition to the United States, and that the headquarters town of Brenham was originally a German settlement, you might think the company would have a built-in sensitivity to cultural differences among its stakeholders. Not so. The company issued its one-size-fits-all announcements in English only. There is no evidence Blue Bell spent any time at all analyzing the needs or expectations of stakeholders spread across twenty-three states.

Did Blue Bell acknowledge diverse levels of risk tolerance?

No. From the beginning, Blue Bell appears to have believed that the only real question among its stakeholders was, "How soon can I buy more Blue Bell?" The company may have been correct to some extent. Blue Bell is more than a product in Texas; it is a passion. For many Texans, their outrage focused on an inability to buy Blue Bell, and not on the potential for acquiring an illness. But what about outside of Texas, in the other twenty-two states that Blue Bell served? Blue Bell treated its entire base of customers as if they were all as passionate about the ice cream as Texans. Moreover, Blue Bell consistently played upon its long history of zero product recalls while downplaying any indications that its plants were contaminated and the outbreak could continue to spread.

Did Blue Bell involve the public in dialogues about risk?

No. At every turn during the outbreak and the recall, Blue Bell held its stakeholders at arm's length. Company executives attempted to minimize the financial effects of the recall by pulling products out of the market in stages, sometimes without alerting consumers, and thus risking public health in twenty-three states. Even when the company finally recalled all of its products from the market, it provided little in self-efficacy messages to warn consumers of the dangers of listeriosis or to protect them from the dangers or mitigate their effects. The company spoke clearly on the issues that it considered important, such as when consumers could expect Blue Bell products to return to stores. However, the company spoke with little empathy for those who became ill or died after eating its products. Company executives all but ignored the victims of the outbreak and their families.

Instead, they apologized for the inconvenience of depriving customers of Blue Bell products.

Did Blue Bell present risk messages with honesty?

In general, no. As evidence of the outbreak unfolded, and Blue Bell's complicity became apparent, the company did its best to avoid acknowledging the overall risk to its customers. The company's focus was more on re-establishing business-as-usual and less on protecting the public from contaminated products.

Did Blue Bell meet risk perception needs by remaining open and accessible to the public?

Partially. Company executives and their marketing teams were more than willing to listen to customers who expressed concern about the absence of Blue Bell products in stores. However, they paid little attention to critics who suggested that the little creamery in Brenham was acting more like a corporate behemoth than a family-owned enterprise. On the technical level, the company limited public access by answering its hotline only during business hours. It posted its announcements and FAQs online and only in English, limiting access to only those stakeholders who read English and have access to the web. It made little effort to reach out to news media, other than to list a media contact on its news releases and public announcements. It also provided company spokespeople upon request as well as some background information and a handful of useful visuals. However, the company shielded the company's chief executive officer from journalists. It also avoided any public forum, such as a news conference, that would allow reporters to ask questions and get answers.

Did Blue Bell collaborate and coordinate about risk with credible information sources?

Yes. The company worked closely with state health officials, the CDC, the FDA, and recognized industry experts to identify the problem and a strategy to solve it. However, it failed to assist government agencies in spreading effective risk messages to the public. It also failed to acknowledge to the public that the company had consulted food safety experts outside of the company; in doing so, Blue Bell missed an opportunity to calm stakeholder outrage.

Section 5: Sources for this case study

"A Blue Bell Listeria Timeline - 2010 to 2015." Marler Blog. May 31, 2015. Accessed February 12, 2018. http://www.marlerblog.com/legal-cases/a-blue-bell-listeria-timeline-2010-to-2015/#.

"A statement from Blue Bell CEO and President Paul Kruse," Vimeo. April 20, 2015. Accessed February 09, 2018. https://vimeo.com/125527719.

Abrams, Rachel, and Hiroko Tabuchi. "Listeria Leads to Major Ice Cream Recall." The New York Times, April 22, 2015, Late` ed., sec. B.

Barrett, Patricia, Stephanie Ericson, and Erika Hanes. Blue Bell; People Over Profit: An Analysis of Blue Bell Creameries' Listeriosis Crisis Response. Case study. College of Communication, DePaul University. New York, NY: Arthur W. Page Society, 2016.

"Blue Bell Company Profile." Owler. Accessed January 26, 2018. https://www.owler.com/iaApp/193971/blue-bell-company-profile?onBoardingComplete=true.

"Blue Bell Creameries, L.P. | Company Profile from Hoover's - Companies & Details." Blue Bell Creameries, L.P. | Company Profile from Hoover's - D&B Hoovers. Accessed January 26, 2018. http://www.hoovers.com/company-information/cs/company-profile.blue_bell_creameries_lp.3b90c3f2354f35ca.html.

"Blue Bell Creameries issues product recall." Denver Post (Associated Press), April 21, 2015, BUSINESS sec.

"Blue Bell Creameries recalling all products." USA Today, April 22, 2015, MONEY 1D.

"Blue Bell recalls ice cream for Listeria; blames supplier." Food Safety News. September 22, 2016. Accessed February 28, 2018. http://www.foodsafetynews.com/2016/09/blue-bell-recalls-ice-cream-for-listeria-blames-supplier/#.Wpbd1RPwbUI.

Blunt, Katherine. "FDA says Listeria came from outside supplier, not Blue Bell." Houston Chronicle. February 02, 2017. Accessed February 28, 2018. https://www.chron.com/business/article/FDA-Listeria-came-from-outside-supplier-not-10901700.php.

Center for Food Safety and Applied Nutrition. "Search for FDA Guidance Documents - Draft Guidance for Industry: Control of Listeria monocytogenes in Ready-To-Eat Foods." U S Food and Drug Administration Home Page. Accessed January 26, 2018. https://www.fda.gov/RegulatoryInformation/Guidances/ucm073110.htm.

Centers for Disease Control and Prevention. "Washington: Updated Notice to U.S. Hospitals and Long-Term Care Facilities: Patients at Risk of Listeriosis from Certain Blue Bell Brand Ice Cream Products." News release, April 22, 2015. US Official News.

Collette, Mark. "Blue Bell, industry, flout listeria guidelines." Houston Chronicle. June 22, 2015. Accessed February 12, 2018. https://www.houstonchronicle.com/news/houston-texas/houston/article/Blue-Bell-industry-flout-listeria-guidelines-6340771.php#photo-7856349.

Collette, Mark. "Blue Bell ice cream CEO retires, but Kruse name persists." Houston Chronicle. February 20, 2017. Accessed January 26, 2018. http://www.houstonchronicle.com/business/retail/article/Blue-Bell-ice-cream-CEO-retires-but-Kruse-name-10946511.php.

"Company Overview of Blue Bell Creameries, LP.", Bloomberg.com. Accessed January 26, 2018. https://www.bloomberg.com/research/stocks/private/snapshot.asp?privcapid=4238 094.

Covello, V. and Allen, F. (1988). Seven Cardinal Rules of Risk Communication. Retrieved January 5, 2018 from https://archive.epa.gov/care/web/pdf/7_cardinal_rules.pdf

Dingus, Gary. "A year after listeria scandal, Blue Bell still battling back." Mystatesman. Austin American-Statesman. September 17, 2016. Accessed January 26, 2018. http://www.mystatesman.com/business/year-after-listeria-scandal-blue-bell-still-battling-back/f6lbTDX8fpXFEAhl1aFdWO/.

Dingus, Gary, and Claudia Grisales. "What's next for Blue Bell?" Austin American-Statesman, April 22, 2015, Main sec.

Elkind, Peter . "How ice cream maker Blue Bell blew it." Fortune. September 25, 2015. Accessed January 26, 2018. http://fortune.com/2015/09/25/blue-bell-listeria-recall/.

Houck, Brenna. "Blue Bell Fined $850K Over Deadly Listeria Outbreak." Eater. July 30, 2016. Accessed February 28, 2018. https://www.eater.com/2016/7/30/12332368/blue-bell-ice-cream-fine-listeria-outbreak.

"Listeria Food Poisoning." AboutListeria.com. Accessed January 26, 2018. http://www.about-listeria.com/.

"Listeria (Listeriosis)." Centers for Disease Control and Prevention. June 29, 2017. Accessed January 26, 2018. https://www.cdc.gov/listeria/index.html.

"Listeriosis." World Health Organization. Accessed February 20, 2018. http://www.who.int/ith/diseases/listeriosis/en/.

"More Listeria Illnesses Linked to Blue Bell Ice Cream - Texas, Oklahoma, Kansas and Arizona." Marler Blog. April 21, 2015. Accessed February 12, 2018. http://www.marlerblog.com/legal-cases/more-listeria-illnesses-linked-to-blue-bell-ice-cream-texas-oklahoma-kansas-and-arizona/.

Newman, Jesse. "Texas Investor Sid Bass to Lend Blue Bell Creameries Up to $125 Million." Wall Street Journal (New York City), July 16, 2015. Accessed February 13, 2018. https://www.wsj.com/articles/texas-investor-sid-bass-to-lend-blue-bell-creameries-up-to-125-million-1437080757.

New Mexico Department of Health. "New Mexico: Blue Bell Recalls All Products Due to Listeria Concerns." News release, April 21, 2015. US Official News. Accessed February 13, 2018.

O'Neil, Carolyn. "Food recalls indicate better detection methods." Atlanta Journal-Constitution, April 22, 2015, LIVING sec. D.

Ramirez, Steve. "Las Crucens cope with Blue Bell ice cream recall." Las Cruces Sun-News, April 21, 2015, NEWS sec.

"Recalls, Market Withdrawals, & Safety Alerts - Blue Bell Ice Cream Recalls Select Products Containing Chocolate Chip Cookie Dough Pieces Purchased From Outside Supplier Aspen Hills Due To Possible Health Risk." Office of Regulatory Affairs. U S Food and Drug Administration Home Page. September 21, 2016. Accessed January 26, 2018. https://www.fda.gov/safety/recalls/ucm522045.htm.

Robinson-Jacobs, Karen. "Texas-based Blue Bell recalls two ice cream flavors over Listeria concerns." Dallasnews.com. September 21, 2016. Accessed February 28,

2018. https://www.dallasnews.com/business/retail/2016/09/21/blue-bell-recalls-ice-cream-listeria-concerns.

US Food and Drug Administration. "Washington: Blue Bell Creameries Voluntarily Expands Recall to Include All of its Products Due to Possible Health Risk." News release, April 22, 2015. US Official News.

World Health, and Food and Agriculture Organization of the United Nations. "Risk assessment of Listeria monocytogenes in ready-to-eat foods : interpretative summary." Apps.who.int. January 01, 1970. Accessed January 26, 2018. http://apps.who.int/iris/handle/10665/42874.

The text of the company's news release announcing the total-product recall is reproduced here at it is no longer available on the company's website.

For Immediate Release

Consumer Contact: 979-836-7977

For Frequently Asked Questions click here.

BLUE BELL CREAMERIES VOLUNTARILY EXPANDS RECALL TO INCLUDE ALL OF ITS PRODUCTS DUE TO POSSIBLE HEALTH RISK

BRENHAM, Texas, April 20, 2015 – Blue Bell Ice Cream of Brenham, Texas, is voluntarily recalling all of its products currently on the market made at all of its facilities including ice cream, frozen yogurt, sherbet and frozen snacks because they have the potential to be contaminated with Listeria monocytogenes, an organism which can cause serious and sometimes fatal infections in young children, frail or elderly people, and others with weakened immune systems. Although healthy individuals may suffer only short-term symptoms such as high fever, severe headaches, stiffness, nausea, abdominal pain and diarrhea, Listeria infection can cause miscarriages and stillbirths among pregnant women.

"We're committed to doing the 100 percent right thing, and the best way to do that is to take all of our products off the market until we can be confident that they are all safe," said Paul Kruse, Blue Bell CEO and president. "We are heartbroken about this situation and apologize to all of our loyal Blue Bell fans and customers. Our entire history has been about making the very best and highest quality ice cream and we intend to fix this problem. We want enjoying our ice cream to be a source of joy and pleasure, never a cause for concern, so we are committed to getting this right."

The products being recalled are distributed to retail outlets, including food service accounts, convenience stores and supermarkets in Alabama, Arizona, Arkansas, Colorado, Florida, Georgia, Illinois, Indiana, Kansas, Kentucky, Louisiana, Mississippi, Missouri, Nevada, New Mexico, North Carolina, Ohio, Oklahoma, South Carolina, Tennessee, Texas, Virginia, Wyoming and international locations*.

Today's decision was the result of findings from an enhanced sampling program initiated by Blue Bell, which revealed that Chocolate Chip Cookie Dough Ice Cream half gallons produced on March 17, 2015, and March 27, 2015, contained the bacteria. This means Blue Bell has now had several positive tests for Listeria in different places and plants and as previously reported five patients were treated in Kansas and three in Texas after testing positive for Listeria monocytogenes.

"At every step, we have made decisions in the best interest of our customers based on the evidence we had available at the time," Kruse said. "At this point, we cannot say with certainty how Listeria was introduced to our facilities and so we have taken this unprecedented step. We continue to work with our team of experts to eliminate this problem."

Blue Bell is implementing a procedure called "test and hold" for all products made at all of its manufacturing facilities. This means that all products will be tested first and held for release to the market only after the tests show they are safe. The Broken Arrow facility will remain closed as Blue Bell continues to investigate.

In addition to the "test and hold" system, Blue Bell is implementing additional safety procedures and testing including:

- Expanding our already robust system of daily cleaning and sanitizing of equipment
- Expanding our system of swabbing and testing our plant environment by 800 percent to include more surfaces
- Sending samples daily to a leading microbiology laboratory for testing
- Providing additional employee training

Blue Bell expects to resume distribution soon on a limited basis once it is confident in the safety of its product.

Consumers who have purchased these items are urged to return them to the place of purchase for a full refund. For more information consumers with questions may call 979-836-7977 Monday – Friday 8 a.m. – 5 p.m. CST or go to bluebell.com.

News Media Contact: Joe Robertson, 979-830-9830, media@bluebell.com

CASE STUDY: The I.M. Healthy SoyNut Butter E. coli O:157 outbreak and recall of 2017

Executive Summary

During the spring of 2017, federal health officials at the US Centers for Disease Control and Prevention (CDC) and the US Food and Drug Administration (FDA) collaborated with state health agencies to investigate an outbreak of E. coli O157 that eventually infected thirty-two persons in twelve states. Of those thirty-two, twelve were hospitalized and nine developed a form of kidney failure known as HUS. There were no deaths reported.

The case is particularly interesting from a risk communications standpoint because:

- It involves two companies: the distributor of the recalled product and the contract manufacturer whose substandard production practices most likely led to the contamination and the outbreak.
- The recall caused the bankruptcy of the distributor.
- The manufacturer had several opportunities to assist FDA in the process of informing stakeholders about how to avoid the contaminated product, but remained silent.
- The manufacturer resisted initial attempts by FDA to investigate its production practices.
- FDA carefully outlined the steps the manufacturer would need to take to keep its manufacturing facility open. However, the manufacturer met only a few of the steps and essentially forced FDA to shut down the facility.
- FDA officials came under heavy public criticism because they declined to release the list of outlets that sold or served the contaminated product.

Section 1: Background

1-A. About the companies: SoyNut Butter Company and Dixie Dew Products

The outbreak and recall involved two companies: The SoyNut Butter Company of Glenview, Illinois, and its contract manufacturer, Dixie Dew Products, Inc., of Erlanger, Kentucky.

Founded in 1996, the SoyNut Butter Company made and distributed food products that were free of peanuts or tree nuts, catering to institutions and consumers concerned with food allergies.

In October 2012, the company said in a news release that its peanut butter substitute, I.M. Healthy SoyNut Butter, was served monthly to more than two million children in educational institutions, daycare facilities, and Head Start programs across the United States (Marketwire, 2012). I.M. Healthy SoyNut Butter was served in schools, park districts, camps, daycare facilities, and other institutions that serve or care for children, including 1,600 KinderCare Learning Centers throughout the United States, the company said. The privately owned company also said it sold its products in leading supermarket chains, in more than 1,400 specialty natural nutrition and health food stores across the United States as well as through online retailers.

In the 2012 announcement, the company boasted of its commitment to food safety, quoting its vice president of research, development, and quality: "We take great measures to ensure the quality and safety of our products including the testing of each batch of SoyNut Butter for salmonella and other contaminants. We process multiple batches of SoyNut Butter daily with each batch tested for salmonella bacteria. We've never had an issue."

SoyNut Butter Company President Stephen Grubb added, "Providing an all-natural, nutritious product that parents, educators and caregivers of children can trust and rely on is at the core of our business."

It was SoyNut Butter that recalled I.M. Healthy SoyNut Butter from the market in 2017. However, the focus of this case study is Dixie Dew Products, which manufactured the I.M Healthy brand for SoyNut Butter, and which was eventually identified as the actual source of the 2017 E. coli outbreak that led to the recall, according to federal health authorities. Founded in 1934, Dixie Dew manufacturers customized products for the food industry, specializing in contract packaging and private labels. Dixie Dew primarily produced caramel and chocolate sauces, fillings and toppings. "Developed and perfected over three generations, we take great pride in producing the highest quality products available," the company said in an online profile. The company employed fewer than twenty workers and generated annual revenue of about $2.4 million (Zoominfo, February 2018; LexisNexis, February 26, 2018; Kentucky Directory of Manufacturers, 2018).

1-B. About the pathogen: Escherichia coli O157

E. coli are bacteria found in the colon of warm-blooded animals. Most are harmless. A few can cause food-borne infections. Among the most dangerous is the E. coli that produce Shiga toxin. These are known as STECs: Shiga-toxin E. coli. An estimated 265,000 STEC infections happen each year in the United States. E. coli O157 causes about 36 percent of these infections and is easily differentiated biochemically from other E. coli strains.

The most common sources of STECs are products made from ground meat that are raw or undercooked; raw milk; and vegetables contaminated with feces. Examples of foods implicated in outbreaks of E. coli O157:H7 include undercooked hamburgers, dried cured salami, unpasteurized fresh-pressed apple cider, yogurt, and cheese made from raw milk.

STECs are sensitive to heat and can be eliminated from food products simply by cooking them thoroughly. STECs can grow in temperatures ranging from 7 °C to 50 °C, with an optimum temperature of 37 °C. Some STECs can grow in acidic foods, down to a pH of 4.4, and in foods with a minimum water activity (aW) of 0.95.

STECs are destroyed by thorough cooking of foods; all parts must reach a temperature of 70 °C or higher. Prevention requires control measures at every stage of the food chain from farm to fork. This includes production, processing, manufacturing, and preparation.

The strain can infect anyone of any age. Older children and young adults can become very ill. But the ones most likely to develop severe illness are the very young and the very old.

The incubation period for an STEC infection is usually three to four days after exposure but may be as brief as one day or as long as ten days. Symptoms begin slowly with mild stomach pain or diarrhea, and may worsen over several days.

Symptoms vary, but may include stomach cramps, diarrhea, bloody diarrhea, or vomiting. Fever is usually low grade: less than 101°F or 38.5°C. People generally recover within seven days. Caregivers should treating the symptoms with antibiotics or anti-diarrheal medications, as these can actually increase the risk of kidney failure.

Doctors diagnose STEC infections through lab tests of stool samples.

STEC infections usually come and go without medical treatment. However, especially in young children and senior citizens, an STEC infection may lead to a form of kidney failure known as haemolygic uraemic syndrome, or HUS. As many as 10 percent of patients with STEC infection may develop HUS, usually in about seven days after the first symptoms appear.

Symptoms of HUS include a decrease in the frequency of urination, general tiredness, and a loss of pink color in cheeks and the inside of the lower eyelids, acute renal failure, haemolytic anaemia, and thrombocytopenia (low blood platelets).

Anyone who shows signs of HUS should seek professional medical care, as their kidneys may stop functioning and they could develop other serious problems. Most HUS patients will recover within a few weeks. Some suffer permanent damage, with fatalities occurring in 3 percent to 5 percent of cases.

Overall, HUS is the most common cause of acute renal failure in young children. It can lead to seizure, stroke, coma, or other neurological complications in 25 percent of HUS patients.

1-C. About the outbreak

Here is how detection of the outbreak unfolded from March 2017 to May 2017, say CDC's public summary, FDA reports, company announcements, and reports from news media outlets.

March 2017

CDC announces on March 3 that it is working with FDA, public health agencies, and state-level regulators to investigate a multi-state outbreak of Shiga toxin-producing Escherichia coli O157:H7 infections. Using its PulseNet network of laboratories, CDC has identified the strain through the techniques of pulsed-field gel ecectrophoresis (PFGE) and whole genome sequencing (WGS). The strain's DNA "fingerprint" is new to the PulseNet database.

The early stages of the investigation have confirmed twelve cases of infection in five states, CDC says. Six persons have been hospitalized and four have developed HUS. Eleven of the twelve are younger than age 18 years. Illnesses began as early as January 6, 2017.

On March 7, CDC updates the count to sixteen confirmed cases in nine states. Fourteen of the sixteen are younger than age 18 years. The investigation now focuses upon a potential source. In interviews with fifteen of the ill persons, or their family members, all report contact with I.M. Health brand SoyNut Butter. Nine report they ate the product at home during the week before onset of symptoms. Two say they attend facilities that serve the product. Four say they attend child-care centers that serve the product.

On March 21, CDC increases the count to twenty-three confirmed cases in nine states. Ten of the ill have been hospitalized and seven have developed HUS. Twenty of the twenty-three are younger than age 18 years. Twenty of the twenty-three also report contact with I.M. Health brand SoyNut Butter at home, at a facility, or at a child-care center during the week before they became ill.

Meanwhile, lab tests have identified the strain of E. coli O157 in opened containers of I.M. Health brand SoyNut Butter taken from homes of ill persons in California, Oregon, and Washington. Also, health officials in California isolated the strain in unopened containers collected from retail locations. PFGE testing then identified the strain found in all of the containers as having the same DNA fingerprint as the strain isolated from the sick people.

On March 30, CDC increases the total number of cases to twenty-nine in twelve states. Twelve have been hospitalized and nine have developed HUS. Start dates for the illnesses fall between January 4 and March 13. Investigators interview twenty-eight of the twenty-nine patients or their families. Twenty-one report eating I.M. Healthy brand SoyNut Butter at home during the week before they became ill, or attending an institution that served the product, or attending a childcare facility that served the product or a related product, I.M. Healthy brand granola coated with SoyNut Butter.

May 2017

On May 2, CDC declares an end to the outbreak. The final count comes to thirty-two cases in twelve states: Arizona (four cases), California (five), Florida (two), Illinois (one), Massachusetts (one), Maryland (one), New Jersey (one), Oregon (eleven), Virginia (two), Washington (two), and Wisconsin (one). Twelve persons spent time in a hospital and nine developed HUS, but CDC received no reports of death. Of the thirty-two cases, twenty-six were in people younger than eighteen years: 81 percent.

Though the outbreak was officially concluded, CDC issued this warning to consumers: "Although the outbreak investigation is over, illnesses may continue for some time. The recalled SoyNut Butter products have long shelf lives and may still be in people's homes or in institutions. Consumers who don't know about the recalls could continue to eat the products and get sick."

Based on its analysis of epidemiologic, laboratory, and trace-back evidence, CDC says, the most likely source of the outbreak, is I.M. Healthy brand SoyNut Butter.

1-D. About the product recall

The product recall takes place almost in tandem with the CDC's updates to the public about the outbreak.

On March 4, the day after the CDC's initial announcement, the SoyNut Butter Company uses a news release to inform consumers that it is recalling I.M. Healthy Original Creamy SoyNut Butter. The news release is for the most part straightforward and unflinching. It says:

- The recalled product may be contaminated with E. coli O157:H7.
- It was "distributed in multiple states and may have been purchased in stores or through mail order."
- It was also served in childcare centers and schools in several states.
- SoyNut's news release provides consumers with clear, actionable information on how to identify the suspected products:
  - o   15-ounce plastic jars with best-by dates of July 5, August 30, and August 31, 2018.
  - o   Individual-portion cups with a best-by date of August 8, 2018.
  - o   Four-pound plastic tubes with best-by dates of November 16 and July 25, 2018.

In addition, SoyNut actively assists CDC and FDA with alerting consumers to the dangers of the E. coli bacteria:

- Most healthy people will recover within a week, but some may develop HUS.
- HUS most frequently develops in young children and the elderly.
- It can lead to serious kidney failure and perhaps death.

The news release outlines the epidemiological evidence that the product is to blame for the outbreak. It urges consumers to avoid eating the suspected product and instructs to return the product to its place of purchase to receive a full refund. It provides a toll-free number for both consumers and journalists, though the phones are answered only on weekdays during normal business hours.

However, the news release offers no apology to the sickened consumers or their families, expresses no regret, and accepts no responsibility, moral or legal. It contains no comment from the ownership or the chief executive, and there is no indication of a news conference to answer questions from reporters.

Unfortunately for SoyNut, the company cannot slow the pace of events. On March 7, as the CDC updates the count of reported cases to sixteen, SoyNut expands its recall to all varieties of I.M Health SoyNut Butters as well as all varieties of I.M. Health Granola products. On March 10, the company expands the recall again to include all varieties of Dixie's Diner Club brand Carb Not Beanit Butter.

On March 24, an unrelated company called ProSports Club recalls its 20/20 Lifestyle Yogurt Peanut Crunch Bars because they contain SoyNut Butter provided by The SoyNut Butter Company.

CDC warns consumers to avoid consuming any variety or size of I.M. Healthy brand SoyNut Butter, the brand's granola, or Dixie's Diner Club brand Carb Not Beanit Butter, regardless of date purchased or the best-by date. The agency urges consumers to throw out any opened product, even if it was eaten or served, and no one fell ill: "Put it in a sealed bag in the trash so that children, pets, or other animals can't eat it." CDC also urges consumers to check their pantries for the products, which can have shelf lives of up to two years.

The succession of recalls overwhelms the small company, which declares Chapter 7 bankruptcy on May 12 with less than $50,000 in assets and millions of dollars in debt.

1-E. About the facility closing

As the distributor of the contaminated product, The SoyNut Butter Company, stumbles toward its almost inevitable bankruptcy, the manufacturer that actually contaminated the product remains silent about its involvement in the outbreak. Even SoyNut declines to identify its supplier to the public. The secrecy ends on March 28, when the FDA announces it has suspended the Food Facility Registration for Dixie Dew Products, Inc., of Erlanger, Kentucky.

In a March 27 letter to Dixie Dew's president, Robert C. Carl, the FDA says it has "determined that food manufactured, processed, packed, received, or held by your facility has a reasonable probability of causing serious adverse health consequences or death to humans, and that your facility created, caused, or was otherwise responsible for such reasonable probability."

More specifically, the letter says, the FDA's judgment is based on three factors:

1. Food products made at the facility have been identified as "the likely source of a multistate outbreak of pathogenic E. coli."
2. An FDA inspection of the facility, held between March 3 and March 15, found "insanitary conditions" that may have contaminated the firm's ready-to-eat products.
3. Though Dixie Dew has taken some corrective actions following the inspection, "we do not believe your response to date is adequate to address the risks caused by your facility."

During its March 3-15 inspection, FDA says, it observed the following:

- A "clear liquid substance" dripping from a hole in the ceiling tile and splashing onto the manufacturing equipment.
- Forklifts operating outside for waste disposal and inside the facility, including the production and packing room for the SoyNut Butter: "Your Plant Manager states that these forklifts are never cleaned."
- Hand-wash stations that lacked soap or hot water; the heating tank had been out of commission for two years.
- A heavy buildup of SoyNut Butter on food contact surfaces, floors, walls, and ceilings: "Additionally, your firm informed the investigators that the last full clean of the soy nut butter production room was in approximately December 2015."
- A fine-mixing machine that was shutting off once or twice daily during production due to amperage overload.
- A thermometer "that has never been verified for accuracy" and thus could not verify that the product had reached a sufficient temperature to kill bacteria.

Moreover, FDA says later, Dixie Dew employees initially resisted the FDA inspection on March 3: "Dixie Dew refused to allow FDA investigators access to the facility's environmental sampling and production records; the FDA subsequently issued a Demand for Records under section 414 of the Federal Food, Drug, and Cosmetic Act. After receiving the Demand for Records, Dixie Dew provided FDA investigators with the necessary records."

Dixie Dew responds to the inspection report on March 20 with promises to take corrective actions. FDA found the company's response to be insufficient. FDA says in the March 27 letter to Dixie Dew, "Given the epidemiological findings showing your food products are the likely source of an outbreak of E. coli O157:H7 and the current condition of the facility, FDA concludes that unless and until Dixie Dew has completed and implemented certain correction actions, food manufactured, process, packed, received, or held at the Dixie Dew facility has a reasonable probability of causing serious adverse health consequences or death to humans or animals."

On March 28, FDA issues a suspension order to close the facility, using the agency's authority under the 2011 FDA Food Safety Modernization Act

On March 30, FDA posts a safety alert on its website. "The Suspension Order applies to the entire facility," the alert says. "While the order is in effect, no food product may leave the facility for sale or distribution. The FDA will reinstate Dixie Dew's food facility registration only when the agency determines that adequate grounds do not exist to continue the suspension of registration."

On May 12, SoyNut files for Chapter 7 bankruptcy.

More than a year later, Dixie Dew follows suit.

1-F. About the FDA's withholding of information

Compounding the overall situation is the FDA's decision to treat SoyNut's list of distribution outlets—primarily retail stores and childcare centers—as trade secrets. The Washington Post reports, "This interpretation differs from that of other agencies in the federal food safety system, an overlapping and often illogical network of regulatory fiefdoms. The system, which is responsible for keeping food free of bacteria and other pathogens, frequently has to weigh the very real interests of private food companies against potential risks to the public. In the case of releasing retailer lists during major outbreaks, the FDA has historically sided with business, ruling that such lists constitute confidential commercial information" and thus should not be available for public consumption (Dewey, 2017)."

Moreover, the FDA declines for several weeks to reveal the name of the contract manufacturer who made the recalled products: "Consistent with law, FDA releases information, including (confidential corporate information), to the extent necessary to effectuate a recall. We have no evidence at this time challenging the effectiveness of this recall (Beach, March 21, 2017)."

1-G. Stakeholder reaction

The E. coli outbreak, the product recall, and the facility closing generated little news coverage in major media. Why? Perhaps because both The SoyNut Butter Company and Dixie Dew Products were small private companies with few prospects of going public, or because the I.M. Healthy brand was hardly a household name, or because soy nut butter remains a fringe product. The March 28 suspension order against Dixie Dew received less than 100 words from the Associated Press and the brief appears to have received little play nationally. The companies involved in the outbreak may have appreciated this lack of news coverage, but it almost certainly put more consumers (especially children) at risk of consuming the product and contracting the infection.

On the legal front, the Chicago Tribune reported one lawsuit filed in California against The SoyNut Butter Company by the family of an eight-year-old boy who, according to the suit, was sickened and hospitalized as a result of eating the tainted product. Seattle attorney Bill Marler claimed to represent another seventeen victims of the outbreak.

Meanwhile, the FDA came under scrutiny for its policy of withholding the names and locations of outlets that served or sold the I.M. Healthy brand. US Rep. Rosa DeLauro of Connecticut's Third District publicly praised FDA's decision to shut down the Dixie Dew plant. But she also condemned the FDA's policy to withhold the names and locations of stores that sold the I.M. Health products and schools that served them. "While the FDA make the right decision in shutting down the Dixie Dew plant, the agency should take another step forward and reverse its policy of withholding the names and locations of stores and schools where recalled food products are sold," she said in a statement. "As we have seen with Dixie Dew, it is irresponsible to rely on the good faith of food corporations to provide all the necessary recall information. Americans deserve to know these details to ensure their health and safety." DeLauro is a longtime advocate for stronger food safety legislation and a senior member of the House appropriations subcommittee, which controls federal funding for agencies like the FDA.

1-H. Timeline: March 2017—November 2018

- March 2—The FDA and CDC advise the owners of The SoyNut Butter Company that evidence identifies their products as the source of the multistate outbreak of E. coli O157:H7.
- March 3—CDC announces it is working with the FDA, state health officials, and local authorities to investigate the outbreak, which now totals twelve reported cases in five states. Meanwhile, FDA officials arrive at Dixie Dew Products' manufacturing plant in Erlanger, Kentucky, to begin almost two weeks of food safety inspections. Dixie Dew is the outsourced supplier of I.M. Healthy SoyNut Butter, though neither FDA nor The SoyNut Butter Company reveal this to the public.
- March 4—SoyNut expands the recall to include fifteen-ounce plastic jars with best-by dates of July 5, 2018, August 30, 2018, and August 31, 2018, as well

as individual cups with a best-by date of August 8, 2018, and four-pound plastic tubs with best-by dates of November 16, 2018 and July 25, 2018.

- March 7—CDC updates the total to sixteen cases in nine states. SoyNut recalls all lots of I.M. Healthy SoyNut Butter and I.M. Healthy Granola in all flavors and sizes.
- March 10—SoyNut again expands its recall to include all best-by dates of Dixie Diner's Club brand Carb Not Beanit Butter, which is available only through direct purchase from the company.
- March 20—Dixie Dew responds to the FDA's inspection report. The company agrees to some of the FDA's changes, but fails to respond to all of them.
- March 21—CDC increases the count to twenty-three cases in nine states; lab tests confirm that the strain of E. coli isolated in the sick people matches that found in containers of I.M. Healthy SoyNut Butter products.
- March 24—An unrelated company, Pro Sports Club, recalls its 20/20 Life Styles Yogurt Peanut Crunch bars because they contain Soy Nut Butter from The SoyNut Butter Company.
- March 28—The FDA issues a suspension order against Dixie Dew, effectively shutting down the plant until the company complies with the agency's standards for food safety.
- March 30—CDC again raises the total number of confirmed cases to twenty-nine in twelve states.
- May 4—CDC declares the outbreak is over, but warns households, retailers, and institutions to remain vigilant to any products that may remain on shelves.
- May 12—SoyNut declares Chapter 7 bankruptcy.
- November 29, 2018—Dixie Dew Products Inc. files for Chapter 7 bankruptcy.

Section 2: Mapping the messages

2-A. Assessing the outrage

From this point, we will focus on how strong outrage management enhanced with message mapping might have helped Dixie Dew Products avoid a facility shutdown. The odds are that no amount of outrage management would have saved The SoyNut Butter Company, which was far too small to survive such an extensive recall of its products. To its credit, SoyNut clearly attempted to assist the FDA in warning consumers about the threat of the E. coli pathogen in its contaminated product, but the company was likely doomed by the scope of the recall. On the other hand, Dixie Dew—for all its many, many sins—had the opportunity to avoid a crippling shutdown of its only manufacturing plant if it had simply managed the outrage of its only vital stakeholders in the E. coli outbreak: officials of the FDA.

How might have Dixie Dew managed this feat? By taking two commonsense steps toward helping the FDA complete its investigation quickly and with minimal obstruction.

First, Dixie Dew could have opened up its records upon request to the FDA rather than forcing the agency to waste time securing a court order to view the documents. Did Dixie Dew executives really believe the FDA would simply retreat? The action was a pointless aggravation that served only to increase outrage within the FDA, which was already feeling heat for its policy of withholding Dixie Dew's identify from the public, and for declining to announce locations of stores that sold the I.M. Healthy brand and institutions that served the product.

Second, Dixie Dew could have made a concerted effort to meet the standards that FDA set for the plant in its inspection report. Given the condition of the plant, and its role in the multistate outbreak, did Dixie Dew executives really believe that FDA would accept anything short of total compliance to the standards outlined in the inspection report? Was this a sad attempt at a bluff? The FDA clearly said: Meet these standards or we will shut you down. What result did Dixie Dew expect?

Instead, Dixie Dew attempted to stonewall part of the investigation, and then tried to bargain with FDA officials on food safety standards. These actions sealed the company's fate by raising the outrage within the agency.

2-B. Identifying stakeholders

Starting on March 3, the day that FDA officials showed up at the Dixie Dew plant, the only stakeholders that truly mattered to Dixie Dew's survival were those same officials. Dixie Dew should have done everything possible to assist the investigation, to warn the public of the E. coli outbreak, and to remedy the standards within its manufacturing plant. By helping the FDA, Dixie Dew stood a decent chance of earning some goodwill among FDA officials and avoiding a total shutdown of production.

2-C. Building the nine message maps

For this exercise, we will assume that Dixie Dew is in position to fully support The SoyNut Butter Company's March 4 recall of fifteen-ounce plastic jars with best-by dates of July 05, 2018, August 30, 2018, and August 31, 2018, as well as individual cups with a best-by date of August 08, 2018, and four-pound plastic tubs with best-by dates of November 16, 2018 and July 25, 2018. Clearly, the hammer is going to come down hard from the FDA. The question is, how hard? At this point, Dixie Dew still has a chance to influence how much damage it will suffer. Its best opportunity is to assist the investigation, accept moral responsibility for the situation, and help the FDA warn consumers through a risk communications strategy of acknowledge and improve.

Map 1: The Overarching Map

As an initial survival strategy, Dixie Dew could have assisted federal health officials in getting the word out about the E. coli outbreak and its connection to the recalled products. In the early stages of the investigation, this was clearly the most pressing task on behalf of public health. Doing so could have earned the manufacturer some badly needed goodwill with federal regulators, who had the power to shut down all of Dixie Dew's operations and effectively kill the company. Beyond that, helping to alert consumers was the clearly ethical course, considering Dixie Dew's role in contaminating the recalled products.

Map 1: The Overarching Map		
Stakeholders: General public and news media		
Question: What does the public most need to know about this recall?		
Key Message 1	**Key Message 2**	**Key Message 3**
Our client, SoyNut Butter Company, is recalling I.M. Healthy SoyNut Butter.	The products may contain E. coli bacteria.	Consumers should return products for full refunds.
Supporting information 1.1	**Supporting information 2.1**	**Supporting information 3.1**
Look for 15-ounce plastic jars best-by dated July 5, August 30, or August 31, 2018.	They were sold in multiple states in stores or by mail.	Avoid eating or serving the products under any conditions.
Supporting information 1.2	**Supporting information 2.2**	**Supporting information 3.2**
Individual cups with a best-by date of August 8.	They were also served in childcare centers and schools.	Check shelves for any stored products.
Supporting information 1.3	**Supporting information 2.3**	**Supporting information 3.3**
4-pound tubs with best-by dates of November 4 or July 28, 2018.	Children and seniors are at risk of kidney failure.	Questions? Call 1-800-Dixie-Dew or visit DixieDew.com.

(Fig. 1)

The Overarching Map serves as the primary guide for delivering risk messages during a news conference or a stakeholder meeting. It is also where the company's public spokesperson returns after bridging from a challenging question.

We should deliver the message map using Covello's Triple T Model:

1. Tell your audience what you are going to tell them: State your key messages from your overarching message map. Keep in mind you want to keep this message at less than nine seconds for broadcast media and twenty-four words for print media.
2. Tell them more: State the first key messages and then state the three supporting messages. Do the same with the second and third key messages and their supporting messages.
3. Tell them what you just told them: Repeat your three key messages.

Here is how Dixie Dew's spokesperson (preferably the CEO) might have delivered the overarching message map using the Triple T Model:

- Step 1: Tell your audience what you are going to tell them. Read the key messages on Tier Two from left to right.
  - ○ "Our client, SoyNut Butter Company, is recalling I.M. Healthy SoyNut Butter. The products may contain E. coli bacteria. Consumers should return products for a full refunds."
- Step 2: Tell them more. Read each column from top to bottom.
  - ○ "Our client, SoyNut Butter Company, is recalling I.M. Healthy SoyNut Butter. Look for 15-ounce plastic jars best-by dates July 5, August 30, or August 31, 2018; individual cups with a best-by-date of August 8; or four-pound plastic tubs with best-by dates of November 4 and July 28, 2018
  - ○ "The recalled products may contain E. coli bacteria. They were sold in multiple states in stores or by mail. They were also served in childcare centers and schools. Children and the elderly are at risk for kidney failure.
  - ○ "Consumers should return the products for a full refund. Avoid eating or serving the products under any conditions. Check shelves for any stored products. Questions? Call 1-800-Dixie Dew or visit DixieDew.com."
- Step 3: Tell them again. Read Tier Two from left to right.
  - ○ "To repeat: Our client, SoyNut Butter Company, is recalling I.M. Healthy SoyNut Butter. The recalled products may contain E. coli bacteria. Consumers should return the products for a full refund."

Map 2: The Recall Map

This map explains exactly why SoyNut recalled the products while also acknowledging Dixie Dew's involvement as the contract manufacturer of the products. The first column puts the focus on the problem with the product, the second focuses on the product's connection with the outbreak, and the third on Dixie Dew's role and what actions it is taking.

Map 2: The Recall Map		
Stakeholders: General public and news media		
Question: Why are you recalling your product?		
Key Message 1	**Key Message 2**	**Key Message 3**
Tests found E. coli O157:H7 in I.M. Healthy SoyNut Butter.	CDC has connected the butter with a disease outbreak.	We manufactured the product for SoyNut Butter Company.
Supporting information 1.1	**Supporting information 2.1**	**Supporting information 3.1**
These bacteria may release toxins into the bloodstream.	The outbreak includes California, Oregon, Arizona, New Jersey, and Maryland.	We are working with FDA to find the contamination source.
Supporting information 1.2	**Supporting information 2.2**	**Supporting information 3.2**
The bacteria may cause kidney failure.	CDC has confirmed 12 cases of infection.	We are consulting experts in food safety.
Supporting information 1.3	**Supporting information 2.3**	**Supporting information 3.3**
Children and seniors are most at-risk.	Eleven cases are younger than age 18.	We will follow their lead on improving our facility.

(Fig. 2)

Map 3: The Situation Map

The federal investigation is still in its early stages. Executives at Dixie Dew might want to act as if they know more than they do and are more certain of the outcome than they are. This is a mistake. Overconfidence and over-reassurance tend to drive up stakeholder outrage. Better to be honest about uncertainty and to stick to the facts about which there is little debate. Better to strike a hopeful tone than one that stakeholders (particularly the FDA) might interpret as arrogant or defiant. It also helps to acknowledge that Dixie Dew is cooperating with federal health officials, seeking their advice, and following their lead.

Map 3: The Situation Map

Stakeholders: General public and news media

Question: How did this happen?

Key Message 1	Key Message 2	Key Message 3
We are unsure what led to the contamination.	Our in-house testing failed to detect the bacteria.	Meanwhile, we are working with the FDA and other experts.
Supporting information 1.1	**Supporting information 2.1**	**Supporting information 3.1**
FDA is investigating our facility.	We are looking at new tests and procedures.	We will follow their advice on improving our plant.
Supporting information 1.2	**Supporting information 2.2**	**Supporting information 3.2**
We are cooperating fully with FDA and state officials.	We will look at better training for our employees.	The FDA will monitor our progress.
Supporting information 1.3	**Supporting information 2.3**	**Supporting information 3.3**
We will disinfect our plant.	We will adopt a test-and-hold policy for all products.	We have asked FDA to report our progress to the public.

(Fig. 3)

Map 4: The Contamination Map

　　With this map, we intend to help stakeholders (through the news media) better understand how the contamination was found and identified. Better here to cite findings from government health authorities than to suggest Dixie Dew ran its own tests. Leaning on the CDC and the FDA adds credibility to the risk messages.

Map 4: The Contamination Map		
Stakeholders: General public and news media		
Question: How did you discover the contamination?		
Key Message 1	**Key Message 2**	**Key Message 3**
CDC detected the bacteria and connected it to the outbreak.	CDC found a DNA fingerprint to make the connection.	FDA is inspecting our plant for contamination.
Supporting information 1.1	**Supporting information 2.1**	**Supporting information 3.1**
We learned of the investigation on March 3.	The agency used advanced diagnostics.	We will follow FDA's advice on what to do next.
Supporting information 1.2	**Supporting information 2.2**	**Supporting information 3.2**
We immediately opened our facilities to investigators.	It also used its PulseNet network.	Meanwhile, we are testing all of our other products.
Supporting information 1.3	**Supporting information 2.3**	**Supporting information 3.3**
We are cooperating fully with health officials.	Interviews with the sick and their families indicate SoyNut Butter is the source.	And we are holding all recently made products at our plant.

(Fig. 4)

Map 5: The Pathogen Map

This map provides facts about E. coli O157:H7—what it is, how it infects people, and why it is a risk to human health. It is easy to let this map become too technical. Keep the language simple and remember that most US stakeholders read at an eighth-grade level.

Map 5: The Pathogen Map

Stakeholders: General public and news media

Question: What are the effects of the pathogen and its disease?

Key Message 1	Key Message 2	Key Message 3
The pathogen is Shiga toxin-producing Escherichia coli O157:H7	People acquire it by eating contaminated food.	An estimated 95,000 infections occur in the United States annually.
Supporting information 1.1	**Supporting information 2.1**	**Supporting information 3.1**
These bacteria are often found in animal feces.	The most common vectors are contaminated meat, milk, or vegetables.	Death occurs in less than 5 percent of cases.
Supporting information 1.2	**Supporting information 2.2**	**Supporting information 3.2**
Humans, animals, and utensils may transmit the bacteria.	The food vectors are contaminated with infected feces.	As many as 10 percent will develop kidney failure called HUS.
Supporting information 1.3	**Supporting information 2.3**	**Supporting information 3.3**
It is the most common of Shiga toxin-producing E. coli.	The bacteria survive because food is raw or undercooked.	HUS is the most common cause of acute renal failure in children.

(Fig. 5)

Map 6: The Avoidance Map

The messages in this map are aimed at helping consumers help themselves by avoiding the contaminated food. It also includes some basic information on what to do if someone has consumed the recalled product. Note the map repeats some information from the other maps. This is fine, since repetition is useful in reinforcing important messages during a high-stress situation. It's also inevitable, since we can't be sure which question reporters or stakeholders will ask first.

Map 6: The Avoidance Map		
Stakeholders: General public and news media		
Question: What can people do to avoid the pathogen?		
Key Message 1	**Key Message 2**	**Key Message 3**
CDC says to avoid eating I.M. Healthy SoyNut Butter.	For refunds, return products to where you bought them.	If you have eaten the product, watch for symptoms.
Supporting information 1.1	**Supporting information 2.1**	**Supporting information 3.1**
Look for 15-ounce plastic jars best-by dated July 5, August 30, or Aug. 31, 2018.	Be sure to check all storage shelves.	These include stomach cramps, diarrhea, bloody diarrhea, vomiting, and low fever.
Supporting information 1.2	**Supporting information 2.2**	**Supporting information 3.2**
Also, individual cups with a best-by date of August 8.	To dispose of products, put them inside two plastic bags.	Most people recover within 7 days.
Supporting information 1.3	**Supporting information 2.3**	**Supporting information 3.3**
And 4-pound plastic tubs with best-by dates of November 4 and July 28, 2018.	Then place the bag inside a garbage can with a secure lid.	Avoid antibiotics or anti-diarrheals, which may promote kidney failure.

(Fig. 6)

Map 7: The Disease Management Map

This map is also a self-efficacy map designed to give consumers the information they need to make decisions about managing the disease. The map presents two scenarios. One, if the symptoms are mild. Two, if the disease becomes serious.

Map 7: The Disease Management Map		
Stakeholders: General public and news media		
Question: What can sick people do to manage E. coli O157:H7 and its symptoms?		
Key Message 1	**Key Message 2**	**Key Message 3**
Mild symptoms generally appear within 2 days after infection.	Most healthy people will recover in 5 to 7 days.	Children and seniors are at a higher risk.
Supporting information 1.1	**Supporting information 2.1**	**Supporting information 3.1**
These include stomach cramps, diarrhea, vomiting, and low fever.	Doctors diagnose the disease with a stool sample.	They may develop hemolytic uremic syndrome, or HUS.
Supporting information 1.2	**Supporting information 2.2**	**Supporting information 3.2**
The disease becomes serious if it enters the bloodstream.	Avoid antibiotics or anti-diarrheals, which may promote kidney failure.	Watch for low urination, tiredness, and pale cheeks.
Supporting information 1.3	**Supporting information 2.3**	**Supporting information 3.3**
This happens in less than 5 percent of cases.	See a doctor if diarrhea is persistent or bloody.	Those who develop HUS should be hospitalized, CDC says

(Fig. 7)

Map 8: The Future Map

This is Dixie Dew's opportunity to look toward the future even as the investigation is unfolding. The tone should be hopeful, not overly confident. To manage outrage within FDA, it's important for Dixie Dew to acknowledge that it likely played a role in the outbreak, and that it plans to listen carefully to the FDA's guidance and to follow it closely. This will require the management to swallow its collective ego, but is absolutely necessary if the company hopes to avoid a shutdown of its manufacturing facility.

Map 8: The Future Map		
Stakeholders: General public and news media		
Question: What are you doing to avoid future contamination in your products?		
Key Message 1	**Key Message 2**	**Key Message 3**
We are in the early stages of the FDA's investigation.	We are following the FDA's lead.	We will follow the FDA's recommendations.
Supporting information 1.1	**Supporting information 2.1**	**Supporting information 3.1**
The FDA is inspecting our plant for contamination.	We have shut down production.	We will listen to their advice.
Supporting information 1.2	**Supporting information 2.2**	**Supporting information 3.2**
They are also looking at our records.	We are withholding our products from the marketplace.	We will improve our facility and methods.
Supporting information 1.3	**Supporting information 2.3**	**Supporting information 3.3**
We expect a full report within a few weeks.	We are testing all of our products for contamination.	The FDA will monitor and report on our progress.

(Fig. 8)

Map 9: The Make It Right Map

This map presents Dixie Dew's plan for making restitution to a broad range of consumers. On one end are customers who simply want their money back. On the other end are those who have suffered serious harm as a result of E. coli infection caused by the recalled products made at Dixie Dew's plant. It is vital to both acknowledge the company's role in the outbreak and to sincerely apologize for any errors that led to the contamination. This is no time to play games with language. Even if its lawyers scream, Dixie Dew must at the very least accept moral responsibility, as the products clearly came from its plant. A firm commitment to "making things right" is essential to bringing stakeholder outrage down to a manageable level.

Map 9: The Make It Right Map		
Stakeholders: General public and news media		
Question: What are you doing to make things right?		
Key Message 1	**Key Message 2**	**Key Message 3**
Our client SoyNut Butter Company is offering refunds.	We are working with FDA, state agencies, and other experts.	We are working to locate the ill and their families.
Supporting information 1.1	**Supporting information 2.1**	**Supporting information 3.1**
The recall covers specific products.	We are seeking the source of the contamination.	We apologize for our role in this outbreak.
Supporting information 1.2	**Supporting information 2.2**	**Supporting information 3.2**
You will find an up-to-date list at our website, DixieDew.com	We will eradicate the bacteria from our facility.	We will pay medical bills for anyone our products made ill.
Supporting information 1.3	**Supporting information 2.3**	**Supporting information 3.3**
Please return these products to your store or distributor.	We will adopt new technology and methods to maintain a clean facility.	We are ready to discuss fair compensation.

(Fig. 9)

You probably noticed some repetition from map to map. This is inevitable as each map looks at the same situation from a different perspective. It is also appropriate to have some repetition on important points to improve the chances of cutting through the mental noise. Remember, the template prompts are there to suggest an approach to framing our messages. Each risk controversy has its own specific details to manage. And there is never a perfect message map.

As you study these examples, note how each follows the rules of high-stress communication:

- The key messages are arranged as sound bites of twenty-seven words or fewer.
- Each key message is reinforced by three supporting messages.
- Each message is written for an eighth-grade reading level.
- Each map attempts to emphasize the positive over the negative without overly reassuring stakeholders.
- As appropriate, each map admits uncertainty.

- Each map aims to put the most important information first and last, following Covello's primacy rule.
- The messages avoid words like "no," "not," and "never."
- When possible, each map cites expert sources to enhance the credibility of the risk messages.
- The majority of the maps employ the acknowledge-and-improve strategy to calm stakeholder outrage.

Section 3: Composing the preamble

We use the preamble to set the stage for our message maps during a public presentation, such as a news conference or a stakeholder meeting in which we will discuss the outbreak and the recall. These events can prove vital to the management of stakeholder outrage. When our company causes or is suspected of causing harm to its stakeholders, the company's top executive should have the courage to answer questions directly from journalists or stakeholders. During a foodborne outbreak, our first priority should be to protect the health of our consumers. In addition, a well-crafted preamble provides our communications teams with pre-vetted language that we can use in other communications, such as news releases, backgrounders, open letters, advertisements, websites and videos.

Using the three-part template established by Covello, Minamyer and Clayton (2007), and applying risk communication concepts from risk communicators Vincent T. Covello and Peter M. Sandman, here is a version of a preamble that Dixie Dew's top executive, President Robert C. Carl, might have delivered at a news conference to announce the March 4 recall.

Part 1: The statement of concern

"Good morning. My name is Robert C. Carl and I serve as the president of Dixie Dew Products Inc. We are a small company with about twenty employees. We make customized products for the food industry and specialize in contract packaging and private labels. One of our clients, The SoyNut Better Company of Glenview, Illinois, announced today that it is recalling specific packages of its I.M. Healthy SoyNut Butter because federal health officials have connected those products with an ongoing outbreak of E. coli infection. Since we manufactured the product, Dixie Dew has a clear responsibility to warn consumers about this situation. For more than three generations, we have taken great pride in producing the highest quality products available. This is a very sad day for us and we ask your forgiveness as we work closely with federal and state health officials to bring an end to this outbreak.

Part 2: The statement of intent

"Moving forward, we will act in an open and transparent manner. We are cooperating fully with the US Food and Drug Administration to identify the source of the contamination. We are listening carefully to FDA officials, we are following their instructions, and we will accept their findings. FDA will monitor our progress and will report to the public. In addition, we are seeking advice from leading US experts in food safety to improve our facility, our technology, and our methods. We have clearly failed to serve the best interests of our client and their customers. We pledge to do better.

Part 3: The statement of purpose

"Today we join our client, The SoyNut Butter Company, in announcing a recall of I.M. Healthy SoyNut Butter. The recalled products may contain E. coli bacteria. Consumers should return these products for a full refund. Again, SoyNut Butter Company is recalling I.M. Healthy SoyNut Butter. Look for 15-ounce plastic jars best-by dates July 5, August 30, or August 31, 2018; individual cups with a best-by-date of August 8; or four pound plastic tubs with best-by dates of November 4 and July 28, 2018. The recalled products may contain

E. coli bacteria. They were sold in multiple states in stores or by mail. They were also served in childcare centers and schools. Children and seniors are at risk for kidney failure. Consumers should return the products for a full refund. Avoid eating or serving the products under any conditions. Check shelves for any stored products. For more information, call 1-800-Dixie Dew or visit DixieDew.com. To repeat: Our client, SoyNut Butter Company, is recalling I.M. Healthy SoyNut Butter. The recalled products may contain E. coli bacteria. Consumers should return the products for a full refund."

"We are now ready to answer as many of your questions as we can."

Section 4: Conclusion—An analysis based on best practices

As a final step, we will now consider Dixie Dew's messages and actions during the outbreak and recall through the lens of nine best practices for risk communication, as outlined in the 2009 book Effective Risk Communication: A Message-Centered Approach, written by four communication scholars – Timothy Sellnow of the University of Kentucky, Robert Ulmer of the University of Arkansas, Matthew Seeger of Wayne State University, and Richard Littlefield of North Dakota State University. These best practices are based on extensive research and are designed to lead a risk controversy toward mitigation and eventual resolution.

Did Dixie Dew infuse risk communication into policy decisions?

No. Indeed, Dixie Dew appears to have had no policy for dealing with foodborne risks, other than to lay low and hope no one noticed its role in the E. coli outbreak. Both the SoyNut Butter Company and the FDA enabled this approach until March 28, when the FDA shut down the Dixie Dew manufacturing facility.

Did Dixie Dew treat risk communication as a process?

No. Dixie Dew made no attempt to help the FDA or SoyNut warn the public about the outbreak or about the contaminated product.

Did Dixie Dew account for the uncertainty inherent in risk?

No. The company made only a minimal effort to meet FDA standards for keeping its plant open. Dixie Dew's overall response to the situation indicates the management expected the crisis to just go away.

Did Dixie Dew design messages to be culturally sensitive?

Judging from the online record as well as news coverage, Dixie Dew made no attempt to communicate with consumers about the outbreak or the recall.

Did Dixie Dew acknowledge diverse levels of risk tolerance?

No. The company made no public acknowledgement of stakeholder outrage.

Did Dixie Dew involve the public in dialogues about risk?

No. The company ignored the risk to the public.

Did Dixie Dew present risk messages with honesty?

No. Dixie Dew presented no messages to the public.

Did Dixie Dew meet risk perception needs by remaining open and accessible to the public?

No. The company made no attempt at transparency or accessibility with the public or with the news media. At one point, it even tried to block the FDA from examining its food safety records.

Did Dixie Dew collaborate and coordinate about risk with credible information sources?

No. Dixie Dew apparently made zero effort to collaborate with FDA, CDC, or state health officials.

Section 5: Sources for this case study

Beach, Coral. "Beach Beat: Public's right to know should trump trade secrets." Food Safety News. April 02, 2017. Accessed March 01, 2018. http://www.foodsafetynews.com/2017/04/beach-beat-publics-right-to-know-should-trump-trade-secrets/#.WphVMpPwbUI.

Beach, Coral. "CDC says soy nut butter outbreak over - but threat continues." Food Safety News. May 06, 2017. Accessed March 01, 2018. http://www.foodsafetynews.com/2017/05/cdc-says-soy-nut-butter-outbreak-over-but-threat-continues/#.WphUc5PwbUI.

Beach, Coral. "Dozens sick from soy nut butter; FDA mum on manufacturer." Food Safety News. March 22, 2017. Accessed March 01, 2018. http://www.foodsafetynews.com/2017/03/138648/#.WphWRZPwbUI.

Beach, Coral. "FDA shuts down soy nut butter maker linked to E. coli outbreak." Food Safety News. April 01, 2017. Accessed March 01, 2018. http://www.foodsafetynews.com/2017/03/fda-shuts-down-soy-nut-butter-maker-linked-to-e-coli-outbreak/#.WphVkJPwbUI.

Beach, Coral. "SoyNut Butter Co. bankrupt because of E. coli outbreak." Food Safety News. May 17, 2017. Accessed March 01, 2018. http://www.foodsafetynews.com/2017/05/soynut-butter-co-bankrupt-because-of-e-coli-outbreak/#.WphSz5PwbUI.

Beach, Coral. "Tainted soy butter spurs recalls one by one; FDA remains mum." Food Safety News. March 26, 2017. Accessed March 01, 2018. http://www.foodsafetynews.com/2017/03/tainted-soy-butter-spurs-recalls-one-by-one-fda-remains-mum/#.WphV2pPwbUI.

Bomkamp, Samantha. "Glenview-based SoyNut Butter files for bankruptcy after possible E. coli contamination." Chicagotribune.com. May 17, 2017. Accessed March 06, 2018. http://www.chicagotribune.com/business/ct-soynut-butter-bankruptcy-0518-biz-20170517-story.html/.

Center for Food Safety and Applied Nutrition. "Outbreaks - FDA Investigated Multistate Outbreak of E. coli O157:H7 Infections Linked to SoyNut Butter." U S Food and Drug Administration Home Page. May 4, 2017. Accessed March 01, 2018. https://www.fda.gov/Food/RecallsOutbreaksEmergencies/Outbreaks/ucm544964.htm.

Dewey, Caitlin. "FDA Won't Reveal Stores That Sold Recalled Food." The Washington Post, March 15, 2017, Suburban ed., sec. A.

Dixie Dew Products, Inc. Company information. Zoominfo. February 2018. Accessed March 5, 2018. Zoominfo.com.

Dixie Dew Products, Inc. Company information. LexisNexis Corporate Affiliations, February 26, 2018. Accessed March 5, 2018.

"E.coli (Escherichia coli)." Centers for Disease Control and Prevention. January 25, 2018. Accessed March 05, 2018. https://www.cdc.gov/ecoli/index.html.

"E. coli." World Health Organization. Accessed March 05, 2018. http://www.who.int/mediacentre/factsheets/fs125/en/.

"FDA Suspends Food Facility Registration of Dixie Dew Products, Inc." U S Food and Drug Administration Home Page. March 30, 2017. Accessed March 22, 2018. https://www.fda.gov/Food/RecallsOutbreaksEmergencies/SafetyAlertsAdvisories/ucm549734.htm.

Hansel, Mark . "Dixie Dew Products in Erlanger remains shut down by FDA for violations, implication in ecoli outbreak." North Kentucky Tribune. April 28, 2017. Accessed March 6, 2018. http://www.nkytribune.com/2017/04/dixie-dew-products-in-erlanger-remains-shut-down-by-fda-for-violations-implication-in-ecoli-outbreak/.

Hines, Richard. "E Coli Outbreak: Erlanger Plant Had 'grossly Insanitary Conditions'." News NKY. May 30, 2017. Accessed March 22, 2018. http://newsnky.com/e-coli-outbreak.html.

"IMPORTANT BANKRUPTCY NOTICE, U.S. FOOD AND DRUG ADMINISTRATION NOTICE." I. M. Healthy - SoyNutButter - Bankruptcy and Health Notice. Accessed March 01, 2018. https://www.soynutbutter.com/.

"Kentucky Directory of Manufacturers." ThinkKentucky. March 6, 2018. Accessed March 6, 2018. http://www.thinkkentucky.com/kyedc/kpdf/Facilities_by_Product_or_Service.pdf.

"Kentucky Eastern Bankruptcy Court Case 2:18-bk-21495 - Dixie Dew Products, Inc." Inforuptcy. November 29, 2018. Accessed December 20, 2018. https://www.inforuptcy.com/filings/kyebke_302020-2-18-bk-21495-dixie-dew-products-inc.

Marler, Bill. "I.M. Healthy and Dixie Dew E. coli Outbreak Update - What Shoes to Drop Next?" Food Poison Journal. April 04, 2017. Accessed March 01, 2018. http://www.foodpoisonjournal.com/food-poisoning-information/i-m-healthy-and-dixie-dew-e-coli-outbreak-update-what-shoes-to-drop-next/.

Meadows, Jonah. "After E. Coli Outbreak Glenview-Based SoyNut Butter Files For Bankruptcy." Glenview, IL Patch. May 18, 2017. Accessed March 22, 2018. https://patch.com/illinois/glenview/e-coli-outbreak-bankrupts-glenview-based-soynutbutter.

"Multistate Outbreak of Shiga toxin-producing Escherichia coli O157:H7 Infections Linked to I.M. Healthy Brand SoyNut Butter (Final Update)." Centers for Disease Control and Prevention. March 30, 2017. Accessed March 01, 2018. https://www.cdc.gov/ecoli/2017/o157h7-03-17/index.html.

"ORDER: Suspension of Food Facility Registration Notice of Opportunity for Hearing." Stephen M. Ostroff to Robert C. Carl, President Dixie Dew Products, Inc. March 27, 2017. In US Food and Drug Administration. Accessed March 22, 2018. https://www.fda.gov/downloads/AboutFDA/CentersOffices/OfficeofFoods/CFSAN/CFSANFOIAElectronicReadingRoom/UCM549757.pdf.

"SoyNut Butter Company Feeds Two Million Children Monthly; Offers Nut Free Alternative to Peanut Butter." Marketwired. October 4, 2012. Accessed March 06, 2018. http://m.marketwired.com/press-release/soynut-butter-company-feeds-two-million-children-monthly-offers-nut-free-alternative-1709517.htm.

Trotter, Greg. "Glenview-based SoyNut Butter sued after 12 infected in E. coli outbreak." Chicagotribune.com. March 06, 2017. Accessed March 06, 2018. http://www.chicagotribune.com/business/ct-soynut-butter-recall-0307-biz-20170306-story.html.

CASE STUDY: The Cadbury Schweppes salmonella outbreak and chocolate recall of 2006

Executive Summary

During the summer of 2006, Britain's top chocolate-maker Cadbury Schweppes announced that it would recall more than one million candy bars distributed in the United Kingdom. At first, other than the scale of the recall, the announcement appeared routine. But over the next few days, the recall—or rather, Cadbury's actions before and during the recall process as well as the subsequent government investigation and prosecution—sparked significant levels of stakeholder outrage among Britain's regulators, customers, investors, politicians, and the news media.

Two government health agencies soon revealed to the British news media how Cadbury had detected a rare strain of salmonella in its candy bars during its production process, had made a deliberate decision to put the bars on store shelves across England during the run-up to the important Easter season, and yet had failed to inform the government of its actions. Only when UK health professionals detected an outbreak of salmonella, and approached Cadbury with evidence that its products had triggered the outbreak, did the company issue a recall. Cadbury publicly declined to accept responsibility for the outbreak for more than a year, thus generating angst and anger in Britain that lasted long past the actual recall.

This case study examines the story of the Cadbury chocolate scare by conducting a close reading of more than 300 contemporary news articles concerning the UK salmonella outbreak of 2006, which were identified via a LexisNexis search; by providing a summary of the case; and then by selecting and organizing the pertinent facts of the case into a timeline narrative.

It then demonstrates the process of producing a set of message maps combined with a public statement that may have improved Cadbury's position during its dispute with Britain's food safety regulators.

Section 1: Background

1-A. The company: Cadbury Schweppes plc

Like many Quakers living in England during the early 19th century, John Cadbury chose to enter the business world. He had little choice, as British universities and England's military rejected Quakers as non-conformists (Dellheim, 1987). Business offered one of the few available paths for Quakers to thrive. So in 1824, the twenty-two-year-old Cadbury opened a grocery in Birmingham. He sold tea and coffee as alternatives to alcoholic beverages. He also sold cocoa and drinking chocolate, which proved so popular that nine years later he decided to focus on manufacturing them. By 1842, he was selling sixteen lines of drinking chocolate in powder or cakes. In 1847, John brought brother Benjamin into his growing firm to create Cadbury Brothers, and constructed a large factory in the city's center. In 1854, the brothers received a Royal Warrant as official suppliers of cocoa and drinking chocolate to Queen Victoria.

Despite this royal testimonial, the company fell into decline and the brothers dissolved their partnership in 1861, leaving control of retail and manufacturing to John's sons, twenty-five-year-old Richard and twenty-one-year-old George. This marked the turning point in the company's fortunes. Charles Dellheim writes in his 1987 analysis of the Cadbury business culture, "Three main influences formed George and Richard Cadbury's beliefs: the Quaker ethic, which shaped their views of the nature and purpose of business; the experience of turning around a failing firm; and an exposure to the social problems of an industrial city."

After five years of struggle, this second generation of Cadburys introduced the breakthrough that would eventually establish their company's dominance in the United Kingdom. In 1866, they adopted a cocoa press developed in Holland that produced a purer form of cocoa, which the Cadburys branded as Pure Cocoa Essence, the United Kingdom's first unadulterated cocoa. This process provided the Cadburys with the raw materials for manufacturing a wide range of chocolate confections. They began to produce "fancy chocolates" to complete head to head with sweets imported from France. By featuring paintings created by Richard Cadbury, the company made its product packaging more attractive, thus inventing the genre of chocolate-box art; today, collectors prize the elaborate boxes the Cadburys distributed across England during the Victorian and Edwardian eras. "Their efforts were particularly successful because they anticipated and helped create the vogue for 'pure' foods in England," Dellheim writes (1987), "a vogue given parliamentary sanction by the passage of the Adulteration of Food Acts in 1872 and 1875."

In 1875, Cadbury's launched a new product—the Cadbury Easter Egg—that would make its brand synonymous with happy childhoods and family values throughout England. Made from dark chocolate, these first-ever chocolate eggs featured a smooth surface containing sugarcoated chocolate drops. By 1878, now with 200 employees, Cadbury's became desperate to expand its operations. "The need for greater accommodation for the rapidly growing business, and a desire to secure improved conditions for the work-people, led to the removal of the factory to a distance of about four miles south of the city," Brandon Head writes in his 1903 account of the cocoa industry. In 1879, the Cadburys constructed a factory on fourteen acres, four miles south of Birmingham, near the Birmingham Canal and a recently completed railway. This combination would give the company better access to milk and cocoa. They renamed the estate Bournville. "The move to the countryside was unprecedented," Delheim writes (1987). "Their contemporaries generally saw it as an unwise, not to say daft, choice, given the practical difficulties of providing transportation for workers and goods."

Before long, the Cadburys introduced a series of innovations and reforms that cemented the company's reputation as politically progressive. The new factory included heated dressing rooms for workers. The Cadburys negotiated special fares for workers who traveled from the city to the factory by rail. George Cadbury acquired 120 acres near the factory and began the design and construction of a model village with 313 cottages and houses for his workers, planning "almost every aspect of the village, from houses and roads to parks and trees (Dellheim, 1987)." Concerned with the health and physical fitness of their workforce, the Cadburys built several parks, pools, and other recreational features to encourage walking, swimming, and outdoor sports. To discourage drunkenness among workers, George Cadbury prohibited pubs from his village. In 1907, Cadbury donated the entire estate to the Bournville Village Trust, having "no desire to rule Bournville like a latter-day feudal magnate (Dellheim, 1987)."

The Cadburys also are credited with significant social reforms, such as half-day holidays on Saturdays and full holidays on bank holidays. They opened medical and dental offices, and established a pension fund, for their workers. In 1918, the Cadburys established democratically elected work councils—one for the men and one for the women—to deal with working conditions as well as issues of safety, health, education, training, and social life.

As a growing company, Cadbury's proved equally aggressive in the marketplace. In 1905, the company challenged the Swiss dominance of milk chocolate with a bar that included more milk than any other at the time: The Cadbury Dairy Milk. "Here too, purity was the key," Delheim writes (1987). "Cadbury's used fresh milk rather than powdered milk. There was a 'glass and a half of milk in every half-pound bar' of C.D.M. The name 'Cadbury' was written on each square."

Over the coming decades, through a combination of new products, effective advertising, and strategic acquisitions, Cadbury's emerged as England's King of Chocolate. In 1969, Cadbury (having dropped the possessive from its company name) became an international behemoth when it merged with the beverage giant Schweppes. The merger effectively cut off the company from its Quaker roots. Yet the Cadbury family retained some power within the new mega-company until 1993, when Sir Dominic Cadbury resigned as the group's chief executive.

By 2003, the company ranked first worldwide in sweets and fourth in chocolate. Its overall brand portfolio of confections and beverages included Cadbury, Trident, Dr Pepper, Halls, Schweppes, Dentyne, Bassett's, Snapple, Orangina, Bubblicious, Hawaiian Punch, and 7 Up.

That same year, 51-year-old Todd Stitzer became the first foreign-born CEO of Cadbury Schweppes. Though he had worked his way steadily up the corporate ladder for more than two decades, Stitzer came under close scrutiny (and some outright distain) from Britain's investment elites. "He's like every American businessman you've ever met or seen or heard about," Marketing Today said in a 2004 profile, with a "meticulous appearance and manner and his tendency to use management speak," but also "a relaxed charm, clarity of vision and solidity. … He's not British, he's not a Cadbury, he's not a Sir."

Britain's investment establishment, known as the City, had assumed Cadbury COO John Brock would succeed John Sunderland as Cadbury's CEO. "Stitzer, in charge of strategy and from a legal rather than a marketing background, was not at the top of the pundit's list," Marketing Today said. On the other hand, the profile said, "As a go-getter with a social conscience, (Stitzer is) really from the same mould as the firm's Quaker founding fathers."

1-B. About the chief executive: Todd Stitzer

Born in New Jersey, raised in New York, Stitzer enjoyed what he described as "a middle-class American childhood." His father directed a YMCA and encouraged his son to follow him. "This means that at an early age he was taught the importance of giving and of serious thought," Marketing Today reported. "His family cared for others and had strong Christian beliefs—not unlike the founding fathers at Cadbury's, in fact."

He first attended Springfield College, "the training ground for future YMCA and aid workers in Massachusetts." However, Stitzer had also long admired an uncle who practiced law in upstate New York. "I thought the combination of skills required of a lawyer were right for me—writing, thinking and verbal skills—plus lawyers did a lot for the community," he told Marketing Today. He soon switched to Harvard University, where he earned a bachelor's degree, and then attended Columbia Law School in New York, where he received his law degree.

In 1973, Stitzer joined the Manhattan law firm Lord, Day & Lord as an associate, and focused his practice on mergers and acquisitions. One of his major projects was to advise New York City Mayor Ed Koch on the restructuring of the city's $3.2 billion debt. While he enjoyed the M&A work, the hours were brutal, and the pay failed to match his contributions to the firm. "I billed more hours than anyone else at the firm for three years in a row," Stitzer said in a 2007 interview with the Columbia Law School's press office. Lord, Day & Lord conformed to the "Marxist theory of surplus value," he told Marketing Today. "The associates worked very hard, the partners made all the profits. ... My wife used to call them Lord, Day & Night. I was there all the time."

Lord, Day & Lord served as the lead firm in the United States for Cadbury Schweppes, and Stitzer frequently advised the company's executives. In 1983, Cadbury offered Stitzer a position as assistant general counsel, a move that would allow Stitzer to live in Connecticut and spend more time with his wife and children. Meanwhile, his law firm informed Stitzer that he was only five years through an eight-to-ten-year process that might eventually allow him to become a partner. He took Cadbury's offer.

"I had a strong interest in the social helping professions, what with my family background." Stitzer told Marketing Today. "There's a huge connection, however, with Cadbury Schweppes, which has a heritage of caring about people and of community and of the greater good. My background and mindset fit with everything Cadbury Schweppes stands for." And yet, London's The Guardian would report in 2009, Stitzer's favorite book was Ayn Rand's Atlas Shrugged, a novel "which rejects religion and supports laissez-faire capitalism and individual rights."

Following the advise of Development Director Dominic Cadbury, the ambitious Stitzer soon steered his career away from Cadbury's legal department and toward its marketing and sales group. He moved to London in 1991 as group development director and returned to the United States in 1993 as vice president for marketing and strategic planning. He told Management Today (Blackhurst, 2009), "I adopted the fire-hose method of management. I stood with my mouth open and they poured into it." The Daily Telegraph in London describes Stitzer as a "furious note-taker; a former colleague refers to Stitzer's management style as 'leading with his head down (Sibun, 2010).'" Stitzer's progress over the coming decade was sure and swift, but often his moves were "not for more money, but to add to his knowledge and to further his career," according to the Marketing Today profile. He became the chief operating officer for Cadbury Beverages in North America in 1995. In 2000, he joined Cadbury's main group board as chief strategy officer. In 2003, in a move that stunned London's financial establishment, he became CEO for Cadbury Schweppes. That same year, Stitzer managed Cadbury's $4.2 billion acquisition of US-based chewing gum-manufacturer Adams from Pfizer to create the world's largest maker of chocolate and other confectionaries. By purchasing Adams, Cadbury added Trident sugar-free gum, Dentyne Ice chewing gum, and Halls cough lozenges to its product portfolio, and instantly became the world's second largest manufacturer of chewing gum (Ball, 2002; Confectionary News, 2002). "Stitzer was chosen, you realize, because he has a bit of everything: the American (more than two-thirds of [Cadbury's] business is in the US); the time-served employee; the ambitious; the humble," Marketing Today said in its profile. "Stitzer's style is to consult, to seek advice, then to act. He is not an autocratic leader."

"Being a principled leader is a part of my life and it's been that way ever since I was a little kid," Stitzer told the Daily Telegraph (Sibun, 2010). "Cadbury is a principled company, it's been that way since 1824. So there was this wonderful accident of Cadbury and Todd Stitzer coming together in 1983 and that's been a great thing for me." But Marketing Today (Blackhurst, 2010) was highly critical of Stitzer's bearing: "It is a pity, though, that he allows this straightforwardness to be clouded by the sort of management gobbledygook that can leave the listener cold. ... In America, excess verbiage may be acceptable and commonplace. It is not in Britain. ... Such language can leave the speaker open to ridicule and hostility." As a lawyer, Marketing Today said, Stitzer "was taught that no word can go unchecked, no statement can go without being fully defined." The Daily Telegraph (Sibun, 2010) concurred: "Stitzer's relationship with the City has never been easy. ... (his) formal, Ivy League bearing has not always sat well with hard-nosed, cynical British investors and analysts." Still, in January 2006, the Times of London (Jameson, 2006) portrayed Stitzer as "the real life Willie

Wonka" from Roald Dahl's children's story, Charlie and the Chocolate Factory, a book rooted in a teenaged Dahl's daydreams of working at a Cadbury factory. In that article, Angela Jameson of The Times found a duality in Stitzer that reflected both of the book's central characters. She wrote, " … chip away at the grey suit and white shirt exterior and there is more of the young Charlie, the boy so anxious to please his guardians, than the mercurial Wonka."

1-C. The pathogen: salmonella Montevideo

A rare strain of non-typhoid salmonella bacteria, salmonella Montevideo enters the body through the consumption of contaminated food or water, or of fecal material. Though commonly considered a contaminant of food animal products, in recent years salmonella bacteria in fresh produce have caused several serious US outbreaks. Food products known to trigger salmonella outbreaks include meat, poultry, eggs, milk and dairy products, fish, shrimp, spices, yeast, cocoanut, sauces, freshly prepared salad dressings, cake mixes, cream-filled desserts, toppings, dried gelatin, peanut butter, cocoa, tomatoes, peppers, cantaloupes and chocolate, according to the US Food and Drug Administration (2012).

The US Centers for Disease Control and Prevention estimate more than 1 million cases of non-typhoid salmonella occur each year in the United States (2013). In England and Wales, the government's estimates put annual cases at around 8,500 (Public Health England, 2016).

Clinical features: Salmonella may infect anyone of any age, but is especially harsh when contracted by those with weak immune systems: the very young, the elderly, people with HIV or a chronic illness, or who are undergoing chemo or immunosuppressive therapy or other medications. Exposure may cause issues with the stomach and intestines, including nausea, vomiting, diarrhea, cramps, and fever. Symptoms generally appear between six and seventy-two hours after exposure. They usually subside in four to seven days, with the worst symptoms lasting fewer than two days. The disease leads to death in less than 1 percent of cases in otherwise healthy adults. The percentage may climb to 3.6 percent among the elderly (WHO, 2015).

There exists no standard treatment for salmonellosis, the illness caused by an infection of the salmonella bacteria. In severe cases, treatment is symptomatic, with an emphasis on rehydration and electrolyte replacement. Antimicrobial therapy is not recommended for mild or moderate cases.

Preventive measures include cooking food thoroughly; washing hands after handling raw food; separating raw food from cooked food; and refrigerating food at 40 degrees F or below.

1-D. The outbreak

Between March 1 and June 19, 2006, the United Kingdom's Health Protection Agency documented eight confirmed cases of salmonella Montevideo among infants younger than one year and twenty-two cases among children younger than age four, according to Scotland on Sunday (Gray, 2006). Looking for clues to the cause, the agency analyzed all samples of the bacterium it had received during the previous months.

On June 16, 2006, scientists at the United Kingdom's Health Protection Agency identified salmonella contamination in samples of chocolate crumb received from a private lab representing an unidentified confectionary firm. The agency approached the lab for more information and was told the source of the samples was confidential. The HPA then alerted the Food Standards Agency. Only when FSA officials approached the lab did its client, Cadbury Schweppes, admit to the contamination.

Cadbury then actively and openly resisted the FSA's insistence upon a significant recall, and rejected the government's opinion that the company should have alerted regulators to the contamination immediately. Cadbury claimed that only 5,000 bars were made with the contaminated chocolate. However, the FSA demanded a much larger recall. Cadbury's delay in reporting the contamination angered agency officials, who told the Telegraph, "Under food hygiene law, having salmonella in a ready-to-eat food such as chocolate is unacceptable and can pose a health risk (Derbyshire, 2006)."

1-E. The recalls

On June 23, 2006, Cadbury Schweppes recalled seven chocolate products from grocery shelves across the United Kingdom, in consultation with the Food Standards Agency: the chocolate button Easter Egg, Dairy Milk Turkish, Dairy Milk Caramel, Dairy Milk Mint, Dairy Milk 8 Chunk, 1 kg Dairy Milk, and the Freddo bar (AFX News). At more than 1 million items, the recall represented one third of Britain's daily consumption of Cadbury chocolate.

Cadbury swiftly positioned the recall as a "precaution," telling the Daily Mirror (2006, June 24): "The levels are significantly below the standard that would be a health problem. There is no evidence anyone has been sick through eating this chocolate." The HPA disagreed, confirming to the Sunday Times in London (2006, June 25) that "molecular fingerprinting tests" showed that the bacteria causing the outbreak were the same as those found in the Cadbury samples. Agency statisticians had suspected that chocolate might be the vector for the disease, since so many of the reported cases were found in children. The reported fifty-three cases could have been ten times higher in reality, the agency told the Times, because most salmonella cases go unreported: "We cannot be 100 percent sure that Cadbury's products caused the disease, but it's a strong possibility."

Over time, health officials identified three ways in which Cadbury's errors led to the outbreak.

First, Cadbury apparently failed to repair a leaky pipe at its Marlbrook, Herefordshire, plant where it manufactured the chocolate crumb, a key ingredient for creating chocolate candy. The Hereford Magistrate's Court brought charges against Cadbury "related to the state of repair of a drainage pipe and roof vent, the layout of the factory, the provision of drainage facilities and the cleaning and disinfection of equipment, including conveyors and storage silos (The Guardian, 2007, July 3)." It is possible that rats, mice, or wild birds, any of which may carry salmonella, may have been watering at the leaky pipe and contaminated the plant (The Times, 2006, June 24).

Second, Cadbury changed its food safety standards in 2003, apparently under the mistaken impression that there are safe levels of salmonella contamination for chocolate crumb. Routine tests were taken three times a day, every eight hours, to check for contamination of ingredients, of the production line, and of finished products. A private laboratory handled the analysis of the tests, detected the salmonella contamination, and alerted Cadbury.

The factory set its alert system to withdraw any product contaminated at ten parts per million per ten grams (The Times, July 24, 2006). Unfortunately for Cadbury and its consumers, chocolate is an ideal vehicle for salmonella because the high levels of fat and sugar preserve the bacteria and carry it into the intestine, according to microbiologists (Sunday Times, 2006, June 25). Sir Huge Pennington, a bacteriologist at Aberdeen University in Scotland, told the Associated Press, "The fat in chocolate actually preserves the salmonella from the normal intestinal defenses, so you don't have to eat very many salmonellas to get infected. It's about a thousand times less than if you're eating it from traditional sources like meats (2006, June 25)."

The Food Standards Agency said in an official report that Cadbury's food safety system was unreliable, outdated, and underestimated the level and likelihood of salmonella contamination (The Guardian, 2006, July 24). The report also said Cadbury's risk assessment erred when it drew parallels between the threshold for salmonella infection and the thresholds for infection by other micro-organisms that may be found in chocolate. The agency says: "We think (Cadbury) made a mistake in assuming there was a safe level of salmonella in a product like chocolate. Our view is there isn't. (Associated Press, July 4, 2006)"

Third, knowing that the crumb contained salmonella, Cadbury chose to distribute the contaminated products throughout England. Cadbury later confirmed it failed to approach the situation as a crisis, but instead decided informally that the contamination levels were too low to warrant a crisis footing, and to move forward with production (Leake and Walsh). The Daily Telegraph reported, "The court heard that in early 2006 the problem was so endemic that Cadbury staff were dealing with 'daily' salmonella-related problems, and were referring to instances of contamination by an alphabetical series of codewords rather than using what they referred to as the 's-word' (Bitten, 2007)."

The Birmingham Crown Court in 2007 fined Cadbury £1 million (about $2 million US) for its role in the salmonella outbreak of 2006: £500,000 for putting unsafe chocolate for sale to the public, £100,000 on each of two other charges, and £50,000 for each of six offenses at its Herefordshire factory (AFX News, 2007, July 16). The Health Protection Agency held Cadbury directly responsible for thirteen of the known fifty-six reported cases of the Montevideo strain of salmonella in 2006 (The Mirror, 2007, July 22). Of the fifty-six cases, thirty-seven were "possibly" caused by Cadbury products, while thirteen of those were "certain," the Mirror said (MacLean, 2007). Because the illness rate fell after Cadbury withdrew seven brands from the marketplace, the agency found that "consumption of Cadbury Schweppes's products was the most credible explanation."

At the urging of the Food Standards Agency, Cadbury agreed to a comprehensive cleaning of all production lines at the Marlbrook plant (The Guardian, 2006, July 27). Cadbury also agreed to destroy any chocolate testing positive for salmonella, however small (Western Daily Press, 2006, July 27), and to release products only after test results returned negative (Birmingham Daily Mail, 2006, July 27).

In addition, Cadbury appeared to become more aggressive in launching recalls. In February 2007, Cadbury voluntarily recalled its chocolate Easter eggs after learning that the product might pose a danger to consumers with nut allergies, the Birmingham Post reported (Revill, 2007).

1-F. Stakeholder reaction (timeline analysis)

Day 1: June 23, 2006—Cadbury Schweppes announces it has recalled seven chocolate products from grocery shelves across the United Kingdom, according to AFX News. In a decision made in consultation with the UK's Food Standards Agency, Cadbury recalls the chocolate button Easter Egg, Dairy Milk Turkish, Dairy Milk Caramel, Dairy Milk Mint, Dairy Milk 8 Chunk, 1 kg Dairy Milk, and the Freddo bar. The company frames the recall as a precautionary measure while admitting some of these products "may contain minute traces of salmonella," according to AFX News. In a prepared statement, the company says, "Cadbury has identified the source of the problem and rectified it, and is taking steps to ensure these particular products are no longer available for sale."

Day 2: June 24, 2006—A dispute erupts between Cadbury and the UK's Food Standards Agency, says the Daily Mirror of London (Sayid, 2006). Cadbury waited for five months to alert the agency that the company distributed contaminated chocolate in more than 1 million candy bars. Cadbury claims the health risks were so "minimal" there was no legal need to inform the agency immediately, the Mirror said. Cadbury tells the Mirror: "This is a precaution. The levels are significantly below the standard that would be a health problem. There is no evidence anyone has been sick through eating this chocolate." But the Food Standards Agency challenges Cadbury's version of events. "They should have told us earlier," the agency says. "Cadbury is duty bound by the Food Hygiene Act to inform us straightaway of any contamination. They failed to do so for almost six months. It doesn't matter how small the risk. … Having salmonella in chocolate can pose a health risk. We wouldn't recall these products just for fun."

Simon Baldry, managing director at Cadbury, tells the Birmingham Evening Mail that there was "no need" to take the chocolate products off the market when contamination was discovered in January. "Our products were perfectly safe," Baldry says. "We'd gone through our rigorous testing process … We'd identified that these were only minute traces." The products are contaminated with a rare strain of the bacteria salmonella Montevideo. Reported cases of the strain have quadrupled in recent months, the Mail says. The UK's Health Protection Agency tells the Mail if there were a decline in salmonella Montevideo following the product recall, it would be "strong evidence" of a link. Each year, Cadbury's plant in Marlbrook generates 97,000 metric tons of chocolate crumb, which are transported to Cadbury factories in Bourneville, Birmingham, and Somerdale (near Bristol) to be blended with cocoa butter, and thus turned into milk chocolate. Cadbury declines to discuss the cost of the recall, but sets up a helpline for concerned customers, and provides a recall procedure to exchange products for refund vouchers.

The Guardian in London reports that Britain's consumers may have already eaten as many as half of the contaminated candy bars during the previous six months, which may have triggered food poisoning in more than forty people. The Food Standards Agency accuses Cadbury of failing to report that a leaking wastewater pipe at the company's Marlbrook plant contaminated the chocolate crumb: "It was found in January, but they didn't tell us until Monday. In the interim, products have gone out into the market. There was a window when they knew they had a problem in their factory." Cadbury corrected the problem sometime in March, meaning the company had produced contaminated products for about forty days, the Guardian says. The Health Protection Agency discovered the problem while investigating an outbreak of salmonella Montevideo among more than forty people. The agency found an exact match with the strain found in bacteria samples found in the Cadbury chocolate, but so far has proven no causal link. Salmonella bacteria affect the stomach and intestines, causing symptoms that include diarrhea, constipation, nausea, headache, stomach cramps, and fever, which generally clear up in seven days without treatment. Severe cases can lead to complications, such as arthritis. Cadbury says: "We found the cause of the problem, fixed it, and subsequent tests proved we were completely clear. … We are aware they have been looking at salmonella prevalence, and that you could say the strain found in our product is similar to the one they found. The scientific evidence was that the level found (in the chocolate) was way below the level that would cause illness (Vasagar, 2006)."

The Food Standards Agency is asking Cadbury to explain why it failed to alert the agency after discovering salmonella at its Marlbrook plant in January, the Times of London reports. Meanwhile, the Health Protection Agency says it has found about forty-five cases of salmonella poisoning since March, compared to fourteen cases between March and June 2005 "The watchdog is particularly irritated that even though Cadbury disclosed on Monday the presence of the bug in chocolate, it took the company until Thursday evening to agree to a recall," according to the Times. Cadbury sells more than 1 billion pounds of chocolate annually in the United Kingdom. The recall was the equivalent of a third of Britain's daily consumption of Cadbury's chocolate. "While the cost to the company," the Times says, which manufactures 2,500 products, is expected to be low, the damage to its reputation could be significant." It is possible that rats, mice, or wild birds, any of which may carry salmonella, may have been watering at the leaky pipe and contaminated the plant. Routine tests were taken three times a day every eight hours to check for contamination of ingredients, of the production line, and of finished products. A private laboratory handled the analysis of the tests, detected the salmonella and alerted Cadbury. The lab found 0.3 parts of a million in the contaminated chocolate. The factory's alert system would have withdrawn any product at ten parts per million per ten grams, Cadbury tells the Times. "We have followed the regulations," a Cadbury spokeswoman says. "The (Food Standards Agency) will have to decide if we need a new regulation and we are willing to work with them on that (V. Elliott, 2006)."

The Daily Telegraph in London reports: "The contamination was made public only after the Health Protection Agency noticed a puzzling rise in salmonella Montevideo cases. Last year, 14 cases were confirmed between March 1 and June 19. This year 45 were scattered across the country. More than half affected children under four." Looking for clues, the agency analyzed all samples of the bacterium it had received during the previous months, including those sent by Cadbury. The agency approached Cadbury's independent lab, and was told the source of the samples was confidential. Only when officials from the Food Standards Agency approached the lab did Cadbury admit to the contamination. Cadbury claimed 5,000 bars were made with the contaminated chocolate. But the Food Standards Agency demanded a much larger recall. Cadbury's delay in reporting the contamination angered agency officials, who told the Telegraph, "Under food hygiene law, having salmonella in a ready-to-eat food such as chocolate is unacceptable and can pose a health risk (Derbyshire, 2006)."

Day 3: June 25, 2006—Lyndon Simkin, a brand-marketing scholar at Warwick University, expresses surprise that Cadbury made a decision to ship the contaminated candy. "What the company had done is strange given its Quaker background of caring for workers," Simkin tells the Sunday Mercury. "Cadbury is much-loved because of very clever brand-building work, like sponsoring 'Coronation Street' (a long-running British TV soap opera). It has homely connotations and people trust it and have great loyalty to it." He predicts that the salmonella controversy "… in a few weeks, it will be forgotten," unless people can prove they got sick from eating the products (Allen, 2006).

Cadbury European President Matthew Shattock tells the Mercury that the traces of salmonella detected in the chocolate crumb were "minute" and that the candy recall is purely precautionary. "The highest level we found was one-thirtieth of the level at which we would raise an alert as to a food safety issue," Shattock says (Allen, 2006).

Between March 1 and June 19, the Health Protection Agency documented eight confirmed cases of salmonella Montevideo among infants younger than one year and twenty-two cases among children younger than age four, according to Scotland on Sunday (Gray, 2006).

Cadbury's European president Matthew Shattock says that only fourteen samples of the chocolate crumb showed minute traces of contamination – out of 7,000 samples tested – according to Wales on Sunday. Since then, no trace has been found in 17,000 samples tested, he says: "Our products are perfectly safe to eat and we have no evidence that anyone has been ill from eating them (Wales, 2006)."

Cadbury announces plans to bury 250 tons of chocolate bars and Easter eggs in landfills across Britain. The candy, which was recalled from shops and warehouses, weighs about the same as thirty-three double-decker buses, according to the Daily Mail, and is equivalent to one-third of Britain's daily consumption of Cadbury chocolate. All wrappers and packaging have been removed, and Cadbury is discouraging children from searching for the candy on a "Willie Wonka hunt" (Leake, 2006).

The Daily Mail reveals that an independent lab alerted the Health Protection Agency to the contamination as early as January, but the information was not passed on to the Food Standards Agency. Members of Parliament call for a government investigation into Cadbury's delayed reports to the government. "We need a proper explanation from ministers about what went wrong," says Liberal Democrat Bob Russell. "There has been a communication breakdown and, clearly, the current rules are not being operated properly (Leake, 2006)."

The Independent (Carrell, 2006) publishes the following timeline of events:

- June 16: The Health Protection Agency finds contaminated samples from an unidentified confectionary firm.
- June 19: The Health Protection Agency alerts the Food Standards Agency, which approaches the private lab for the name of the client. The lab alerts Cadbury, which then calls the Food Standards Agency and admits contamination had taken place.
- June 21: Cadbury agrees to share additional information about affected products.
- June 22: Cadbury denies a cover-up, but agrees to a product recall.

Cadbury European President Matthew Shattock tells the Independent: "Our responsibility is the welfare of our consumers and I can reassure you that our products are perfectly safe to eat (Carrell, 2006)."

In the Sunday Mirror (Hayward, 2006), officials at the Food Standards Agency express surprise that Cadbury failed to report the contamination earlier: "We will be in talks with local environmental and trading standards officers this week to see if any action is taken." Massive fines are a possibility. Meanwhile, officials at the Herefordshire council's health department tell the Sunday Mirror, "Cadbury's compliance with the Food Safety Act will be part of the ongoing investigation." Cadbury European President Matthew Shattock replies, "We are absolutely confident these minute levels of salmonella would not have made anyone ill."

Journalists at the Sunday Herald report buying Cadbury's recalled products readily in England stores. Cadbury says it is "working all hands on deck" to complete the recall. Officials at the Food Standards Agency say, "The ultimate responsibility lies with the manufacturer." Meanwhile, Sir Hugh Pennington, president for the Society for General Microbiology, tells the Herald that DNA testing could trace the strain to Cadbury. "The only safe level of salmonella in chocolate is zero," he says (J. Johnson, 2006).

Britain's Parliament is demanding a "full and public explanation" of the Cadbury recall, the Sunday Independent in Ireland reports. Richard North, a food safety advisor, tells the Independent: "Cadbury is being disingenuous. It has only withdrawn its products because it has been found out." Cadbury sent nine samples of chocolate crumb to an independent lab, which detected salmonella, then passed the samples on to the Health Protection Agency without identifying the source. The agency says it received the samples between early February and late May (Harrison, 2006).

The Health Protection Agency confirms that "molecular fingerprinting tests" show that the bacteria causing the outbreaks were the same as those contaminating Cadbury products, according to the Sunday Times in London. Agency statisticians suspected that chocolate might be the vector for the disease, since so many of the reported cases were in children. The reported fifty three cases could have been ten times higher in reality, the agency tells the Times, because most salmonella cases go unreported: "We cannot be 100 percent sure that Cadbury's products caused the disease, but it's a strong possibility." Chocolate is the ideal vehicle for salmonella because the high levels of fat and sugar preserve the bacteria and carry them into the intestine, microbiologists tell the Sunday Times. "This meant that serious illness could be caused by what appeared to be mere trace elements of the bacterium," the Sunday Times said. Food safety consultant Michael Kane says the rules for food safety are established under the Global Food Standard and the British Retail Consortium: "They say that as soon as salmonella was detected the company should have instituted a crisis management procedure, including recalls of any potentially hazardous products and warning relevant authorities." Cadbury confirms it failed to approach the situation as a crisis, but instead decided informally that the contamination levels were too low to warrant a crisis footing, and to move forward with production. The Herefordshire's environmental standards department last inspected the factory in fall 2005 (Leake & Walsh).

Sir Hugh Pennington, a bacteriologist at Aberdeen University in Scotland, tells the Associated Press: "The fat in chocolate actually preserves the salmonella from the normal intestinal defenses, so you don't have to eat very many salmonellas to get infected. It's about a thousand times less than if you're eating it from traditional sources like meats."

Day 4: June 26, 2006—A member of the British Parliament, Liberal Democrat Bob Russell, tells the Birmingham Post: "It seems extraordinary than Cadbury, or whoever makes these decisions, decided to withdraw these products so far down the line when there were concerns about this some months ago." Meanwhile, the Straits Times reports that Cadbury is recalling its chocolate bars in Singapore.

The Birmingham Evening Mail (Authi, 2006) reports that "thousands" have called Cadbury's salmonella hotline.

The Bulldog Reporter, a trade publication serving the US public relations industry, quotes a Cadbury spokesperson: "There are minute traces of salmonella, which are significantly below those (levels) which scientific standards say present any hazard. There's no connection between our product and anybody becoming ill from it. ... We've taking this precautionary step because our consumers are our highest priority. We apologize for any inconvenience caused."

Day 6: June 28, 2006—Cadbury suspends its £10 million annual sponsorship of "Coronation Street," one of the longest-running scripted television programs in the world, second only to the US soap opera "As the World Turns," the Birmingham Post says. This marks the first time in ten years that the program will air without Cadbury advertising, says the Western Daily Press (Morgan, 2006). Cadbury originally wanted to replace its ads, which promoted a wide range of Cadbury products, with a message designed to "reassure" customers. But broadcasting rules in the United Kingdom prohibited the plan, says the trade publication Marketing (Bowery, 2006).

Day 8: June 30, 2006—Times columnist Mike Hume questions the need for the Cadbury recall: "An epidemic it ain't. In any case, the Cadbury's chocolate produced in January is likely to have long since been scoffed. So what is withdrawing a million different bars months later supposed to be a 'precaution' against?" He continues: "Cadbury is big enough to defend itself. It is the rest of us I am worried about, living in a superstitious society where it is deemed wise to bury tonnes of perfectly good foodstuff, and where government agencies treat us like milky children in need of protection from hypothetical evils, and too much chocolate." In the same issue, the Times reports that a baby, a child, and an adult have been admitted to hospitals with new cases of the salmonella Monteverdi strain, also known as SmvdX07. The Health Protection Agency raises the count of cases to thirty-one in England and Wales since March 1, with the most affected group being two-year-olds. The agency says it first noticed an uptick in cases on May 22.

Business columnist Sheila O'Flanagan of the Irish Times writes: "Purely precautionary would have been doing something about it back in January. The current recall isn't precautionary. It's slamming a stable door after the horse has not only bolted but done a lap of the track. ... What on earth were they thinking when they allowed salmonella infected product onto the shelves? ... The 'we know best' mentality isn't one that works when you have to deal with anxious consumers. ... An arrogant company, suggesting that they considered the problem, but didn't think it worth dealing with, will not find the public very sympathetic. ... Nevertheless, confidence in the brand has been shaken. And it's not because something bad happened—problems always occur. It's because the directors sat around and discussed it and decided that the profitability trade off was probably worth a few people getting sick—and that's always the wrong decision."

The Burton Mail reports, "Tests by food safety officers have found that half of shopkeepers visited in Burton have ignored the food hazard warning for various Cadbury's chocolate products." The East Staffordshire Borough Council sent another written warning to all shopkeepers after finding the initial recall had been ignored in about half of local stores. Rob Morgan, head of environmental health, tells the Mail: "In this case after we informed the shop owners, everybody was happy to take the products off the shelves. They all said they weren't aware, which is quite a surprise (Powles, 2006)."

Day 9: July 1, 2006—The Guardian reports: The Health Protection Agency called the Food Standards Agency on June 16 to express its concerns about a potential salmonella outbreak. Since March 1, the Health Protection Agency has received an unusual number of samples with the Montevideo strain, which is usually found in hotter regions of the world. The cases were scattered geographically rather than clustered, as is the case with most food poisonings. Half the victims were under two. Officials at Health Protection suspected a nationally distributed product marketed to children. Their investigation focused on nine samples from an anonymous company, all of which arrived in early February. The lab refused to identify the source, so Health Protection turned to Food Standards to use its powers to get the source's name. The agencies learned that Cadbury's Herefordshire factory sent the contaminated crumb to its Bourneville factory, where it was stored in a silo, and later mixed with other batches. About thirty brands were made during the period that the contaminated crumb was in the factory. Birmingham authorities are sifting through Cadbury warehouses in search of contaminated stock. Herefordshire authorities are also investigating whether the contamination might have come from a nearby dump about a half-mile from the Cadbury plant. The dump contains rotting chicken feathers, animal parts, and feces.

Concerned the crumb may have found its way into the full line of chocolate products, the Food Standards Agency ordered testing for thirty more lines of Cadbury products, the Guardian reports. An agency spokesman says, "There may be contamination in other Cadbury products." A Cadbury spokeswoman responds: "We are testing product lines four times a day, and environmental health are checking so they can feel as confident as we do about our testing regime. We have tested all products and found no salmonella." Kath Dalmeny, policy expert for the independent watchdog group The Food Commission, says: "It seems Cadbury has been arrogant enough to rely on its reputation to get it through a crisis rather than taking immediate action (Lawrence, 2006)."

The Grocer, a trade publication, interviews several players within the industry to comment on Cadbury's position in the wake of the recall (Carmichael, 2006):

- Paul Osborne, a confectionary buyer for Hancocks C&C, says: "Cadbury has been quite lucky in one way. Most of the affected products don't have direct rivals, so there's no alternative for people to switch to."
- David Arkwright, branding consultant at MEAT, says: "Brands like Cadbury's are like human beings and are forgivable, but they have to earn that. I'm confident that Cadbury can be forgiven, but it would have to present itself as penitent and this must be done purposefully. I'm not sure they've done that as much as they ought, should and could, but it's a brand with huge equity and public affection and that can outweigh any momentary negative."
- Paul Cousins, director of Catalyst marketing consultants, says: "In the short term, the effects will be noticeable: some people are nervous. There'll be a short-term dip in sales, but in the long term I don't think it'll make much difference."

On the day of the recall, Cadbury Schweppes chairman Sir John Sunderland—though not acting quite like himself—gave an upbeat keynote address to the annual luncheon for the Biscuit Cake Chocolate & Confectionary Association, according to The Grocer. Sunderland reminded his audience of the positive role that his industry plays in the lives of ordinary Britons, providing safe, affordable, quality food. He closed by telling his audience they would hear more about food safety that afternoon. A few hours later, Cadbury announced it would recall 1 million candy bars (Carmichael, 2006).

Day 10: July 2, 2006—Cadbury publicly rejected suggestions that it should recall more of its products due to the salmonella scare, according to AFX News. Through a spokesman, Cadbury says, "We're not recalling any more products. Environmental health officers have tested a number of other products, which is perfectly normal. We've tested tens of thousands of products and they've all come up negative so we do not believe there is any reason to recall any other products."

Day 11: July 3, 2006—Analysts estimate the scare will cost Cadbury Schweppes £25 million, according to the Daily Mail: £5 million in recall costs, with the rest in lost sales during to a loss of consumer confidence (Poulter, 2006).

Day 12: July 4, 2006—The Food Standards Agency says in an official report that Cadbury's food safety system is unreliable, outdated, and underestimates the level and likelihood of salmonella contamination. Birmingham food safety team leader Nick Lowe tells the Guardian, "What we and Cadbury are doing with testing is just at the needle-in-haystack level." Cadbury's response: "At all times we have acted in good faith and we do not challenge the views of the expert committee or the environmental health officers. We will be changing our procedures in light of their advice (Lawrence, 2006)."

The agency's report also says Cadbury's risk assessment erred when it drew parallels between the threshold for salmonella infection and the thresholds for infection by other micro-organisms that may be found in chocolate, according to the Associated Press. The agency says: "We think (Cadbury) made a mistake in assuming there was a safe level of salmonella in a product like chocolate. Our view is there isn't."

Day 13: July 5, 2006—The Daily Mail reports that Cadbury informed the Food Standards Agency of a similar contamination incident in 2002, but had yet to submit paperwork with details, such as the affected products or factories. "I don't know if it was a cynical move by Cadbury," an agency spokesman tells the Mail, "but we would have expected to be informed about it as soon as it happened." The agency also criticized the company's approach to detecting contamination, telling the Mail (Levy, 2006): "Cadbury's risk assessment does not address the risk of salmonella in chocolate in a way that the (FSA's independent Advisory Committee on the Microbiological Safety of Food) would regard as a modern approach to risk assessment. We can't rule out the possibility that other products are affected."

The 2002 incident at the Marlbrook plant involved the same rare strain of salmonella, the Food Standards Agency tells the Independent (Hickman, 2006). The Herefordshire County Council says it was not informed of the incident.

Cadbury detected the strain in two products—Cadbury's Dairy Milk and Brazil Caramel—as long ago as 2002, but failed to notify government authorities, the Guardian reports (Lawrence, 2006). Cadbury told the Food Standards Agency it destroyed the products at the time. Cadbury tells reporters it was unable to identify the source of that contamination.

Several tankers of chocolate crumb from the Marlbrook plant tested positive for the rare strain during a three-week period in 2006, the Guardian reports. However, Cadbury's just-in-time production system allowed the tankers to leave and the contents to be mixed at other factories before the test results were completed. A tanker left the plant every hour, but results were not available for twenty-seven to twenty-nine hours, rendering "the test meaningless," said Andrew Tector, head of environmental health in Herefordshire. A Cadbury spokeswoman tells the Guardian: "Under the legislation, it is left to the manufacturer to determine their testing protocols. We did this based on sound independent science. At all times we acted in good faith (Lawrence, 2006)."

In a statement published in the Birmingham Evening Mail, Cadbury tells the news media that it will continue to seek guidance from the Food Standards Agency and environmental health officers: "However, we welcome the confirmation by the FSA that they believe 'proportional action was taken by recalling seven products.'"

"The PR plan was too little, too late for Cadbury. The day it discovered salmonella in its chocolate, it should have set the PR wheels in motion," Ruth Shearn, managing director of RMS PR, tells the trade magazine Marketing.

Day 14: July 6, 2006—The outbreak could be the first in a series of health scares in the food industry, Marketing Week speculates. An anonymous industry insider says, "I can't imagine that Cadbury is the only company that tests for salmonella in this way." Cadbury responds that its detection tests are based on "hard science."

Investment bankers JP Morgan speculates in a research note that the outbreak will cost Cadbury in excess of £30 million (about $55.4 million US), according to AFX News: "The recall has received a growing and increasingly negative amount of media coverage damaging the brand image and the corporate reputation," the note says. Morgan recommends investors avoid Cadbury until the "situation is clarified." Cadbury responds that it is "far too early to tell" what the eventual costs would be, and adds "… you can't estimate what the sales impact might or might not be." The company says it plans to address the issue when it publishes interim results for the second half.

Day 15: July 7, 2006—At the urging of the Food Standards Agency, Cadbury agrees to a comprehensive cleaning of all production lines at the Marlbrook plant, according to the Guardian. Third-party companies used chocolate crumb from the Marlbrook plant to manufacture chocolate products, the Guardian says (Lawrence and Meikie, 2006), but the Food Standards Agency is unable to provide a list of those companies.

Cadbury agrees to destroy any chocolate testing positive for salmonella, however small, according to the Western Daily Press. A spokesman for the Food Standards Agency says, "We are not saying the whole plant is contaminated but salmonella is a very difficult thing to get rid of and the dry powder can get in all the cracks so the best thing to do is have a complete overhaul, start from scratch and clean the whole place up (Hughes, 2006)."

Cadbury also agrees to release products only after test results return negative, says the Birmingham Daily Mail.

Day 16: July 8, 2006—The Times of London explains to its readers the science behind salmonella as a threat to food safety and human health: Large numbers of salmonella will interfere with the function of the digestive tract. The bacteria prevent the body from absorbing water normally, and the liquid is passed out as diarrhea. It takes roughly a million salmonella cells to make a person noticeably ill. However, as few as 2,000 can cause illness if taken in chocolate. The fat in the chocolate protects the bacteria from digestive acids. Chocolate is a perfect vehicle to carry the cells into the small intestine. Chocolate is not submitted to high temperatures during the manufacturing process that would normally kill salmonella. Exceptional care must be taken to make sure that the raw ingredients are free of the bacteria before the process begins. "Salmonella infection is so common that we might have been unaware of Cadbury's problems," the Times says, "had the variety of bacterium involved—Montevideo—not been so rare (Parry, 2006)."

Cadbury dismisses speculation that more companies could be drawn into the scare, according to a story in the Birmingham Post, which identifies several third-party companies who buy chocolate crumb from Cadbury, including Premier Chocolate, Premier Beverages, and British Sugar. None received the contaminated crumb, Cadbury says. The Food Standards Agency confirms Cadbury's story: "We have no reason to believe (the crumb) would have been contaminated."

Day 17: July 9, 2006—The Sunday Express in London (L. Johnson, 2006) reports that Chris Huhne, an environmental spokesman for the Liberal Democrats, is demanding legal action against Cadbury: "This looks like a case of corporate cover-up when what was needed was an honest owning-up. Cadbury's should be prosecuted to ensure all food manufacturers know safety must come first. Its failure to notify the FSA is a clear break of its legal duty." Jerry Morris, a food expert at the Chartered Institute of Environmental Health, agrees that Cadbury should answer to the public: "We would want to know the reasons why Cadbury's risk assessment differs from that of the government experts."

Catherine Henderson, 62, of County Antrim in Northern Ireland, tells the Sunday Express (L. Johnson, 2006) that she was in a hospital isolation ward for five days after eating a Cadbury Caramel. "I never thought you could get ill like that from chocolate," she says. "I didn't think I would come out alive. … I am not looking for money. I just feel the company should have been more responsible in informing people." Solicitors at Irwin Mitchell have taken her case. A Cadbury spokeswoman denies the company withheld information about the contamination and says Cadbury's had scientific evidence to show "levels of the bug found were too low to pose a risk."

Day 19: July 11, 2006—Sallie Booth, an attorney with the Irwin Mitchell law firm representing salmonella victim Catherine Henderson, tells the Belfast News Letter: "As chocolate is targeted mainly at children, the measures taken by Cadbury's should have been ultra-rigorous."

Day 24: July 16, 2006—The pollster Brand Index says Cadbury has lost the confidence of consumers, according to the Sunday Telegraph in London (Murray-Watson, 2006). Just before the scare began, Cadbury posted a brand score of 44; after the outbreak, the score fell to 22. Brand Index monitors the reputations of hundreds of organizations. The brand score is based upon responses to questionnaires. Chief executive Stephan Shakespeare tells the Telegraph: "The loss of confidence in Cadbury is the greatest we have seen since we started

Brand Index nine months ago. The issue has gone right into the core of the public consciousness."

Day 25: July 17, 2006—Cooking columnist Julia Watson says in a dispatch from United Press International: "How appropriate that (Cadbury) are now paying a far higher price than they would have done had they behaved as though their customers were indeed their highest priority as soon as they discovered the leaking water pipe."

Day 29: July 21, 2006—The Health Protection Agency reports that Cadbury products were the probable cause of a national outbreak of salmonella Montevideo, the Guardian Unlimited says, with fifty-six cases documented since March. The agency's outbreak control team (OCT) obtained detailed food histories of fifteen victims; of them, thirteen (or 85 percent) had consumed Cadbury products. The agency says, "After carefully considering all the available evidence the OCT concluded that consumption of products made by Cadbury Schweppes was the most credible explanation for the outbreak of salmonella Montevideo." Cadbury responds: "We are sorry to hear that people have been unwell. We've already announced that we have changed our protocols because we understand that the consumers' desire for no risk at all is paramount. Any product showing any traces of salmonella will be destroyed."

UK government investigators comment on the Cadbury recall in a report published in the Communicable Disease Report Weekly: "No other common brands, retail outlets, catering chains or single food types were identified as common factors (Associated Press, 2006, July 21)."

Day 30: July 22, 2006—The Independent in London reports that Cadbury says it will consider compensation for outbreak victims. The Health Protection Agency says it has identified forty-nine primary cases of salmonella Montevideo since March 1. Of those, thirty-seven are of the same strain – SmvdX07 – found in the Cadbury products. The agency estimates the reported cases represent between 111 and 185 total cases linked to Cadbury products. Cadbury declines to say whether it agrees with the HPA's conclusions. A Cadbury spokeswoman tells the Independent: "If any people come forward, we will take their situation seriously and consider their case (Hickman, 2006)." David Standard of the law firm Irwin Mitchell tells the Scotsman in Glasgow: "Confirmation of the causal link between Cadbury's products and this rare and serious form of salmonella means the case strengthens for those willing to take legal action (Jamieson, 2006)."

Day 37: July 29, 2006—The Birmingham Evening Mail reports that Cadbury will tell investors in its half-year report that the salmonella scare will cost the company at least £30 million. Of that, £5 million is the result of the recall of 1 million chocolate bars. Cadbury has yet to indicate how much the scare has affected sales in the seven weeks since the contamination became public. There is also no assessment of how much the company may pay in related legal costs (Morley, 2006).

Day 38: July 30, 2006—Andrew Wood, an analyst at New York brokerage Sanford C. Bernstein, tells the Independent: "Public recalls are not unusual in the food industry. So why has this one garnered so much attention? For a start, salmonella in chocolate doesn't seem to jive, and they have known about it since January. (Cadbury's) reputation has suffered." Thayne Forbes, joint managing director of the brand experts Intangible Business, agrees: "For Cadbury, this is a really serious PR problem because it affects children and it's a health issue. They should be taking a proactive approach, be seen to be giving advice and putting in place quality control, and I really don't see them doing that. ... They are trying to downplay the effects, while I would say they should be trying to establish a quick, concerted and extensive programme to sort it out. Otherwise, it looks like they don't really care (Townsend, 2006)."

Day 39: July 31, 2006—Stockbrokerage ABN Amro estimates a £25 million drop in sales for Cadbury, leading to a £15 million drop in profits, according to the Western Daily Press in Bristol (Buckland, 2006).

Day 41: Aug. 2, 2006—Five of the seven brands that Cadbury recalled are scheduled to return to store shelves, coinciding with the release of Cadbury's 2006 interim results, according to a report from Agence France Presse.

According to the Birmingham Evening Mail, Cadbury Schweppes CEO Todd Stitzer is telling investors that chocolate sales have plunged 14 percent since the scare began. He expects a total bill of at least £26 million. Half is due to the recall, the rest to manufacturing improvements and dealing with news media. Insurance will cut the total bill by about £6 million. Despite these costs, the well-diversified company posted a 24 percent boost in pre-tax profits (£402 million) for the six months leading to July 30, 2006 (Morley, 2006).

Cadbury CEO Stitzer defends Cadbury's decision not to inform the Food Standards Agency when the company discovered the contaminated crumb, according to an AFX News report. "We felt that we were acting in accordance with what the law specifies so we didn't feel that we were doing anything wrong," Stitzer says. "Clearly, in conversations with the FSA they had a different view and we've changed our processes because we don't want consumers to have any possible concern about our processes and our products (AFX International Focus, 2006)."

"We clearly caused concern to our consumers and we are truly sorry for that," Stitzer tells the Evening Standard (Miller, 2006) in London. The company plans to spend £5 million in advertising and marketing to reassure customers.

The overall market for candy in the United Kingdom fell by 7 percent during July because of a major heat wave, according to Market Watch. Cadbury's market share fell by 1.1 percent during the first four weeks of the second half, thanks to the heat combined with the recall. Shares for Cadbury Schweppes rose 3 percent in morning trading after the first-half results were released (Lagorce, 2006).

The company's first-half profits beat the consensus among analysts, who expected profits to come in at between £376 million and £398 million. Cadbury said the seven product lines that were recalled represent less than 3 percent of British sales and about 0.5 percent of group sales, Agence France Presse reports.

Claire Collingwood, a trader at CMC Markets in London, tells the Associated Press, "The main reason behind the share price jump was the relief that the cost of its recall was not as much as the market has feared." David Lang at Investec says, "The burning question is how the consumer treats Cadbury at Christmas (Stringer, 2006)."

Brand surveys indicate that consumer confidence in Cadbury is returning to normal, says Simon Nixon at breakingviews.com: "The company still shows a worrying refusal to admit it has done anything much wrong." Cadbury stands by its original protocols, has apologized only for the "concern" the outbreak has generated, and continues to cast doubt on the idea that Cadbury is the source of the outbreak. "Cadbury's stance suggests either complacency or confirms the threat of legal action—from consumers and regulators—remains real," Nixon writes.

Day 42: Aug. 3, 2006—CEO Todd Stitzer continues to defend Cadbury's pre-outbreak protocols, the Times of London reports, but he admits Cadbury has upgraded to a "zero presence testing" system since the scare began. In addition, Cadbury has modified some of its operations (including transportation of chocolate crumb) to improve hygiene, Stitzer says. He also says that local plant managers followed company procedures, and that he made no changes to management at the Marlbrook facility. Stitzer played down the effect of the outbreak on a slump in sales since June 23, putting the blame instead on Britain's recent heat wave. He says the company expects minimal damage to Cadbury's reputation or sales (Klinger, 2006).

Cadbury says it will resume sponsorship of "Coronation Street" in the fall with a £5 million deal, according to the Birmingham Mail (Morley, 2006).

Cadbury Schweppes Chair John Sunderland says he and the board learned about the salmonella issue just two days before the recall, the Mail reports (Morley, 2006). The Times says that CEO Todd Stitzer did not know about the salmonella problem until "some time after its discovery (Klinger, 2006)."

CEO Todd Stitzer tells the Mail (Morley, 2006): "Although we have always acted in good faith throughout, we have caused concerns and for that I am extremely sorry."

In an opinion piece for the Guardian, journalist Nils Pratley writes, "It would be different if Cadbury screwed up again, but British consumers, by and large, are forgiving."

Day 44: Aug. 5, 2006—Cadbury has sent letters of apology to 28,000 convenience stores in its distribution channel, The Grocer reports. The letters thank the stores for their support and for helping to execute the recall "as quickly and efficiently as possible." The letter adds: "… we are taking all the necessary steps to put this right at both our manufacturing sites and in the eyes of the public."

Day 66: Aug. 27, 2006—The Food Standards Agency will bankroll an investigation of the Cadbury chocolate factory by the Herefordshire council, the Sunday Telegraph reports. The money will come from a £200,000 fighting fund and "will help expedite a prosecution of Cadbury," according to the Telegraph. "Prosecution will mean that the company receives further negative publicity, possibly just as it enters the key Christmas sales period (Northedge, 2006)."

Day 96: Sept. 26, 2006—Staff members at the Food Standards Agency are annoyed by the lack of cooperation from Cadbury, according to documents acquired under the UK's Freedom of Information Law, the Belfast Telegraph reports (Hickman, 2006). The agency staff privately considered that Cadbury has posed an unacceptable risk to the public. Meeting minutes show that staff members were unhappy with a lack of response for requests for information that would have helped the government better deal with the outbreak. Also, a request for Cadbury's risk assessment went unfulfilled. "All requests for information have to be reinforced," the document said.

Day 99: Sept. 29, 2006—The Food Standards Agency's Advisory Committee on Microbiological Safety of Food (ACMSF) is calling for Cadbury to implement a "robust" Hazard Analysis Critical Control Point system at its manufacturing plants, according to the trade publication Process Engineering. But Cadbury claims it already has such a system at all factories. The article says that Cadbury relied on end-product testing that ACMSF found unsuitable for food safety. "The company wrongly drew parallels between the threshold for salmonella infection and the threshold for infection by other micro-organisms found in chocolate," the article says. "(but) there is no minimum infection dose for salmonella."

Day 116: Oct. 16, 2006—Stockbrokers in England are turning negative on Cadbury as the share price slips by 6p to 551.5p, the Guardian Unlimited reports. Merrill Lynch goes from buy to neutral; JP Morgan drops its rating as well, and tells its clients: "Cadbury has been struggling to regain positive sales momentum in UK chocolate since the announcement of its product recall (over salmonella) on 23 June. If the authorities were to take legal action, Cadbury could face another PR nightmare and we believe serious bad press could result in further pressure on sales —with serious financial consequences if that were to happen during the Christmas season."

Day 126: Oct. 26, 2006—Cadbury's chocolate sales have dropped by 5 percent since the beginning of July 2006, as compared to same period in 2005, the Evening Standard in London reports. Cadbury has blamed a recent heat wave for slow sales, but both summers were unusually hot for Britain. Meanwhile, consumer confidence in the brand has returned, Cadbury claims, citing rising sales for a new product called Flakes. Cadbury CEO Todd Stitzer "stressed the importance of the returning confidence in the Cadbury name among British consumers in the run up to the crucial Christmas season," the Evening Standard says (Armitage, 2006).

A new ACNielsen research report says Mars—the manufacturer of Snickers, Twix, and Milky Way—has overtaken Cadbury as the market leader in British chocolate, with a 33.7 percent share vs. Cadbury's 31.3 percent share, according to the Evening Standard. Cadbury CEO Todd Stitzer disputes the report, claiming Cadbury owns a 3 percentage-point lead over Mars in 2006 year-to-date sales of chocolate. He accused the Financial Times, which broke the story, of a "totally overzealous interpretation" of a single month's figures, and says public confidence in Cadbury products has returned to pre-contamination levels. The coming Christmas season accounts for 35 percent of Cadbury's annual sales in the United Kingdom (Armitage, 2006).

Day 127: Oct. 27, 2006—"Cadbury is not the only one suffering; the whole UK confectionery market has been down 5 (percent) since the beginning of July," the Daily Mail reports (Brown, 2006). The Birmingham Post quotes Cadbury CEO Todd Stitzer: "Had it not been for the continued long, warm spell, the group would have met its targets for revenue and margin grown. … The UK confectionary market, which accounts for 15 percent of our group sales, has been weak, but we think the weather had a greater effect than the recall difficulties." Around 70 percent of Cadbury's sales come from the Americas and the Asian Pacific. Chris Huhne, a Liberal Democrat who served as the Department for Environment, Food and Rural Affair's "shadow secretary," tells the Post: "Cadbury has paid the price for its failure to quickly tackle contamination in its plants, and then for failing to own up quickly and put things right. … It is another object lesson that in areas concerning public health, companies cannot be too careful with their reputation, and also that regulators need to be tough and vigilant (Pain, 2006)."

Day 130: Oct. 30, 2006—Cadbury tells analysts that the company will no longer forecast profitability growth, saying it will increase operating margins "over time" while avoiding specifics, the Associated Press reports.

Day 135: Nov. 4, 2006—ACNielsen now says that Mars' usurping Cadburys for dominance of the British chocolate market "was a blip," according to the Grocer. The value of Cadbury's top-seven chocolate lines is significantly higher than the top-seven lines of Masterfoods (owner of Mars): £670 million to £560 million. In related news, a survey by YouGov says consumer confidence in Cadbury is also recovering. "Trust in the (Cadbury) brand plummeted directly after the salmonella scare but has steadily risen since, although it is still not up to pre-salmonella levels," the Grocer says.

Day 136: Nov. 5, 2006—CEO Todd Stitzer spent the previous week making presentations to investors and analysts in London and New York, the Sunday Times reports. The result? The share price fell 3.7 percent. Stitzer says the response was predictable, the result of a lot of information in a short time. "Stitzer is confident that in Britain, Cadbury's chocolate can recover from the trauma of the salmonella episode," the Sunday Times says. "A raft of new products is to be launched between now and Christmas. … Stitzer predicts that in Britain there will be big increases in sales of dark and premium chocolate (Laurence, 2006)."

Day 173: Dec. 12, 2006—Cadbury has raised its estimate of the costs it incurred during the salmonella outbreak to £30 million ($59 million US), according to Agence France Press. The change reflects "higher manufacturing and facility rectification and remediation costs," the company said in a statement.

Day 177: Dec. 16, 2006—"The award for cock-up of the year," The Grocer says, "could go to no one else but Cadbury for its management of the salmonella scare."

Day 235: Feb. 12, 2007—Cadbury is recalling its chocolate Easter eggs after learning that the product might post a danger to consumers with nut allergies, the Birmingham Post reports (Revill, 2006). Liquid chocolate used in the eggs was mistakenly "manufactured on a line that has also been producing chocolate which contains nuts," a Cadbury spokesman tells the International Herald Tribune. The products are "perfectly safe" for consumers without nut allergies, Cadbury says (Nayeri, 2006). Phil Stern, a consumer behavior scholar at Warwick Business School, tells the Post: "As an alternative to withdrawing the products, they could have asked the retailers to put stickers on the eggs, saying they may contain nuts. But they chose not to do that. They did not consider that to be reliable enough, and decided to recall the products. That is the most responsible decision they could have taken." The Post says, "Cadbury's promptly action was a textbook action in dealing with the crisis, added Dr. Stern. The key, apparently, is to acknowledge the issues, and point out if possible that it is not the result of some systematic failure, but rather a one-off (Revill, 2006)."

Day 243: Feb. 20, 2007—Cadbury announces a major investment program in the United Kingdom following "2006 results which were below market expectations," AFX News reports, by launching Trident gum in Britain. Cadbury's share of the UK market has recovered to 34 percent by the end of 2006, about where it stood before the salmonella scare. "Our market share has recovered in the fourth quarter and, in particular, over the Christmas season," CEO Todd Stitzer says. "(The salmonella outbreak) is not something you'll hear us talking about again." He added that February's nut-allergy recall had been "immaterial" to sales and profits, but declined to discuss pending legal actions under the UK's environmental health laws. Cadbury has learned important lessons from its problems in 2006, Stitzer says. "We're profiting from those learnings, taking them and applying them to our business going forward so that we can be a bigger, stronger business," he says. "Our record stands for itself."

Credit Suisse reiterates its "underweight" rating on Cadbury, with a target of 520 pence, citing future pressure on earnings based on the company's investment plans, AFX News reports. Citigroup rates Cadbury a buy at 620 pence, and considers the salmonella scare to be a short-term problem.

Day 265: March 14, 2007—US corporate raider Nelson Peltz reveals he owns a 3 percent stake in Cadbury, making him the company's fourth-largest investor, the Guardian reports. On that news, market value for Cadbury climbs by more than £1 billion. Rumors say Peltz plans to break up Cadbury. England's unions express outrage; about 2,000 of Cadbury's UK workforce (3,500) belong to the Transport and General Workers Union (Finch, 2006).

Day 267: March 16, 2007—Following pressure from shareholders, the New York Times says, Cadbury announces plans to separate its beverage unit from its candy unit. The beverage unit includes Dr Pepper, Seven Up, Canada Dry, all Schweppes brands, all Mott's juices, and Hawaiian Punch (Werdigier, 2006). "Once separated, both businesses could fall prey to bids from rivals or private equity companies," says the Times. The Daily Telegraph says, "It's the biggest strategic move since its merger with Schweppes in 1969." CEO Todd

Stitzer insists the de-merger is the "culmination of a two- or three-year process (Wallop, 2006)." This contrasts with Stitzer's statement less than a year before, just after Cadbury purchased the Dr Pepper/Seven Up Bottling Co. for £198 million, as the investment community anticipated a potential demerger of Cadbury and Schweppes: "There is nothing to read into our future strategy from today's deal. We have done this because it is the right thing for our beverage business and will help it continue to grow. (English, 2006)."

Day 269: March 18, 2007—Critics of the decision to split Cadbury Schweppes into two companies say the move could make Cadbury vulnerable to a hostile takeover. CEO Todd Stitzer disagrees, telling the Sunday Times: "We would expect to be the transformer rather than the transformed (Laurence and Rushe, 2007)."

Day 306: April 24, 2007—The Birmingham City Council levies three charges against Cadbury, each punishable by unlimited fines, or up to two years in prison, or both, according to the Western Main: putting unsafe contaminated chocolate on the market between January 19 and March 10, 2006; failing to inform relevant authorities about the dangers; and, failing to identify the hazards posed by the contamination. Cadbury is summoned to appear before the Birmingham Magistrates' Court on June 15, 2007. Cadbury responds with a written statement: "We have fully co-operated with the authorities throughout their inquiries and we will examine the charges that have been brought. As there is now legal action pending, it would be inappropriate for us to comment further (Barnett, 2007)."

Day 358: June 15, 2007—In a ten-minute hearing, Cadbury's attorney entered guilty pleas to the three charges brought before the Birmingham Magistrates' Court, the Associated Press reports. In a statement of the hearing, Cadbury said: "Mistakenly, we did not believe that there was a threat to health and thus any requirement to report the incident to authorities. We accept that this approach was incorrect."

Day 376: July 3, 2007—Cadbury attorneys appear in Hereford Magistrates' Court to face charges under UK food and hygiene regulations, according to the Associated Press. "The company did not enter a formal plea," the Associated Press says, "but its lawyers said that the chocolate-maker intended to plead guilty to six counts of contravening food hygiene regulations." The charges "related to the state of repair of a drainage pipe and roof vent, the layout of the factory, the provision of drainage facilities and the cleaning and disinfection of equipment, including conveyors and storage silos," the Guardian reports. The hearing was adjourned until July 13 and moved to the Birmingham Crown Court.

Day 386: July 13, 2007—A prosecutor for the Birmingham City Council told the Birmingham Crown Court that a change in Cadbury's testing systems led to the outbreak of salmonella poisoning, the Guardian says (Smithers, 2007). Cadbury entered guild pleas to all six charges.

Prosecutor Barry Berlin told the court that Cadbury altered its system in 2003 to allow "safe levels" of salmonella to enter their chocolate-making processes, according to the Birmingham Evening Mail. Cadbury allowed the changes to its system to save money and cut back on waste, the prosecutor said. Cadbury detected the presence of salmonella in its products in January 2006, but failed to report it until June despite regularly scheduled visits from local authorities to the chocolate plant in Herefordshire every two months, he said. Berlin "insisted there should be no salmonella in ready-to-eat products at all," the Mail reported. "He said the problem with chocolate and salmonella was that the fat in chocolate preserved the organism." Cadbury "sought to save money from wastage by allowing a tolerance for salmonella in their food," Berlin told the court, according to the Press Association. Berlin presented the court with research literature about salmonella. "Cadbury knew perfectly well, we submit, that outbreaks of salmonella had been associated with very low levels in chocolate," the prosecutor said. The Local Government Chronicle quotes

Berlin as telling the court: "There is no dispute that there is a linkage between the chocolate that was distributed by Cadbury and the poisoning that took place later on."

Anthony Scrivener, QC, defense attorney for Cadbury, describes Cadbury as a reputable company that made an error, according to the Derby Evening Telegraph. "At no time did it close eyes to the risks or choose to accept any risk," he tells the court. "Nothing was destroyed or hidden—Cadbury believed it had nothing to hide." He points out that Cadbury's tests for salmonella detected (at its highest point) a level that is still 100 times less than the level that Cadbury believed to be dangerous to human health. "Negligence we admit," Scrivener says, "but we certainly do not admit that this was done deliberately to save money and nor is there any evidence to support that conclusion."

The Daily Telegraph (Bitten, 2007) reports, "The court heard that in early 2006 the problem was so endemic that Cadbury staff were dealing with 'daily' salmonella-related problems, and were referring to instances of contamination by an alphabetical series of codewords rather than using what they referred to as the 's-word.'"

The Western Daily Press says, "It also emerged in court that some of those who were taken ill after eating the chocolate needed hospital treatment. One person began to vomit blood, a 61-year-old woman lost 10lb in weight and another woman was so ill she could not attend her sister-in-law's funeral."

After the hearing, Cadbury issues a statement: "Quality has always been at the heart of our business, but the process we followed in the UK in this instance has been shown to be unacceptable. We have apologized for this and do so again today. In particular, we offer our sincere regrets and apologies to anyone who was made ill as a result of this failure (Western Daily Press, 2007)."

Day 387: July 14, 2007—The Derby Evening Telegraph reports, "A Derbyshire child will be awarded a payout after eating Cadbury chocolate and falling ill with salmonella." Cadbury agreed to the compensation, but did not admit responsibility. A judge will decide on the exact sum after consulting a medical expert.

Day 389: July 16, 2007—AFX News reports that the Birmingham Crown Court has fined Cadbury £1 million (about $2 million US) for its role in the salmonella outbreak of 2006: £500,000 for putting unsafe chocolate for sale to the public, £100,000 on each of two other charges, and £50,000 for each of six offenses at its Marlbrook factory. Recorder James Guthrie says in his ruling, "I regard this as a serious case of negligence. It therefore needs to be marked as such to emphasize the responsibility and care which the law requires of a company in Cadbury's position." Sallie Booth, a lawyer who is representing twelve persons affected by the contamination, says: "The 1 million pound fine sends a clear message that companies who have a great deal of responsibility for protecting public health cannot afford to ignore a potentially dangerous situation and cannot take a risk with the public's health." In the day's trading, Cadbury shares fall 0.2 percent on the London Stock Exchange.

The Western Daily Press quotes Recorder Guthrie as saying to the courtroom: "The victims varied from the elderly to the very young and their symptoms varied in severity. Three people needed treatment in hospital and all of them suffered extremely distressing symptoms." Andy Tector, head of environmental health and trading standards service for the Herfordshire Council, says, "We are now confident the factory at Marlbrook is operating within food and hygiene regulations and will continue to work with Cadbury to ensure this remains the case and consumers can be confident the firm's products are safe to eat (Denby, 2007)."

Law firm Irwin Mitchell confirms to The Grocer that it is pursuing civil cases against Cadbury on behalf of twelve individuals who claim to be affected by the contaminated chocolate (C. Williams, 2007).

Cadbury's chocolate tests positive for salmonella thirty-six times between January and February 2006, says the Guardian: "… it was not until the suffering of several victims several months later was linked to Cadbury that the products were pulled from the shelves (R. Williams, 2007)."

Day 395: July 22, 2007—The Mirror reports that a Health Protection Agency investigation holds Cadbury directly responsible for thirteen of the known fifty-six reported cases of the Montevideo strain of salmonella in 2006. Of the fifty-six cases, thirty-seven were "possibly" caused by Cadbury products, while thirteen of those were "certain," the Mirror says (MacLean, 2007). Because the illness rate fell after Cadbury withdrew seven brands from the marketplace, the agency found that "consumption of Cadbury Schweppes's products was the most credible explanation." Cadbury issues a statement: "We are sorry for all those who suffered."

1-F. The aftermath

March 26, 2009—Marketing Week reports that the Cadbury's brand is "the most trusted chocolate producer" in the UK, according to a public option survey published by Reader's Digest: "… no other chocolate comes close to the parent Cadbury brand in terms of trust." Cadbury chocolate enjoys a winning margin of 53 percent over the nearest brand. "Even a widely publicized salmonella scare in 2006 appears to have had no impact on the level of trust people have in Cadbury," the magazine says.

Cadbury's UK marketing director Phil Rumbol tells Marketing Week, "As a company, Cadbury has really clear values that drive how it behaves. In many respects, you cannot separate the company from the brand. Those values of integrity, honesty and striving to do the right thing govern the way Cadbury does business." He says that Cadbury was involved in corporate responsibility "decades before the phrase was coined." How did Cadbury's reputation survive the salmonella scare? Rumbol credits Cadbury for having plenty in "the bank of goodwill." Rumbol says he signed on as Cadbury's marketing director just six weeks before news broke of the salmonella outbreak. "He described a consumer focus group held at the time," Marketing Week reports, "where one member of the group cast aspersions on Cadbury's handling of the issue, prompting the rest of the group to vigorously defend the brand." Rumbol says. "I've never seen that before. … I would hypothesize that level of trust comes from lots of small things that Cadbury has done that we have all experienced; maybe nothing in particular sticks in your mind but you have the overall sense of fairness and decency." It takes "a long, long time for that kind of reputation to build up," Rumbol says (Jack, 2009).

November 30, 2009—The UK trade magazine Management Today ranks Cadbury as Britain's fourth most-admired company.

January 18, 2010—When asked to describe his legacy as Cadbury's first foreign-born CEO, Todd Stitzer tells the Daily Telegraph, "I would like to think that when my time is done here, people will say there was a sea-change in commercial and financial capability. And that we did it in line with our values. If I get some modicum of credit for delivering on both sides of that equation, that would be a great legacy (Sibun, 2010)."

January 19, 2010—After a hostile negotiation that consumed five months, US food conglomerate Kraft Foods agrees to buy Cadbury for £11 billion UK (840p per share), about $19.5 billion US, according to the Evening Standard. The combined companies create the world leader in chocolate and sweets, and the number-two company in the chewing gum market. "The agreed price is 13 times Cadbury's earnings. Cadbury had argued that similar recent takeovers in the sector had been for 14 times earnings or more," the Standard says. CEO Todd Stitzer walks away with a payout worth £7 million (which comes to a little more than two years of compensation): £4 million in cash; £3 million in stock. The Standard says, "He has been highly critical of Kraft throughout the course of the bid, dismissing the American company as an unsuitable partner with low growth prospects." Stitzer and Chairman Roger Carr are likely to be pushed out of the company, the Standard says. Jeremy Batstone-Carr at stockbrokerage Charles Stanley says, "We have to admit surprise at how meekly Cadbury has acquiesced." Andrew Wood at stockbrokerage Sanford Bernstein in New York says, "A year from now, Kraft will be singing the praises of what a great deal they got (English, 2010)."

February 2, 2010—Seventy-two percent of Cadbury shareholders vote to approve the takeover bid. US billionaire investor Warren Buffett criticizes the deal, saying Kraft was "overpaying by using undervalued shares to complete the deal. Buffett's company Berkshire Hathaway is Kraft's largest shareholder. "Kraft sidestepped a vote among its own stockholders by reducing the number of shares to be issued for the deal," the New Zealand Herald reports.

February 3, 2010—The Evening Standard in London reports that Stitzer will leave Cadbury after twenty-seven years with the company. The newspaper estimates that Stitzer will exit with about £20 million in compensation that includes shares and long-term bonuses. Stitzer tells the media that he will take "some time out" to spend with his family, but: "You can be sure my heart will always be a deep Cadbury purple."

March 12, 2010—FT Magazine (a publication of Financial Times) reports in an extensive, behind-the-scenes story on the Kraft acquisition: "When Cadbury employees woke that morning (January 19) to newspaper headlines announcing the impending sale of their employer, many were surprised and angry. Some descendants of Cadbury's founders were, too. They claimed that hedge funds and other short-term investors—which owned close to one-third of the company's stock as the bid battle drew to a close, up from just 5 per cent before Kraft went public with its offer in September 2009—had sold Cadbury out. … Institutional investors, meanwhile, were concerned that Cadbury had given in too easily. Cadbury's second-largest shareholder, Legal & General, issued a statement saying the final price did not 'fully reflect the long-term value of the company' and that it was 'disappointed' management had recommended the offer for an 'iconic and unique British company'."

May 18, 2011—Springfield College announces it will dedicate the new Stitzer YMCA Center on May 19. Established through lead gifts from the Stitzer family, the Stitzer YMCA Center "is a destination site for YMCA professionals and groups from around the world. It includes the national YMCA Hall of Fame, offices of the Association of YMCA Professionals (AYP), the Springfield College Office of YMCA Relations and facilities for YMCA meetings and other programs," the college says in a news release. The college quotes family spokesman Todd Stitzer: "The defining values of the YMCA, and of Springfield College as a premier educator of YMCA leaders, have profoundly influenced our family. It is our hope that this new center will help empower present and future YMCA professionals to maximize their potential in service to all members of our society. And, in honoring the visionaries who shaped the YMCA movement, it will perpetuate their principles."

Section 2: Mapping the messages

2-A. Assessing the outrage

Of the twelve primary factors identified by risk communication consultant Peter Sandman (1993) Cadbury managed to violate at least eleven during the chocolate scare, virtually guaranteeing the company would provoke outrage among its customers, its regulators, London's investment community, the British government, and the news media. Let's now examine these factors one by one:

Voluntary or coerced?—We tend to think of coercion as the result of force, and might at first glance dismiss coercion as a factor in the Cadbury case. After all, no one forces customers to purchase Cadbury chocolate or to consume it. But coercion may also result from fraud. If I tell you that something is "perfectly safe," while my in-house data is telling me that the risk involves at least some hazard, and you find out that I deceived you, then you are likely to feel you have been coerced through fraud, and thus are likely to become outraged.

One could make the case that Cadbury's first mistake—before choosing to distribute contaminated chocolate or resisting the government's attempts to recall its product—was the much earlier decision to alter its detection protocols (based on a shockingly flimsy understanding of salmonella contamination) so the company could cut costs on wasted product (Birmingham Evening Mail, 2007, July 13). However, this decision is not at all surprising.

Corporations are designed to pursue one end, and that is shareholder value. CEOs like Todd Stitzer (for all his expressed admiration of public service) are trained and indeed required to relentlessly pursue shareholder value. "Today, most corporate law scholars embrace some variant of shareholder primacy," legal scholar Stephen M. Bainbridge (2002) says. A leading critic of corporations, former Harvard professor David Korten (2010), agrees. "Any chief executive officer of a Wall Street-traded corporation that puts social or environmental considerations ahead of financial return will soon find himself cast out in disgrace through a revolt of institutional shareholders or hostile takeover."

In 2006, Cadbury was a British-owned company, but its stock traded on Wall Street and its management was clearly concerned with impressing investors in the United States. Moreover, Stitzer is an American lawyer trained in New York City and acclimated to working with (and thinking like) the corporate behemoths of the New York Stock Exchange. Also, following its merger with Schweppes, Cadbury (which had long behaved aggressively in the marketplace, often growing more from acquisition than from marketing) stopped being the quaint, family-operated, Quaker-influenced company of British lore, and became instead an international corporate player. Such companies do not thrive on the world markets without adapting the American notion of shareholder primacy.

This doesn't make Stitzer or most other CEOs "evil," but it does point to a reality of modern business: Every corporation is designed to behave as a sociopath, to pursue its advantages, to "externalize" any cost it can, and to resist attempts by anyone—even government regulators—to rein in the corporation's desire to expand its power, grow its market, pocket higher profits, and increase shareholder value (Bakan, 2012). This is not a political opinion. It is a legal fact.

To recognize this reality is not to brand the corporation as "evil," but rather to fathom that Big Business considers the marketplace to be a battlefield, corporations to be armies, and government to be a nuisance that must be usurped or circumvented whenever possible. This is just how the game is played, not just by custom, but also by law. The shareholder is first in all things. If there is a legal corner to be cut, then it should be cut. The onus is always on government to write the rules that protect the public, enforce them, and punish offenders. This is how a large organization of intelligent, decent, law-abiding people makes the decision to distribute chocolate that it knows is contaminated, and why those same people will later defend their organization's decision with righteous indignation and more than a little hubris.

Natural or industrial?—Salmonella are bacteria and thus are found in nature. Natural things rarely trigger outrage. While people will tend to tolerate cruelty from Mother Nature, they are generally unwilling to accept the same trait in their fellow humans or their organizations. The presence of salmonella or any contaminant in a manufactured food like chocolate is purely industrial, and thus tends to trigger outrage.

This is especially true when an organization chooses to cut costs by ignoring the science behind food safety, which explicitly says that no level of salmonella is safe in chocolate, and then attempts to foster the blame on government regulations. "We followed the rules" will not fly as an excuse for skirting the hard science that is supposed to guide your manufacturing process.

Familiar or exotic?—Both the World Health Organization (2014) and the US Centers for Disease Control and Prevention (2015) rank salmonella as a frequent contributor to foodborne illness in humans worldwide. In the United Kingdom, "salmonella is the pathogen that causes the most hospital admissions—about 2,500 each year" says the UK's Food Standards Agency (2014).

However, in the Cadbury case, the culprit turned out to be an extremely rare (at least, in the United Kingdom) strain, salmonella Montevideo. Indeed, it was the rareness of this strain that pointed the finger at Cadbury as the source of the contamination (Birmingham Evening Mail, 2006, June 24)

Did the exoticness of this specific strain actually trigger outrage among the non-experts? That seems unlikely. While the strain is unusual, the symptoms and the prognosis are the same for more common strains: diarrhea, fever, and abdominal cramps for twelve to seventy-two hours after infection, lasting from four to seven days, with more severe issues for infants, the elderly, and those with weakened immune systems (Centers for Disease Control and Prevention, 2013).

What is unusual about the Cadbury case is the transmission of salmonella bacteria through chocolate. The public is at least somewhat familiar with the presence of salmonella bacteria in meat, poultry, eggs, and raw milk. Food safety advocates in the United States and Western Europe have enjoyed significant success in communicating a simple technique to prevent the bacteria from making us ill: cooking food thoroughly before serving it. This solution does not work for chocolate. Chocolate becomes inedible when raised to the temperatures required to kill salmonella bacteria. Worse yet, salmonella actually thrives in chocolate.

Not memorable or memorable?—Sandman (1993) refers to the memorable as the flipside of the familiar; that is, the more memorable a risk, the more easily one can imagine what can go wrong. Whether a particular risk is memorable depends less on events, and more on the symbols that act upon the public's mind, both consciously and unconsciously. The best source is personal experience, Sandman says; the second best is what we learn through news media.

For example, the headlines in the British press during 2006-07 served to frame the situation for England's reading public:

- The Guardian (London)—Salmonella scare: Chocolate may have poisoned more than 40
- The Times (London)—A million 'food bug' chocolate bars taken off shelves
- The Daily Telegraph (London)—Cadbury's deliberately let salmonella into bars
- The Sunday Independent (Dublin)—Cadbury hid salmonellas for months
- Sunday Express (London)—I'm lucky to be alive, says victim of the chocolate bug

- The Guardian (London)—Poisoned patients and mystery samples – how food detectives traced Cadbury's bug

The stories tend to characterize (mostly through implication) Cadbury and its executive team as greedy at best and evil at worst. Upon this are heaped descriptions of empty shelves in grocery stores (V. Elliott, 2006), and of truck after truck dumping millions of Cadbury bars—weighing about the same as thirty-three double-decker buses—into landfills, followed by dire warnings to the nation's children not to explore the landfills on Willie Wonka-style treasure hunts (Leake, 2006). Such should be expected. "Reporters deal in extremes in stories," crisis consultant James E. Lukaszewski says (2013), "telling stories that have bright, attractive beginnings, very little in the middle, and devastating or climatic endings."

All of this negative imagery directly conflicts with England's long-held image of Cadbury (the company) as a beacon of social justice and Cadbury (the chocolate) as a beloved childhood memory that connects deeply with England's observances of Christmas and Easter. This incongruity reveals itself in the scene described by Cadbury's UK marketing director, in which a consumer focus group shouts down a member who dares to question Cadbury's integrity, even as the salmonella scare makes headlines across Britain (Jack, 2007).

Not dreaded or dreaded?—When we talk about dread, we generally mean apprehension. We dread the things that make us ill or uncomfortable. We dread cancer. We dread hazardous waste and contaminated water. When we perceive that a company is doing something that may cause us to get cancer, or may contaminate our drinking water, we tend to become outraged.

A very close cousin of dread, according to Sandman (1993), is "disgust." Consider the following: Cattle and chickens are common reservoirs of salmonella Montevideo, according to Cornell University (2013), and outbreaks are generally associated with imported spices and live poultry. "Salmonella live in the intestinal tracts of humans and other animals, including birds," the US Centers for Disease Control says (2013). "Salmonella are usually transmitted to humans by eating foods contaminated with animal feces. Contaminated foods usually look and smell normal. Contaminated foods are often of animal origin, such as beef, poultry, milk, or eggs, but any food, including vegetables, may become contaminated."

Now consider this quote from a Cadbury executive: "The highest level we found was one-thirtieth of the level at which we would raise an alert as to a food safety issue (Allen, 2006)." Cadbury hoped this and similar technical information would demonstrate its mastery of the subject matter and thus would calm the situation. But when faced with this sort of information, non-experts are far more likely to respond: "What the hell? Cadbury thinks it's OK to put animal crap in my chocolate?!!!" This results from what Sandman (2012) calls the Yuck Factor; our instinctive aversion to consuming animal feces completely overrides any explanation of just how little feces is in the chocolate. This aversion tends to drive outrage upward.

Chronic or catastrophic?—Non-experts tend to become more concerned about risks that are (or have the potential to become) catastrophic than those that are chronic (Sandman, 1993). In other words, communities are more likely to become upset about things that kill people in large clumps in a short time (like jumbo jets) than about things that kill more people in much smaller clumps over a longer period of time (like family automobiles). With this in mind, where do we place a foodborne pathogen like salmonella on the chronic/catastrophic scale?

"Salmonellosis is one of the most common and widely distributed foodborne diseases, with tens of millions of human cases occurring worldwide every year," according to the

World Health Organization (2013). In the United States and Western Europe, salmonella is less common but still chronic; we are unlikely to eliminate a bacterium such as salmonella as we have a virus such as smallpox.

Americans do a good job generally of keeping salmonella contamination out of pre-packaged foods. In 2014, the Centers for Disease Control recorded ten outbreaks involving products as diverse as poultry, cucumbers, nut butter, spices, cheese, and frozen feeder rodents. However, much risk remains in restaurants and households that fail to adhere to the common standards of food safety.

All that aside, should we consider salmonella particularly catastrophic? Even in an epidemic, the symptoms for salmonella remain typically mild and, while decidedly uncomfortable, usually last for only two to ten days without treatment. Strictly speaking, salmonella would seem an improbable candidate to punch the catastrophic button of community outrage.

However, one may argue that the Cadbury case simulated a catastrophe, as could any food-poisoning case that involves pre-packaged food. Remember, the case came to the attention of UK health authorities only because the Health Protection Agency detected a significant uptick—about forty cases of salmonella Montevideo.across Britain, and asked the Food Standards Agency to investigate. We could reasonably consider this clump of morbidity as a contributing factor in the community outrage that followed Cadbury during and after the recall. This may stretch the logic to the point of breaking, but is worth considering nonetheless.

Knowable or unknowable?—The unknowable factor covers at least three components: uncertainty, expert disagreement, and detectability (Sandman, 1993).

"Uncertainty" refers to the margin of error: How much do we actually know about the risk, and how much do we know about the worst-case scenario? In general, the non-experts are far more comfortable with a dangerous but fairly certain risk than with a safer but less certain risk.

"Expert disagreement" refers to a common situation in public disputes where each side trots out its subject-matter experts. These experts, of course, disagree on whether a specific hazard is dangerous or safe. The non-experts are generally more comfortable with expert consensus than with expert disparity.

"Detectability" refers to whether a specific risk may be perceived with one or more of the five human senses. If we can see it, hear it, smell it, touch it, or taste it, we are less likely to become outraged by a potential hazard. This is one reason why a radiation leak is far more likely to outrage us than a gas leak.

All three components came into play during the Cadbury controversy. First, there was the uncertainty of whether the Cadbury recall had successfully removed all or even most of the contaminated candy from store shelves, especially given news reports that many shopkeepers were oblivious to the recall notice (J. Johnson, 2006; Powles, 2006), as well as Cadbury's steadfast refusal to acknowledge any uncertainty about its testing procedures or its decision-making, such as Cadbury European President Matthew Shattock's early statement that, "We are absolutely confident these minute levels of salmonella would not have made anyone ill (Hayward, 2006)."

Second, there was the expert disagreement between Cadbury (whom one would expect to be an authority on food safety for chocolate) and its government regulators. From the beginning, these experts disagreed on the basic facts of the situation, the proper size of the recall, the degree of Cadbury's culpability, and even the fundamental science behind salmonella contamination in chocolate. Cadbury's experts insisted that the risk to the health of its consumers was "minimal," that the recall was only "a precaution" (Sayid, 2006), that there was "no evidence anyone has been ill from eating this chocolate," and that the contaminated chocolate was "perfectly safe to eat" (Wales, 2006). Meanwhile, experts at the government agencies condemned Cadbury's testing protocols as outdated and unreliable (Lawrence, 2006 July 4), declared that no level of salmonella is safe when found in chocolate (J. Johnson, 2006), and said Cadbury should have approached the situation as a crisis by warning the authorities and issuing an immediate recall of suspected products (Leake, 2006).

Third, there was the lack of detectability, as foods that are contaminated with salmonella "usually look and smell normal. (CDC, 2013)." It was impossible for anyone to examine any Cadbury product with only the five human senses and tell whether it contained any trace of salmonella contamination.

Controlled by me or controlled by others?—Control is all about who implements any given action (Sandman, 1993). Most people feel much safer if they are driving a car rather than simply riding in a car. One of the reasons many people fear air travel is that they must relinquish control to the pilot. In a situation that involves risk, organizations are rarely willing to cede control to a community, preferring that the organizations' experts exert their control. For the experts, this makes sense; for the non-experts, it's often an outrage.

During the first year of the salmonella controversy, Cadbury did its best to maintain control of the situation. It controlled the original distribution of the contaminated product and largely controlled its recall. It kept control of the incriminating test results until the government all but demanded that Cadbury's private lab identify the source of the contaminated sample. It tried to control the decision on how much chocolate to recall and how well to clean its contaminated factory in Marlbrook. It sought control over the direction of the government's investigation. It even attempted to maintain control of the public discourse through its rhetoric, such as the company's early assertion that, "We found the cause of the problem, fixed it, and subsequent tests proved we were completely clear (Vasagar, 2006)." At every turn, Cadbury's attempts to control the situation served only to increase the outrage that fueled the controversy.

Fair or unfair?—Fairness addresses the balance between the distribution of risk and the distribution of benefit (Sandman 1993). In the Cadbury case, the most glaring lack of fairness is the way Cadbury attempted to externalize its costs to its customers by altering its protocols for managing salmonella contamination in its chocolate crumb. First, Cadbury chose to save money by lowering its testing standards for salmonella contamination, thus cutting back on wasted crumb (Birmingham Evening Mail, 2007 July 31). Second, Cadbury allowed its tankers to leave the Marlbrook plant, and allowed its other factories to mix the crumb into Cadbury products, before the company's lab had delivered results from the diagnostic tests, which required up to twenty-nine hours for completion (Lawrence, 2006 July 5). Third, Cadbury had allowed its food safety system to become outdated, and thus unreliable, according to the Food Standards Agency (Lawrence, 2006 July 4). By default, these practices shifted the risk for salmonella contamination onto the unsuspecting consumer while offering clear benefits to Cadbury's bottom line. Such practices, once revealed to the non-expert public, tend to increase community outrage.

Morally irrelevant or morally relevant?—If anyone pushed morality to center stage during the salmonella scare, it was Cadbury, which had long wrapped itself in its Quaker heritage, even well after the Quaker influence had ebbed from its leadership. Moreover, CEO Todd Stitzer had citied Cadbury's Quaker culture as one of the reasons he had left the New York law firm Lord, Day & Lord to work for the British chocolate-maker (Marketing Today, 2006).

Yet, when it came time for that culture to step forward and take moral responsibility for a situation its processes had created, Cadbury shirked. At first, Cadbury executives simply denied the possibility that their candy had anything to do with the outbreak, while knowing full well that Cadbury's own diagnostics had detected the contamination (Sayid, 2006). Next, they publicly parried with regulators over the size of the recall as well as the details of England's food standards laws (Vasagar, 2006; V. Elliot, 2006). Long after the Health Protection Agency found a "molecular fingerprint" that directly linked Cadbury to the outbreak (Leake and Walsh, 2006), CEO Stitzer dodged responsibility, apologized only for causing concern, and insisted that the company had followed UK's food standards laws in good faith when Cadbury decided to accept a level of salmonella contamination that exceeded zero (Daily Mail, 2006 August 3). As Sandman (1993) says, "What makes people angry is not the failure to achieve zero: It is the casualness with which some companies accept that failure." Worse yet, Cadbury didn't simply fail to achieve zero; it very deliberately chose to accept a level of risk higher than zero to save money on wasted product.

Trustworthy or untrustworthy?—From the first day of the crisis, Cadbury attempted to manage the situation by reassuring the British public through the nation's mass media. The company repeatedly cited its "rigorous testing process" (Birmingham Evening Mail, 2006 June 24) based on "sound independent science" (Lawrence, 2006 July 26). A Cadbury spokesperson went as far as to deny any possible connection between the outbreak and the chocolate (Bulldog Reporter's Daily Dog, 2006). Moreover, Cadbury suspended its long-standing sponsorship of a popular television program because the network declined to allow the company to replace its standard product advertisements with reassuring messages about the outbreak and the recall (Bowery, 2006).

Unfortunately for Cadbury, the government agencies that police food safety and public health in the United Kingdom refused to co-operate with the company's reassurances. Instead, the government issued public messages along these lines:

- "Cadbury's risk assessment does not address the risk of salmonella in chocolate in a way that the committee would regard as a modern approach to risk assessment. We can't rule out the possibility that other products are affected (Levy, 2006)."
- "There may be contamination in other Cadbury products (Lawrence, 2006 July 1)."
- "We think (Cadbury) made a mistake in assuming there was a safe level of salmonella in a product like chocolate. Our view is there isn't (Associated Press, 2006 July 4)."
- "We would want to know the reasons why Cadbury's risk assessment differs from that of the government experts (J. Johnson, 2006 July 9)."
- "No other common brands, retail outlets, catering chains or single food types were identified as common factors (Associated Press, 2006 July 21)."

This dynamic points to a recurring theme in Sandman's research: When it comes to managing outrage, not all sources of information are treated as equal. The playing field in any crisis is asymmetrical, Sandman says, and tilts toward those who claim that the hazard in question is real, imminent, and dangerous.

"People know the activists' warnings are probably exaggerated; they generally approve of the exaggeration," Sandman says "People also know the company's reassurances are probably exaggerated, and consider that a much more serious problem. The asymmetry is built in: Exaggerated warnings are a public service, while exaggerated reassurances are a public disservice (2010)."

In Cadbury's case, the company wasn't competing for the public's trust with hyperbolic activists, but rather with generally methodical, understated government regulators. In any situation where the source of a risk is a huge corporation that is attempting to defend its brand and its shareholder value, and its opponents are underpaid government officials who are charged with looking out for the public's welfare, the non-expert community is far more likely to believe the government's experts than the corporation's spokespeople. The result? Every time that Cadbury said "minute traces," and the government said, "no amount is safe," Cadbury lost a little more of the public's trust (The Grocer, 2006 November 4), thus inflaming the community outrage it was attempting to calm.

"Even lay persons recognize that overly-certain projections of risks that fail to acknowledge the inherent uncertainty are simply unrealistic," according to risk communication researchers Timothy L. Sellnow, Robert R. Ullmer, Matthew W. Seeger, and Robert S. Littlefield (2009). "They beg the question, how can anyone know for complete certainty how a risk might develop in the future? These overly certain and reassuring messages also imply that the communicator is not being entirely open and honest regarding the nature of the risk."

Responsive or unresponsive?—Cadbury CEO Todd Stitzer is conspicuously absent from the public discourse until August 2, forty days after the controversy began, and only then to explain to Cadbury investors what effects the chocolate scare might have on company earnings (Morley, 2006). Instead of assuming leadership for the crisis, he sends a succession of relatively minor functionaries to deal with the controversy. This is odd behavior for someone who claims to put public service at the forefront of his thinking, and who claims to value the concerns of his customers above all.

When he finally does take center stage, Stitzer often resorts to a series of non-denial denials:

- "… we've changed our processes because we don't want consumers to have any possible concern about our processes and our products (AFX International Focus, 2006)." Translation: The processes have changed to alleviate concern, but not to address any particular hazard caused by those processes.
- "We clearly caused concern to our consumers and we are truly sorry for that (Miller, 2006)." Translation: Cadbury takes responsibility for causing concern, but not for causing illness, among its customers.
- "Although we have always acted in good faith throughout, we have caused concerns and for that I am extremely sorry (Morley, 2006)." Translation: Whatever Cadbury did, the company did with the best of intentions, but it will admit to nothing. (This "good faith" defense gradually supplanted the "hard science" defense as it became more and more evident to all that Cadbury had embraced defective practices for food safety.)
- "We're profiting from those learnings, taking them and applying them to our business going forward so that we can be a bigger, stronger business. Our record stands for itself (AFX News, 2007)" Translation: The lessons of the salmonella scare add nothing to Cadbury's ability to protect its customers, but rather contribute to future earnings and shareholder value.

Again and again, Stitzer turns down obvious opportunities to provide leadership, choosing instead to respond to questions and challenges in an unresponsive fashion, sidestepping meaningful apology, and inadvertently driving up the outrage at every stage. Indeed, the one direct apology the company made was to its distributors, not its customers (The Grocer, 2006 August 5).

Stitzer's measured comments reflect a preoccupation with the investment community, such as his Oct. 26 statement that "stressed the important of returning confidence in the

Cadbury name among British consumers in the run up to the crucial Christmas season (Armitage, 2006)." The company's overall reticence became so evident that one pundit referred to it as "a worrying refusal to admit (Cadbury) has done anything much wrong (Nixon, 2006)." Indeed, Stitzer's emotions seem to engage with the crisis only when it threatens Cadbury's standing within the market, such as his response to a Financial Times article about an A.C. Nielsen research report that indicated archrival Mars had surpassed Cadbury as Britain's market leader, which Stitzer characterizes as a "totally overzealous interpretation (Armitage, 2006)."

- In addition, there is Cadbury's oft-repeated insistence that the crisis was over before it began, such as the early statement by Cadbury's European president Matthew Shattock—"We are absolutely confident these minute levels of salmonella would not have made anyone ill (Hayward, 2006)"—or its attempts to evade culpability by blaming regulators for its dilemma, such Cadbury's June 24 statement, "We have followed the regulations. The FSA will have to decide if we need a new regulation and we are willing to work with them on that (V. Elliott, 2006)." In early 2007, CEO Stitzer concurred by telling journalists, "Our market share has recovered in the fourth quarter and, in particular, over the Christmas season. (The salmonella outbreak) is not something you'll hear us talking about again (AFX News, 2007)." About two months after Stitzer's statement, the Birmingham City Council levied three criminal charges against Cadbury for its role in the salmonella outbreak, thus forcing Cadbury to continue a conversation that Stitzer had unilaterally declared to be closed.
- Finally, there is Cadbury's reluctance to take even the most sensible actions to protect the public it claimed to care so much about:
- Cadbury received a lab report indicating that it had distributed chocolate contaminated with salmonella, yet waited for five months before sharing this information with the Food Standards Agency (Sayid, 2006), and did so only because the agency had tracked the source of the outbreak to Cadbury's doorstep (Derbyshire, 2006).
- When the agency insisted that Cadbury recall the products, the company resisted, declaring the candy bars to be "perfectly safe" (Birmingham Evening Mail, 2006 June 24).
- When health authorities warned the public about the seriousness of the contamination, and alerted Britons to the growing number of reported cases of salmonella poisoning, Cadbury countered by telling the news media: "Our products are perfectly safe to eat and we have no evidence that anyone has been ill from eating them (Wales, 2006)."

By any standard, Cadbury was unresponsive to the demands of its public. Cadbury so angered its regulators that the Foods Standards Agency dipped into its "fighting fund" to pay for Herefordshire's local investigation of Cadbury's criminal culpability (Northedge, 2006). This extended the controversy well into the next year, produced a public trial that excoriated Cadbury and its food safety practices, played havoc with investor confidence (Guardian Unlimited, 2006), and generated a court fine of £1 million (AFX News, 2007 July 16).

Cadbury could have avoided all of this by cooperating with its regulators from the start. As evidence, consider how Cadbury responded in early 2007, when the company quickly and voluntarily removed from store shelves a large shipment of candy bars that may have come in contact with nuts (Revill, 2007). The 2007 recall quickly dropped out of the news cycle and registered little effect on the company's share price (AFX News, 2007 February 20).

Secondary factors—In addition to the twelve primary factors, Sandman (1993) identifies eight secondary factors. These are factors that may contribute to community outrage, but not as often as the primary factors. Of these eight secondary factors, five appear to apply to the Cadbury case:

- Vulnerable populations: The public is more likely to become outraged if a risk affects the elderly, the very young, the sick, the poor, and the otherwise helpless. During the height of the outbreak, the Health Protection Agency documented twenty-two confirmed cases of salmonella Montevideo among children younger than age four, including eight among infants (Gray, 2006). Indeed, the agency's statisticians suspected chocolate as the vector because so many of the fifty-three documented cases involved children (Leake and Walsh, 2006). Moreover, salmonella is known to present a higher threat to the elderly and to those whose immune systems are damaged or suppressed (WHO, 2013).

- Delayed vs. immediate effects: A risk that lies in wait to strike is more likely to trigger outrage than will an immediate threat. By allowing any level of salmonella contamination into its chocolate crumb, Cadbury created a perverse version of the Golden Ticket hunt made famous by the 1971 motion picture "Willie Wonka and the Chocolate Factory," with this underlying-if-unintended message: "Here are a million chocolate bars, but only a select few are contaminated with a bacteria that will ruin your fortnight and perhaps send you to an emergency room. Have fun, kids!" Is it any wonder that outrage soared among consumers, regulators, politicians, and journalists?

- Identifiability of the victim: Statistical victims will trigger less outrage than will a single, easily recognizable victim. On Day 16 of the Cadbury crisis, a sixty-two-year-old woman from Northern Ireland named Catherine Henderson put a human face on the salmonella outbreak when she began talking to the London news media. "I never thought you could get ill like that from chocolate," she said. "I didn't think I would come out alive (Johnston, 2006)."

- Reduction of risk: The public wants to eliminate the risk, not merely reduce it, whenever possible. Throughout the early stages of the controversy, Cadbury put much effort into attempting to reassure the public that its chocolate could not have caused the outbreak because the amount of detected contamination was "minute" (Allen, 2006). The company sent its European vice president to deliver "reassuring" sound bites, such as: "We are absolutely confident these minute levels of salmonella would not have made anyone ill (Hayward, 2006)." Even if Cadbury had been correct with its interpretation of food safety science (which is wasn't), this was the wrong strategy. Non-experts are happiest when the experts set their goal for acceptable risk at zero; anything that registers greater than zero tends to trigger outrage. "Reduction might be wiser and more cost-effective," Sandman says (1994), "but elimination speaks to the outrage."

- Media attention: The media cannot cause community outrage, but it can amplify existing outrage. The Cadbury case generated 265 non-duplicative newspaper articles, primarily in the United Kingdom, between June 23, 2006 and July 24, 2007, according to a Lexis-Nexis search conducted on March 6, 2015, using the search terms "Cadbury and salmonella."

2-B. Identifying the stakeholders

Clearly, from the beginning of the 2006 chocolate scare, Cadbury Schweppes took a hardline, winner-take-all approach to managing its messages to the government, the investment community, the marketplace, the news media, company critics, consumers, and the general British public. In this section, we will consider options that Cadbury Schweppes could have explored to better manage the British public's outrage and avert damage to its reputation.

For example, before the chocolate scare began, the company could have avoided the crisis almost entirely simply by:

- Maintaining a zero-tolerance protocol for salmonella contamination in its chocolate crumb.
- Reporting contamination of the chocolate crumb at Marlbrook immediately to regulators and seeking guidance from agency microbiologists.
- Responding promptly and openly to the government's requests for information or action.
- Recalling any questionable products from store shelves rapidly, efficiently, and voluntarily.

However, for the purposes of this section, let's begin our analysis on June 19, 2006, the day on which the Food Standards Agency first approached Cadbury's private lab for information about a rare strain of salmonella the agency had found in a sample that came from the company's Marlbrook plant. At this point in the controversy we can make the following assumptions:

- Cadbury has altered its protocols to tolerate what the company's experts consider to be "safe levels" of salmonella contamination in its chocolate crumb (The Press Association, 2007).
- Cadbury's Marlbrook employees are generally aware that salmonella contamination has become endemic at the plant (Britten, 2007).
- At some level within Cadbury, administrators know that the company has shipped chocolate candy that is contaminated with salmonella (V. Elliott, 2006).
- These administrators have decided that the levels of contamination are in line with food safety regulations and thus pose no threat to human health (Lawrence, 2006 July 5).
- These administrators believe there is no reason to alert public health authorities (Sayid, 2006).
- Neither Cadbury CEO Todd Switzer (Klinger, 2006) nor Chairman Sir John Sunderland (Moreley, 2006) appears at this point to be aware of these specific administrative decisions.
- Authorities at the Health Protection Agency (Leake and Walsh, 2006) and the Food Standards Agency (Derbyshire, 2006) suspect that a chocolate product is the source of the outbreak, but have not completely narrowed the field to a specific manufacturer.
- The Food Standards Agency is aware of a similar contamination at Marlbrook in 2002, but has yet to receive formal paperwork about the incident from Cadbury (Levy, 2006).
- The agencies are apparently unaware of Cadbury's current protocols for salmonella contamination (Associated Press, 2006 July 4; Levy, 2006) or of the decision-making process that led to the distribution of contaminated products (Lawrence, 2006 July 5).

All considered, these points are clearly pushing Cadbury toward the precipice of a significant public controversy. It is almost inevitable that the news will create headlines across England.

OK, so it's June 19, 2006. We are top executives at Cadbury Schweppes and we've just learned from our private lab that the Food Standards Agency is asking about a sample from our Marlbrook plant. The sample has tested positive for a rare strain, salmonella Montevideo. We also know that the government is investigating an outbreak of the illness caused by this pathogen. Obviously, Cadbury is going to get pulled into a national debate on food safety, whether we are guilty or innocent. It's time to get moving. With any luck, we have a day or so before the story becomes public. Our first step is to identify our stakeholders for this dispute. More specifically, in Peter Sandman's terminology (2003), who are the attentives and who are the fanatics?

Clearly, the immediate need is to address the stakeholders who are most likely to be affected by the outbreak: consumers who may have purchased and eaten the contaminated chocolate, including those who have become ill (though not necessarily from having eaten Cadbury products). They will become the primary audiences for our messages in the days to come, and—because our customers are spread across the width and breadth of United Kingdom—our best choice is to reach them through mass media, with an emphasis on the nation's newspapers, television and radio. Ideally, we would address stakeholders directly and let the news media report on what we say and do. However, in the case of a foodborne outbreak, we must hope to enlist the news media as allies in getting crucial information to our customers. For immediacy and outreach, there's no other good choice.

Thus, our initial set of message maps will target customers as our primary stakeholders and journalists as our primary medium. Customers who frequently or occasionally purchase Cadbury products are likely to become attentive to these messages. Customers who have consumed Cadbury chocolate within the last few weeks, or who have also become ill with symptoms such as fever, nausea, and diarrhea—though not necessarily because of the chocolate—are also likely to become attentive, and perhaps fanatical (especially when they learn that Cadbury made a deliberate decision to sell the contaminated chocolate to the public).

For the purpose of this exercise, we will focus on messages aimed primarily at Cadbury customers, with the assumption that many of these messages will also inform other significant groups of stakeholders. These include internal stakeholders, such as employees and managers, as well as stakeholders who are vital to the health of our company, such as distributors and investors. This also includes external stakeholders, such as the regulators with whom we must collaborate over the coming weeks and months, as well as food safety experts who not directly connected to the situation, and policymakers in the government, especially members of Parliament and their advisors.

We know from experience that Cadbury is held in high regard throughout England. Our goal is to leverage that goodwill without abusing it. To accomplish this, we should follow the example of our company's founders, and work diligently through this process in the best interests of our customers. Clearly, the best way to protect Cadbury's shareholders in this situation is to protect our customers. This is a rare instance when our corporate responsibility aligns with our social duty.

2-C. Building the message maps

Next, we will work through the message-map process using Cadbury's salmonella outbreak for our source material. Once again, we will assume that today is June 19, 2006, the day when the Food Standards Agency first contacted Cadbury's private lab for information about the salmonella Montevideo contamination found in a sample from Cadbury's Marlbrook plant. Time is short. It is clear that this news will break soon across the nation and will affect Cadbury's reputation, sales revenue, and share prices. However, the company's first priority should be to assist regulators in containing the outbreak and to help consumers avoid the pathogen or manage the illness, even if the company is certain their products are innocent. In the long run, this is the communications strategy that will best serve the company, its share price, its reputation, and thus its stakeholders.

Map 1: The Overarching Map

The first map puts the focus on the information that stakeholders—specifically British consumers and the public at-large—most need to know about the situation. This is our opportunity to frame the story for the news media. However, we should frame the story from a risk communication perspective (how to help the most people avoid the hazard and to manage their outrage) rather than from a traditional public relations perspective (how to minimize the damage to the company and its brand). The good news is that a solid risk communications strategy is almost always our best public relations strategy; it will minimize our unforced errors while mitigating stakeholder outrage toward our company and our brand.

The first key message and its supporting messages alert the public to the recall. The second set explains what's wrong with the candy. The third set gives stakeholders a group of actions to take. The ability to take effective action tends to lower outrage among stakeholders.

Map 1: The Overarching Map		
Category of stakeholder: Cadbury customers and the British public		
Question or concern: What does the public need to know most?		
Key message 1	**Key message 2**	**Key message 3**
Cadbury is recalling 7 chocolate products.	The candy may be contaminated with salmonella bacteria.	Please avoid eating any of these products.
Supporting information 1.1	**Supporting information 2.1**	**Supporting information 3.1**
They are the chocolate button Easter Egg and the Freddo Bar;	The bacteria are a rare strain known as salmonella Montevideo.	Return them to your store for a full refund.
Supporting information 1.2	**Supporting information 2.2**	**Supporting information 3.2**
Dairy Milk bars in caramel, mint, and Turkish delight flavors;	They can cause nausea, diarrhea, and other digestive problems.	For details, please visit our website: Cadbury.co.uk.
Supporting information 1.3	**Supporting information 2.3**	**Supporting information 3.3**
Dairy Milk 8 Chunk and the 1 kilogram Dairy Milk.	Health officials believe our candy has caused an outbreak.	Or call us toll-free at 0-800-818181 any time.

(Fig. 1)

Map 2: The Recall Map

     This map provides an efficient explanation of the circumstances that led to Cadbury's recall. The first key message and its supporting messages focus on the pathogen. The second set connects the pathogen to the outbreak. The third set is designed to calm stakeholder outrage by detailing how we are cooperating with authorities to end the outbreak. Overall, this map addresses Cadbury's uncertainty at this point over its culpability while making it clear the company intends to act responsibly by putting public health first.

Map 2: The Recall Map

Category of stakeholder: Cadbury customers and British public

Question or concern: Why are you recalling the product?

Key message 1	Key message 2	Key message 3
Tests found salmonella bacteria in our chocolate samples.	Our chocolate may have caused an outbreak of salmonellosis in England.	We are cooperating fully with government health officials.
Supporting information 1.1	**Supporting information 2.1**	**Supporting information 3.1**
This strain of salmonella bacteria is very rare.	There are 53 confirmed cases across Britain.	We are recalling 7 Cadbury chocolate products.
Supporting information 1.2	**Supporting information 2.2**	**Supporting information 3.2**
We are unsure how it contaminated our chocolate.	There are no reported deaths.	We are searching for the source of the contamination.
Supporting information 1.3	**Supporting information 2.3**	**Supporting information 3.3**
Salmonellosis endangers children, seniors, and people with low immunity.	22 cases are with children younger than age 4.	We have suspended chocolate production.

(Fig. 2)

Map 3: The Situation Map

   In addressing how this happened, Cadbury's best available option is to simply plead stupidity. How else to explain how one of the world's leading chocolate-makers failed to understand basic food safety? There is no level of salmonella bacteria that is safe in chocolate. Experts in Britain were dumbfounded to learn that Cadbury believed otherwise. So now Cadbury has only two choices: It can let the public believe the company is evil and deliberately put the bacteria in its chocolate, or it can admit that it made a serious error in judgment. The first key message and its supporting messages give a brief explanation of events. The second set explains Cadbury's error. The third set makes it clear that Cadbury understands the error and is working to correct it.

Map 3: The Situation Map

Category of stakeholder: Cadbury customers and British public

Question or concern: How did this happen?

Key message 1	Key message 2	Key message 3
Health officials believe our chocolate crumb started the outbreak.	We knew some crumb contained traces of salmonella.	We erred in thinking the crumb was safe to eat.
Supporting information 1.1	**Supporting information 2.1**	**Supporting information 3.1**
Our Marlbrook plant made the crumb in January.	We changed our food safety protocols in 2003.	We now know zero is the only safe level for salmonella.
Supporting information 1.2	**Supporting information 2.2**	**Supporting information 3.2**
We are searching for the cause of the contamination.	These changes allowed for minimal contamination.	Experts are helping us update our protocols.
Supporting information 1.3	**Supporting information 2.3**	**Supporting information 3.3**
We are disinfecting the Marlbrook plant.	We thought these changes followed current food science.	We are adopting a test-and-hold policy.

(Fig. 3)

Map 4: The Contamination Map

This set of messages is designed to unravel a complex situation. The truth is that Cadbury knew the crumb was contaminated when it shipped out the candy. The company had recently revised its food safety protocols to accept low levels of salmonella contamination on the assumption that the cooking process would deactivate the bacteria. What the company learned from HPA and FSA—and summarily dismissed—was that the bacteria had indeed triggered an outbreak. Rather than fight the obvious, Cadbury would have served itself better by admitting its error and expressing its dismay at learning it had shipped a hazardous product.

Map 4: The Contamination Map		
Category of stakeholder: Cadbury customers and British public		
Question or concern: How did you discover the contamination?		
Key message 1	**Key message 2**	**Key message 3**
We knew some of our chocolate contained salmonella bacteria.	We thought the levels were safe for consumption.	We are horrified to learn that we were wrong.
Supporting information 1.1	**Supporting information 2.1**	**Supporting information 3.1**
HPA found bacteria in samples from our Marlbrook plant.	Our private lab told us about the government's concern.	We are recalling 7 chocolate products.
Supporting information 1.2	**Supporting information 2.2**	**Supporting information 3.2**
They were seeking the source of the outbreak.	We have suspended production at our Marlbook plant.	We are reviewing our protocols with government experts.
Supporting information 1.3	**Supporting information 2.3**	**Supporting information 3.3**
HPA asked FSA to contact Cadbury's private lab.	We will reopen it when FSA is satisfied.	We are thoroughly disinfecting our Marlbrook plant.

(Fig. 4)

Map 5: The Pathogen Map

This map is designed to be purely informational. There are no attempts at self-efficacy or apology. The first set describes the pathogen, the second outlines its effects on people, and the third provides some context on which populations are most at risk. This is a map that could be prepared in advance of a risk controversy in collaboration with subject-matter experts.

Map 5: The Pathogen Map

Category of stakeholder: Cadbury customers and British public

Question or concern: What are the effects of the pathogen and its disease?

Key message 1	Key message 2	Key message 3
The pathogen is called salmonella Montevideo.	It infects people who consume contaminated food products.	England and Wales report about 12,000 cases of salmonellosis annually.
Supporting information 1.1	**Supporting information 2.1**	**Supporting information 3.1**
HSA says it is a rare strain of bacteria.	Symptoms appear within 6 to 72 hours.	Less than 1% leads to death in healthy adults.
Supporting information 1.2	**Supporting information 2.2**	**Supporting information 3.2**
The bacteria contaminate food animal products.	Symptoms generally subside in fewer than 7 days.	However, children and the elderly are at high risk.
Supporting information 1.3	**Supporting information 2.3**	**Supporting information 3.3**
These include dairy-based products, like chocolate.	Symptoms include fever, nausea, diarrhea, cramps, and vomiting.	So are people with weakened immune systems.

(Fig. 5)

Map 6: The Avoidance Map

This map is focused on self-efficacy. That is, giving stakeholders their best available options for avoiding the pathogen and thus the infection. In the case of foodborne illness, the primary option is almost always to avoid consuming the contaminated products. This is handled in the first set of messages. The second set answers the question, "What do I do with the products I've purchased?" If we want to manage outrage, we need to provide a simple method for returning purchases and receiving refunds. A contaminated product is a defective product. Consumers deserve to get their money back with minimal hassles. The third set answers the question, "What if I've already consumed the product?" These messages provide useful information for those who may be ill. They also help to manage outrage among what hospitals call "the worried well," those folks who may not have the infection but are highly concerned about the outbreak.

Map 6: The Avoidance Map

Category of stakeholder: Cadbury customers and British public

Question or concern: What can people do to avoid the pathogen?

Key message 1	Key message 2	Key message 3
For now, avoid eating any Cadbury chocolate.	Return purchased products to your store or contact Cadbury.	If you have eaten the candy, watch for symptoms.
Supporting information 1.1	**Supporting information 2.1**	**Supporting information 3.1**
We have recalled 7 chocolate products.	Do this even if you have eaten part of the product.	These include fever, nausea, cramps, vomiting, and diarrhea.
Supporting information 1.2	**Supporting information 2.2**	**Supporting information 3.2**
You can find a complete list online at Cadbury.co.uk	Look for any products stored at home or your office.	Symptoms usually appear in 12 to 72 hours.
Supporting information 1.3	**Supporting information 2.3**	**Supporting information 3.3**
Or call us anytime at 0-800-818181.	Please alert your family, friends, co-workers, or neighbors.	If you have symptoms, please see your doctor.

(Fig. 6)

Map 7: The Disease Management Map

A companion map to Map 6, this one also focuses on giving stakeholders some power over the situation. It's important to be honest. If the disease is deadly, say so. If it's not, avoid being overly reassuring. It's usually wise to attribute this information to food safety experts or public health officials, based on readily available literature. The first set is focused on the relative hazard of the disease. The second set outlines some potential treatments for mild cases. The third set provides details on which populations are most at risk and how they should respond.

Map 7: The Disease Management Map		
Category of stakeholder: Cadbury customers and British public		
Question or concern: What can people do to manage the disease and its symptoms?		
Key message 1	**Key message 2**	**Key message 3**
Salmonellosis rarely leads to hospitalization or death.	Most healthy people recover without treatment, experts say.	Children, seniors, and people with low immunity are at high risk.
Supporting information 1.1	**Supporting information 2.1**	**Supporting information 3.1**
Symptoms of salmonellosis include fever, cramps, and nausea.	Antibiotics are ineffective for typical cases.	High-risk individuals should see a doctor if they suspect they are ill.
Supporting information 1.2	**Supporting information 2.2**	**Supporting information 3.2**
These usually start within 12 to 72 hours after exposure.	Drink fluids and electrolytes to avoid dehydration.	Hospitalization is likely in high-risk cases.
Supporting information 1.3	**Supporting information 2.3**	**Supporting information 3.3**
They usually end within 4 to 7 days.	Anti-diarrheals may ease cramping, but may prolong the diarrhea.	Death occurs in about 3% of high-risk cases.

(Fig. 7)

Map 8: The Future Map

This map sets the stage for our next actions as we attempt to remedy the problem and to compensate for our mistake. This is also the map that the lawyers will try most to suppress. Attorneys frequently underestimate the need to win in the court of public opinion, and thus the need to mitigate stakeholder outrage. Cadbury attempted to ignore health officials at the national and local levels. It dismissed media coverage. The company disregarded the concerns of Parliament. In the end, Cadbury was forced to acknowledge its mistakes and to seek forgiveness. The brand would have been better served if Cadbury executives had acted with far less hubris and far more remorse. The first set deals with what we are doing now. The second set is focused on what we are doing in the near term. The third set is a list of specific actions we plan to take. In the end, there is no substitute for effective action if we want to reduce outrage and end the controversy.

Map 8: The Future Map

Category of stakeholder: Cadbury customers and British public

Question or concern: What are you doing to avoid future contamination in your products?

Key message 1	Key message 2	Key message 3
We are working with experts to find the cause.	We are reviewing our food safety protocols.	We will improve to meet or exceed government standards.
Supporting information 1.1	**Supporting information 3.1**	**Supporting information 2.1**
The suspected source came from our Marlbrook plant.	We believed the bacteria level in the samples was safe.	We will find and fix the problem.
Supporting information 1.2	**Supporting information 3.2**	**Supporting information 2.2**
Health officials are combing the plant to find the problem.	Experts are telling us we were mistaken.	We will thoroughly clean our plant under official supervision.
Supporting information 1.3	**Supporting information 3.3**	**Supporting information 2.3**
We are shutting down production at the Marlbrook plant.	We pledge to follow all government protocols from today onward.	We will resume production when health officials approve it.

(Fig. 8)

188

Map 9: The Make It Right Map

This final map lets stakeholders know our plan for assisting health officials in their efforts to end the outbreak and for fairly compensating injured stakeholders for any harm we have caused. That's the easy part. For many executives, the hard part is publicly admitting fault, accepting blame, and apologizing for our role in the outbreak. Yet the process of mitigating outrage among stakeholders is never complete without penance (Sandman, 2001, May 4). Making things right requires that we do more than just sign checks. The first set of messages explains our refund process. The second makes it clear that we are working with health officials to end the outbreak. The third set lets the public know we take responsibility, we are sorry, and we are actively seeking to identify any consumers who were harmed so we can work out fair settlements. The emphasis here is to acknowledge our mistakes and to take actions that significantly improve the situation for our stakeholders.

Map 9: The Make It Right Map		
Category of stakeholder: Cadbury customers and British public		
Question or concern: What are you doing to make thing right?		
Key message 1	**Key message 2**	**Key message 3**
We're offering a refund for all returned chocolate products.	We are working with health officials to end this outbreak.	We are seeking consumers who were harmed.
Supporting information 1.1	**Supporting information 2.1**	**Supporting information 3.1**
This includes partially consumed products.	We are recalling 7 chocolate products.	We apologize to anyone who was made ill.
Supporting information 1.2	**Supporting information 2.2**	**Supporting information 3.2**
Return the product to the store where you bought it.	We will safely destroy all returned products.	We will offer fair and quick compensation.
Supporting information 1.3	**Supporting information 2.3**	**Supporting information 3.3**
Or call us at 0-800-818181 for help.	We are working with retailers to remove products from shelves.	If you were made ill, please contact us at 0-800-818181.

(Fig. 9)

Section 3: Crafting the preamble

Our choice of messenger is crucial to successfully delivering our message to our stakeholders. Cadbury chose to use lower-level executives to bring their messages to the news media and to the British public. This was a massive error in judgment. It suggested that the company's top executives were too busy or too insensible to discuss the situation with Cadbury's customers.

Selecting the actual spokesperson should depend upon his or her ability to convey caring and empathy, and not necessarily on expertise and status. We should keep Covello's research in mind during the selection process: Stakeholders under stress are far more concerned with issues of listening, caring, empathy, honesty, and openness than they are in competence and expertise (Covello, 2003).

For the sake of credibility, the best choice would have been a joint news conference featuring top leadership from Cadbury Schweppes, the Health Protection Agency, and the Food Standards Agency. This would have allowed the three organizations to speak from a common set of messages, and would have led to far less confusion and consternation in the news media. It would also have signaled to Parliament and to food safety experts that Cadbury was working with, and not against, its regulators.

We want to deliver the initial information in three stages (Covello, Minamyer and Clayton, 2007): a statement of concern, followed by a statement of intent, followed by a statement of purpose for the event or meeting at which we have chosen to deliver our messages.

The preamble helps us to set the stage for our message maps. We use the preamble to open either a news conference or a town meeting in which we will discuss the outbreak and the recall. Such public events are crucial to managing stakeholder outrage. We must have the courage to answer questions directly from journalists or stakeholders.

In addition, a well-crafted preamble provides our communications teams with pre-vetted language that they can use in other communications, such as news releases, backgrounders, open letters, advertisements, websites and videos.

As an illustration, let's compose a preamble for Cadbury on the day the company announced its product recall. We will assume this is for a news conference.

To start, let's consider: Who should deliver this preamble and the key messages, and then field questions from stakeholders and journalists? In a perfect world, it would be the CEO, Todd Stitzer. However, for the many reasons cited earlier, Stitzer clearly is neither emotionally nor professionally prepared to handle this duty well. The best available choice is likely the board chair, Sir John Sunderland, who is more experienced in public speaking, and has the added quality of actually being British.

So here's the preamble that Sir John might deliver after he is introduced.

Part 1: The statement of concern

Good morning. As chairman of Cadbury Schweppes, I want to apologize on behalf of the entire Cadbury Schweppes family, and express our deep concern for the situation we are about to describe and any harm it may have caused.

Our company has a long tradition of championing food quality in Britain. We take that tradition seriously. Unfortunately, if the government's experts are right, we have failed Cadbury's tradition, our customers, our employees, and our nation.

You will have every right to be angry with us. We should have known better. We should have served you better.

We are deeply sorry for any anger you may feel toward the Cadbury name. We have a duty to live up to that name, and it appears we have failed that duty.

We are saddened and we are humbled by the situation that warrants it. The very idea that we may have allowed the sale of contaminated chocolate to any customer sickens us to the core.

Part 2: The statement of intent

You have our pledge today that we will make this right. We will act honestly and transparently as we work with the government to resolve this situation.

If we are indeed proven to be the actual source of this outbreak, we will establish a fair and just process to compensate those harmed by it. Even if we are not proven to be the source, we pledge to work with government experts to upgrade our food safety standards to meet their expectations.

We will also work closely with national and local authorities to follow a process that allows them to independently measure and monitor the safety of Cadbury products on behalf of you, the British public.

It is what you deserve.

Part 3: The statement of purpose

I am here today to announce that we are recalling seven of our chocolate products from across Britain. We do this at the request of government experts in food safety, who have detected an outbreak of salmonellosis in Britain.

The experts tell us that our chocolate is the source. As a result, we feel it is our moral duty to follow their advice and recall our chocolate products from British store shelves.

Over the next few minutes, I will provide you with the details, as we understand them. I will then answer your questions. To assist me, we have with us today representatives from the Health Protection Agency and the Food Standards Agency.

Here is what we know right now: Cadbury is recalling seven chocolate products. The candy may be contaminated with salmonella bacteria. Please avoid eating any of these products. The seven products are the chocolate button Easter Egg and the Freddo Bar; Dairy Milk bars in caramel, mint, and Turkish delight flavor; Dairy Milk 8 Chunk and the 1 kilogram Dairy Milk. The candy may be contaminated with a rare strain known as salmonella Montevideo. It can cause nausea, diarrhea, and other digestive problems. Health officials believe our candy has caused an outbreak. Please avoid eating any of these products. Return them to your store for a full refund. For details, please visit our website: Cadbury.co.uk. Or call us toll-free at 0-800-818181 any time. To repeat our key messages for today: Cadbury is recalling seven chocolate products. The candy may be contaminated with salmonella bacteria. Please avoid eating any of these products.

We are now ready to answer your questions.

Note how the preamble flows from the statement of concern, to the statement of intent, to the statement of purpose. Also note how the language allows the speaker to express contrition without legally binding Cadbury this early in the investigation. Given that Cadbury already knew that its safety standards would allow some contaminated chocolate to enter the British food system, the smart play is to announce its failure at the same time as its recall, instead of letting the bad news dribble out over the coming days, weeks, and months.

Section 4: Conclusion—An analysis based on best practices

In this final section, we will analyze Cadbury's messages and actions during the outbreak and recall by using nine best practices for risk communication, as outlined in the 2009 book Effective Risk Communication: A Message-Centered Approach, written by four communication scholars: Timothy Sellnow of the University of Kentucky, Robert Ulmer of the University of Arkansas, Matthew Seeger of Wayne State University, and Richard Littlefield of North Dakota State University. These best practices are based on extensive research and are designed to lead a risk controversy toward mitigation and eventual resolution.

For Cadbury, the goal should have been to use a combination of messages and actions to cause their harshest critics to say, "Cadbury has finally accepted our position and is now on the right path." Since this largely involved raising the company's food safety standards for salmonella while compensating those who were injured by the outbreak, while also expressing the company's contrition for having caused the problem, this would have been a relatively small price for Cadbury to pay. Unfortunately, the company's leadership avoided the actions that would have cut the dispute short and spared the company's reputation.

Did Cadbury infuse risk communication into policy decisions?

No. The company made a significant change to its food safety protocols when it decided to accept "minimum levels" of salmonella bacteria in its chocolate. There is no evidence that Cadbury considered how this change might affect its reputation among British consumers or its relationship with government regulators.

Did Cadbury treat risk communication as a process?

No. From the moment the company learned that health officials suspected its chocolate as the source, Cadbury's approach was to reassure the British public that its products had played no role in the outbreak. Oddly, the company did this while knowing that it had distributed candy products made from chocolate contaminated with the same rare strain of salmonella as detected in government tests. Again and again, Cadbury attempted to end its conversation with stakeholders by declaring its products to be "perfectly safe." Again and again, this tactic not only failed but also made the situation worse for Cadbury.

Did Cadbury account for the uncertainty inherent in risk?

No. Indeed, Cadbury acted as if its products posed zero risk to consumers. The company treated its recall as merely precautionary and dismissed the concerns of health officials and food safety experts. From the beginning, Cadbury acted as if knew all the answers as well as all the questions.

Did Cadbury design messages to be culturally sensitive?

No. For almost a year, Cadbury issued messages that served only to infuriate health officials at the national and local levels and to anger members of the British Parliament. It was as if Cadbury were a stranger in its own land.

Did Cadbury acknowledge diverse levels of risk tolerance?

No. Many times over, the company insisted that its interpretation of events was the correct one, and that anyone who disagreed was either misinformed or malicious. It failed to demonstrate any understanding of how non-experts view risk.

Did Cadbury involve the public in dialogues about risk?

No. Cadbury made no effort to establish an ongoing dialogue with concerned stakeholders, other than investors and retailers.

Did Cadbury present risk messages with honesty?

No. Cadbury knew it had sold candy made from chocolate crumb that was contaminated with the same rare strain of bacteria that triggered the outbreak, yet insisted its products could not be the source of the outbreak. Rather than deal with the uncertainty, the company repeatedly attempted to end the discussion by dismissing the concerns of public health officials and food safety experts.

Did Cadbury meet risk perception needs by remaining open and accessible to the public?

No. Cadbury made no attempt to make itself accessible to anyone other than the investment community. It all but ignored health officials, government representatives, the news media, injured consumers, outraged customers, or tort attorneys.

Did Cadbury collaborate and coordinate about risk with credible information sources?

No. Cadbury resisted investigation, ignored advice, and fought bitterly with food safety officials representing the British public. If there was a wrong move to be made, Cadbury made it.

Section 5: Sources for this case study

"$2 million fine for Cadbury." (2007, July 16, 2007). AFX News.

"21.7 million pounds of beef recalled." (2007, September 30). CNN.com Retrieved 24 April 2015 from http://www.cnn.com/2007/US/09/29/meat.recall/

Allen, P. (2006, June 25). "Bosses knew Easter eggs could be contaminated; expert attacks Cadbury's salmonella alert delay." Sunday Mercury (Birmingham).

Armitage, J. (2006, Oct. 26). "Cadbury hits back at Mars top choc claim." Evening Standard (London), p. 41.

Armitage, J. (2006, Oct. 26). "UK chocolate lovers regain their taste for Cadbury." Evening Standard (London), p. 31.

Authi, J. (2005, June 25). "Callers flood choc helpline; Cadbury: Concern grows as agency orders salmonella probe." Birmingham Evening Mail, p. 2.

Bainbridge, S. M. (2002). "Director primacy: The means and ends of corporate governance." Nw. UL Rev., 97, 547.

Bakan, J. (2012). The corporation: The pathological pursuit of profit and power. Hachette UK.

Ball, D. (2002, December 18). "Cadbury Deal to Acquire Adams Bolsters Revenue; Pact for Pfizer Candy Unit Leaves Confectioner With Heavy Debt Load." The Wall Street Journal.

Barnett, L. (2007, April 24). "Cadbury faces salmonella contamination charges." Western Mail, first edition, p. 8.

Belson, K. (2007). "After Extensive Beef Recall, Topps Goes Out of Business." The New York Times.

"Birmingham to prosecute Cadbury over salmonella outbreak." (2007, July 13). Local Government Chronicle.

"Bosses defend reporting delay." (2005, June 26). Birmingham Post, p. 3.

Bowery, Joanna. (2006, June 28). "Cadbury freezes all ads amid salmonella scare." Marketing, p. 1.

Blackhurst, C. (2004). "THE MT INTERVIEW: TODD STITZER-The CEO of Cadbury Schweppes may be an American in charge of a British corporation, but he's from a New York family with a social conscience quite in line with the firm's founding Quakers. And he knows how to market, as the author discovers in conversation with him." Management Today, 42.

"Britain's Most Admired No. 4: Cadbury, Todd Stitzer." (2009, November 30) Management Today.

"British Food Safety Agency criticizes Cadbury for salmonella contamination." (2006, July 4), Associated Press

Britten, N. (2007, July 14). "Cadbury's deliberately let salmonella into bars." Daily Telegraph (London), p. 9.

Brown, T. (2006, Oct. 27). "Cadbury sees sales of chocolate melt away." Daily Mail (London), p. 90.

Buckland, R. (2006, July 31). "Cadbury faces 20 million pound clean-up." Western Daily Press (Bristol), p. 33.

"Cadbury allowed salmonella in its chocolate bars." (2007, July 14) Western Daily Press (Bristol), p. 4.

"Cadbury becomes world leader with Adams acquisition." (2002, December 17). ConfectionaryNews.com. Retrieved April 9, 2015, from http://www.confectionerynews.com/Manufacturers/Cadbury-becomes-world-leader-with-Adams-acquisition.

"Cadbury bosses Todd Stitzer and Roger Carr leave after Kraft takeover." (2010, February 3). Evening Standard (London).

"Cadbury CEO admits unable yet to assess full impact of salmonella scare." (2006, Aug. 2), AFX International Focus.

"Cadbury chocolate's PR meltdown." (2006, Dec. 16). The Grocer, p. 34.

"Cadbury dismisses talk that more products will need to be recalled." (2006, July 2). AFX News.

"Cadbury 'failed to assess' risk." (2006, July 5). Birmingham Evening Mail, p. 3.

"Cadbury hikes cost of salmonella food scare to 30 million pounds." (2006, Dec. 12) Agence France Press.

"Cadbury in court on hygiene charges." (2007, July 3). The Guardian (London).

"Cadbury named over salmonella outbreak." (2006, July 21). Guardian Unlimited.

"Cadbury pleads guilty to 3 offenses in salmonella contamination." (2007, June 15) Associated Press.

"Cadbury Schweppes appears in court on food hygiene charges." (2007, July 3). Associated Press.

"Cadbury Schweppes scraps its forecast for profitability." (2006, October 30). The Associated Press.

"Cadbury Schweppes slips as FTSE hits another high." (2006, Oct. 16). Guardian Unlimited.

"Cadbury Schweppes withdraws seven chocolate products in salmonella scare." (2006, June 23). AFX News.

"Cadbury shareholders approve Kraft deal." (2010, February 2) New Zealand Herald.

"Cadbury talk down salmonella whispers." (2006, July 8). Birmingham Post, p. 5.

"Cadbury to pay out on kid's salmonella case." (2007, July 14). Derby Evening Telegraph, p. 3.

"Cadbury warns over salmonella scare as first-half profits jump." (2006, Aug. 2). Agence France Presse.

"Cadbury writes sweet letters in charm offense on c-stores." (2006, Aug. 5). The Grocer, p. 6.

"Cadbury's pulls Coronation St ads." (2006, June 28). Birmingham Post, p. 1.

Carmichael, M. (2006, July 1). "Cadbury faces meltdown in million-bar product recall." The Grocer, p. 30.

Carrell, S. (2005, June 25). "Unwrapped; How a leaking pipe poisoned Britain's favourite chocolate Cadbury denies a cover-up, as millions of chocolate bars are removed from the shelves six months after contamination was detected." Independent on Sunday (London), p. 11.

"CDC Estimates of Foodborne Illness in the United States." (n.d.). Retrieved March 1, 2015, from http://www.cdc.gov/foodborneburden/2011-foodborne-estimates.html

"Changes 'led to Cadbury scare'." (2007, July 13). Birmingham Evening Mail. City Centre Edition, p. 8.

"Chocolatier faces serious PR crisis in U.K.: Cadbury recalls a million candy bars because of possible salmonella risk." (2005, June 26). Bulldog Reporter's Daily Dog.

Cordes, R. (2006, April 26). "Cadbury takes Dr Pepper." Daily Deal/The Deal.

"Cost-cutting led to salmonella outbreak, court told." (2007, July 13). The Press Association.

Dellheim, C. (1987). "The creation of a company culture: Cadburys, 1861-1931." The American Historical Review, 13-44.

Denby, M. (2007, July 17) "Cadbury's hands out." Western Daily Press, p. 4.

Derbyshire, D. (2006, June 24). "Salmonella scare hits Cadbury's chocolate; A million bars withdrawn from sale." The Daily Telegraph (London), p. 1.

Dorsey, P. (2006, July 21) Stock Strategist: Ten Stocks for the Next Ten Years. McClatchy-Tribune News Service.

Elliott, G. (2006, May 20). "Master of sorry management." The Australian. Retrieved March 25, 2015, from http://www.psandman.com/articles/ausoil12.htm.

Elliott, V. (2006, June 24). "A million 'food bug' chocolate bars taken off shelves." The Times (London), p. 1.

Elliott, V. (2006, June 30). "Three in hospital after being hit by chocolate bar salmonella bug." The Times (London), p. 19.

English, S. (2010, January 19). "Boss gets a sweet send-off after chocolate deal goes through." The Evening Standard (London).

English, S. (2006, April 26). "Cadbury's pounds 198m bottling deal sparks talk of spin-off." The Independent (London), p. 50.

"Firm failed to tell authorities about presence of salmonella." (2007, July 17). Derby Evening Telegraph, first edition, p. 2.

Finch, J. (2007, March 14). "Union anger as American corporate raider takes a bite out of Cadbury Schweppes." The Guardian (London), FINANCIAL section, p. 27.

Finch, J. (2009, November 12). "Cadbury's Todd Stitzer does not believe in sweet surrender." The Guardian (London).

"FOCUS: Cadbury's Salmonella scare could cost company over 30 mln stg." (2006, July 6). AFX International Focus.

"Food safety." (2014, November). Retrieved March 1, 2015, from http://www.who.int/mediacentre/factsheets/fs399/en/

Forsythe, S. (2010). The Microbiology of Safe Food, Second Edition. Chelsea, West Sussex, United Kingdom. John Wiley & Sons Ltd.

"FSA rebuke to Cadbury sparks food sector scare." (2006, July 6). Marketing Week, p. 3.

Gray, R. (2006, June 25). "Cadbury reputation under threat." Scotland on Sunday (Edinburgh).

Harrison, D. (2005, June 25). "Cadbury hid salmonellas for months." Sunday Independent (Dublin).

Head, B. (1903). The Food of the Gods: A Popular Account of Cocoa. RB Johnson.

Hickman, M. (2006, July 22) "Cadbury to consider payouts for victims of salmonella outbreak." The Independent (London), p. 6.

Hickman, M. (2006, July 5). "Cadbury's plant had suffered salmonella outbreak in 2002" (July 5, 2006), The Independent (London), p. 15.

Hickman, M. (2006, Sept. 26). "Reveals: watchdog's poor verdict on Cadbury." Belfast Telegraph.

The History of Chocolate. Cadbury UK. https://www.cadbury.co.uk/the-story Retrieved February 18, 2015.

Hughes, J. (2006, July 7). "Chocolate factory gets deep clean." Western Daily Press (Bristol), p. 2.

Hume, M. (2006, June 30). "Why Willy Wonka would have been in terror of the Food Standards Agency." The Times (London), p. 25.

Jack, L. (2007, March 26) "Trusted brands survey; case study – Cadbury." Marketing Week, p. 19.

Jameson, A. (2006, January 16). "The real-life Willy Wonka savours sweet success at Cadbury Schweppes." The Times (London), p. 46.

Jamieson, A. (2006, July 22). "Cadbury's blamed for salmonella outbreak." The Scotsman (Glasgow), p. 20.

Jivkov, M. (2006, May 20) "Not much fizz in Sch … you know who." The Independent (London), p. 12.

Johnson, J. (2005, June 25). "Food safety: Recall; Cadbury's reputation is on the line as it comes under fire for dragging its heels over a hug discovered months ago." The Sunday Herald (Glasgow), p. 14.

Johnston, L. (2006, July 9) "I'm lucky to be alive, says victim of the chocolate bug." Sunday Express (London), p. 10.

Johnston, L. (2006, July 9) "The secrecy that left a bad taste in the mouth and spoilt a reputation." Sunday Express, p 10.

Klein, P. (2012, December 28). "Three Ways to Secure Your Social License to Operate in 2013." Forbes.com. Retrieved March 25, 2015, from http://www.forbes.com/sites /csr/ 2012/12/28/three-ways-to-secure-your-social-license-to-operate-in-2013/.

Klinger, P. (2006, February 22). "Investors relish profit leap as Cadbury overtakes Mars." The Times (London) p. 44.

Klinger, P. (2006, Aug. 3). "Cadbury estimates cost of salmonella scare at £20m." The Times (London), p. 45.

Korten, D. C. (2010). Agenda for a New Economy: From Phantom Wealth to Real Wealth. San Francisco: Berrett-Koehler, Inc.

Lagorce, A. (2006, Aug. 2). "Cadbury takes salmonella hit, but profit triples on disposals." Market Watch.

Lampel, K., ed. (2012). Big Bug Book: Handbook of Foodborne Pathogenic Microorganisms and Natural Toxins. Washington, D.C.: US Food and Drug Administration.

Laurence, B. (2006, Nov. 5) "Cadbury makes future sweeter." The Sunday Times (London), p, 17.

Laurence, B. and D. Rushe. (2007, March 18) "Cadbury." The Sunday Times (London), Business section, p. 5.

Lawless, J. (2005, June 25). "Cadbury bracing for possible backlash after recalling chocolate over salmonella fears." Associated Press.

Lawrence, F. (2006, July 1) "Cadbury's bug may be in 30 more products: Food watchdog testing all sweets containing contaminated ingredient." The Guardian (London), p. 1.

Lawrence, F. (2006, July 4) "Cadbury's safety checks 'unreliable'." The Guardian (London), p. 5

Lawrence, F., J. Meikle, J. Vidal and S. Henderson. (2006, July 1). "Salmonella outbreak: Poisoned patients and mystery samples – how food detectives traced Cadbury's bug: Experts still testing more than 30 different products: Poultry dump investigated as possible source." The Guardian (London), p. 7

Lawrence, F. (2006, July 5). "Salmonella outbreaks kept secret by Cadbury in 2002." The Guardian (London), p. 3

Lawrence, F. and J. Meikle. (2006, July 7). "Scare over salmonella in chocolate widens: Other food firms bought Cadbury's base ingredient: Company now agrees to clean all production lines." The Guardian (London), p. 5.

Leach, A. (2006, July 30). "So sorry, says Cadbury chief." Knight-Ridder Tribune Business News.

Leake, C. (2005, June 25). "Cadbury's will bury 250 tons of chocolate." The Daily Mail (London), p. 13.

Leake, J. and G. Walsh. (2005, June 25). "Chocolate bug cases spread." The Sunday Times (London), p. 8.

Levy, Andy. (2006, July 5) "Out-of-date salmonella test could extend alert on Cadbury chocolate." Daily Mail (London), p. 2

MacLean, S. (2006, July 22). "Cadbury's bug blame." The Mirror (London), 1 Star Edition, p. 15.

Marks, S. (2006, May 10). "Cadbury gets in its $50m Stride as talk of a Buffett bid fades." London Evening Standard, p 31.

Miller, Robert. (2006, Aug. 2). "Salmonella scare to cost Cadbury's Pounds 20 million." The Evening Standard (London), p. 10.

Morgan, Tom. (2006, June 28). "Coronation Street deal hit by bug." Western Daily Press (Bristol), p. 2.

Morley, C. (2006, Aug. 3). "Cadbury in a Rovers return; INDUSTRY: Link with Corrie resumed after salmonella scandal." Birmingham Evening Mail, p. 6.

Morley, C. (2006, July 29) "Cadbury's pounds 30 m blow; Huge cost of salmonella crisis is revealed." Birmingham Evening Mail, p. 1.

Morley, Chris. (2006, Aug. 2) "Cadbury: We are suffering; SALMONELLA: Choc sales plummeting, boss admits." Birmingham Evening Mail, page 6.

Murray-Watson, A. (2006, July 16). "Salmonella scare diminishes confidence in Cadbury Brand. Sunday Telegraph." (London), p. 2.

Nayeri, F. (2007, Feb. 12). "Cadbury recalls some Easter eggs." International Herald Tribune, p. 14.

"New UK food poisoning figures published." (2014, June 26). Retrieved March 1, 2015, from http://www.food.gov.uk/news-updates/news/2014/6097/foodpoisoning

"News Analysis: Recall bites at Cadbury." (2006, Sept. 29). Process Engineering, p. 10.

Nixon, Simon. (2006, Aug. 2). "A question of trust." Breakingviews.com.

Northedge, R. (2006, Aug. 27). "Watchdog to fund Cadbury case." Sunday Telegraph (London), p. 2.

O'Flanagan, S. (2006, June 30). "Sweet PR talk fails to disguise Cadbury fiasco." The Irish Times (Dublin), p. 4.

Pain, S. (2006, Oct. 27) "Sales down for Cadbury." Birmingham Post, p. 17.

Parry, V. (2006, July 8) "Sweet mystery." The Times (London), p. 2.

"Poison choc firm defiant; Cadbury: Salmonella in January – revealed in June." (2006, June 24). Birmingham Evening Mail, p. 6.

Poulter, Sean. (2006, July 3). "Cadbury salmonella alert has spread to 30 products." Daily Mail (London), p. 20

Powles, D. (2006, June 30). "Danger chocs still on sale." Burton Mail.

Pratley, N. (2006, Aug. 3) "Viewpoint: Cadbury suffers barely a nibble from salmonella." The Guardian (London), p. 26.

Public Health England, "Salmonella Data 2006 to 2015 November 2016." Gov.uk. January 2017. Accessed May 12, 2018.
https://assets.publishing.service.gov.uk/government/uploads/system/uploads/attachment_data/file/598401/Salmonella_2016_Data.pdf.

"Reports of Selected Salmonella Outbreak Investigations." (2014). Retrieved March 2, 2015, from http://www.cdc.gov/salmonella/outbreaks.html

Revill, J. (2006, Feb. 12). "Protect the brand – and don't get egg on your face." Birmingham Post, p. 31.

Ries, A., and Trout, J. (1997). Marketing Warfare. New York City: McGraw-Hill.

Rodgers, S. (2007). "Todd Stitzer's Golden Ticket." Columbia Law School web site. Retrieved February 21, 2015.

"Roundup: Cadbury launches UK marketing offensive to offset salmonella impact." (2007, Feb. 20). AFX News.

"Salmonella-scare chocolate to return to British stores." (2006, Aug. 1) Agence France Presse.

Salmonella. (2013, May 13). Retrieved March 1, 2015, from http://www.cdc.gov/salmonella/general/diagnosis.html.

Salmonella Montevideo. (2013, October 20). Retrieved March 1, 2015, from https://confluence.cornell.edu/display/FOODSAFETY/Salmonella Montevideo.

Salmonella (non-typhoidal). (2013, August). Retrieved March 2, 2015, from http://www.who.int/mediacentre/factsheets/fs139/en/.

Samuel, B. (2000, March 1). "The Cadburys: Quaker Social Reformers." Quakerinfo.com. Retrieved Feb 18, 2015. http://www.quakerinfo.com/ quak_cad.shtml.

Sayid, R. (2006, June 24). "Why the Delay? Storm Over Five-Month Wait for Chocolates Health Alert." The Daily Mirror (London), p. 10.

Sellnow, T. L., R. R. Ulmer, M. W. Seeger, and R. S. Littlefield (2009). Effective risk communication: A message-centered approach. Springer Science & Business Media.

Sibun, J. (2010, January 18). "Cadbury's Todd Stitzer, the confectioner who dislikes sweet talk." The Daily Telegraph (London).

Slovic, P. E. (2000). The perception of risk. Earthscan Publications.

Smithers, R. (2007, July 14). "Cadbury allowed salmonella in chocolate to save cash, court told." The Guardian (London), Home Pages, p. 4.

"Springfield College will dedicate new Stitzer YMCA Center." (2011, May 18) Springfield College website. Retrieved February 21, 2015.

"Stockwatch: Cadbury Schweppes lower, FY pretax before consensus, opinions mixed." (2007, Feb. 20). AFX News.

"The Story of Cadbury." Cadbury Australia. Retrieved February 21, 2015. https://www.cadbury.com.au/About-Cadbury/The-Story-of-Cadbury.aspx.

"Stringer, David." (2006, August 2). Cadbury Schweppes says first-half earnings rises despite costs of British product recall. Associated Press.

Sun Tzu and S.B. Griffith. (1971). The Art of War. Oxford University Press.

Susskind, L. and P. Field (1996). Dealing with an angry public: The mutual gains approach to resolving disputes. Simon and Schuster.

"Testing increased at salmonella plant." (2006, July 7). Birmingham Evening Mail, p. 3.

"The truth about the Mars bar statistics (2006, November 4)." The Grocer, p. 34.

"Topps Meat to close down after meat recall." (2007, October 5) Associated Press

Townsend, A. (2006, July 30). "It never rains but it pours; Two corporate giants, two public relations nightmares. But while BA shares rise above the turbulence, Cadbury will need more than sugar to sweeten the City." Independent on Sunday (London), p. 6.

"U.K. investigators link Cadbury products to 13 salmonella cases." (2006, July 21). The Associated Press

Vasagar, J. (2006, June 24). "Salmonella scare: Chocolate may have poisoned more than 40: Watchdog says Cadbury's should have acted earlier: Contamination cause by leak of waste water." The Guardian (London), p. 3.

Walaski, P. (2011). Risk and Crisis Communication: Methods and Messages. Wiley.

Wales, J. (2006, June 25). "Chocs bosses defend bug scare delay." Wales on Sunday (Cardiff), p. 9.

Wallop, H. (2007, March 16). "Cadbury seeks sweet success with plans to split." Daily Telegraph (London), City Section, p. 5.

Watson, J. (2006, July 17). "Eat to Live: Cadbury under microscope." United Press International.

Werdigier, J. (2007, March 16) "Cadbury plans to separate its drinks and candy units." New York Times, Late Edition Final, Business/Financial section, p. 3.

"When can food be deemed safe?" (2006, July 5). Marketing magazine, p. 15.

Wiggens, J. (2010, March 12). "The inside story of the Cadbury takeover." FT Magazine.

Williams, C. (2007, July 14). "After its trial and punishment, Cadbury now faces civil cases." The Grocer, p. 8.

Williams, R. (2007, July 27). "Cadbury fined £1m for salmonella offenses." The Guardian (London), home pages, p. 5.

"Woman may sue chocolate maker." (2006, July 11). Belfast News Letter (Northern Ireland), p. 6.

About the author

Rusty Cawley, APR is a public relations counsel and risk communicator with experience in issues relating to foodborne, vector-borne, zoonotic, and trans-boundary pathogens. Today, he is the assistant director for Research Communications and Public Relations at Texas A&M University in College Station.

He is Accredited in Public Relations (APR) on behalf of the Public Relations Society of America by the Universal Accreditation Board.

From 2006-14, he managed research communication and risk communication for:

- The Institute for Infectious Animal Diseases (formerly the National Center for Foreign Animal and Zoonotic Disease Defense), a US Department of Homeland Security Science and Technology Center of Excellence as well as a unit of Texas A&M AgriLife Research in The Texas A&M University System.

- The Texas A&M Veterinary Medical Diagnostic Laboratory, a state agency of The Texas A&M University System and one of the busiest labs of its kind in the world, processing thousands of diagnostic tests each day.

Before joining Texas A&M, he was vice president, director of media relations, and a crisis communication counsel for Levenson, which at that time was the largest independent advertising and public relations agency in Dallas-Fort Worth. Clients included Zale Corp., Church's Chicken, Alon USA (Fina brand gasoline), ABC Radio Network, Ascension Health, Cellular One, Coca-Cola Enterprises, Carrier North Texas Corp., Fulbright & Jaworski, Phoenix Corp. (Black-Eyed Pea Restaurants), H-E-B Central Market, the Dallas Center for the Performing Arts Foundation, the Dallas Convention and Visitors Bureau, the Central Dallas Association, the Islamic Association of North Texas, the Town of Addison, Brierley & Partners, and KERA Public Broadcasting.

Prior to his time at Levenson, Cawley spent twenty years as a reporter, editor, and publisher in the news business.

www.ingramcontent.com/pod-product-compliance
Lightning Source LLC
Chambersburg PA
CBHW050458190326
41458CB00005B/1337